THE WORKING FAMILY'S COOKBOOK

Irena Chalmers

BARRON'S

ACKNOWLEDGMENTS

STAFF
Managing Editor: Grace Freedson
Contributors: Stephanie Lyness, Rick Rogers

CREDITS
Photographer: Matthew Klein
Designer: Milton Glaser, Inc.
Food Stylist: Andrea Swenson
Wallcovering by Color House Wallcoverings

All inquiries should be addressed to:
Barron's Educational Series, Inc.
250 Wireless Boulevard
Hauppauge, NY 11788

International Standard Book No. 0-8120-1566-5 (pbk)
                                0-8120-6147-0
Library of Congress Catalog Card No. 92-36589

Library of Congress Cataloging-in-Publication Data

Chalmers, Irena.
    The working family cookbook / by Irena Chalmers.
        p.   cm.
    Includes index.
    ISBN 0-8120-1566-5
    1. Quick and easy cookery.   I. Title.
TX652.C479   1993   92-36589
641.5'55 – dc20   CIP

PRINTED IN HONG KONG
2345 9927 987654321

TABLE OF CONTENTS

INTRODUCTION

Every working parent knows that the period between leaving work and making dinner is not always the idyllic time some like to imagine. It must be only in other households that everyone arrives home at the same minute, full of smiles, brimming with happiness and offering to help.

We are offering to help.

We have the feeling that it is not the actual cooking that is the biggest problem, but rather deciding what to cook. Dreary as it may sound, it really is worth spending a few minutes deciding what you want to buy before setting foot in the market.

Our goal in putting together this book is to suggest new ideas to add to your faithful standbys. Most things can be prepared in less than an hour. Our aim is to keep everyone healthy by using a minimum of fat in the recipes. We have substituted yogurt for cream and sour cream, cut down on the butter and used many of the fresh herbs that have become readily available in stores everywhere. We have included more chicken and fish than beef. There are all kinds of recipes for grains, pastas and a good selection of soups, salads and fruit desserts.

We recommend using fresh ingredients throughout the book. Except for canned chicken broth, tomato paste and such staples, this is the way we like to cook. If you find it more convenient to use frozen vegetables you will readily get the sense of the recipe and know how easily you can adapt it. Certainly frozen peas and spinach and some of the other packaged foods are every bit as good-tasting and nutritious as the fresh vegetables.

Throughout we have offered suggestions for using leftovers as assets, not liabilities. Calvin Trillin, the humorist, claims that throughout his childhood he only ate leftovers and never once saw the original! If you have saved some time by not cooking a meal from scratch, you may want to make everyone feel cared for by adding some homemade cornbread or muffins. The first time you try a new recipe it always seems to take far longer than when you have become familiar with it. After making popovers or biscuits a few times, you will be able to remember the recipe and whip up a batch in no time at all. An even easier solution is to show one of the children how to make them and let them take over this part of the meal. A little praise overcomes a lot of resistance.

Speaking of help, we have also put together some thoughts for the man of the house to consider if he enjoys preparing Sunday brunch, a cook-out, or even a candlelit dinner.

We are well aware that many families cook in the microwave and have included some microwave recipes. Microwave ovens vary greatly in the amount of power they deliver, and there are so many other variables that we have left it to you to decide to what extent you want to microwave other recipes as well. With your experience and familiarity with your own oven, you will be able to look over our directions and know just how they can be adapted.

The pizzas are included for fun and because we hope you will experiment with some unusual toppings. We have also cooked up some burgers made with turkey as well as others using lean ground beef. We completed our collection with some old-fashioned desserts, summer and winter drinks, suggestions for children's birthday parties and a few ideas for lunch-box or anytime healthy snacks. We hope this book will find a handy place in your kitchen and that its pages will be well thumbed by everyone in the family.

IRENA CHALMERS

CHOOSING THE RIGHT HERBS AND SPICES

BEEF	allspice, bay leaves, bouquet garni, cayenne pepper, celery seed, cloves, coriander, garlic, mace, marjoram, mustard, nutmeg, oregano, paprika, parsley, pepper, rosemary, sage, thyme
CAKES AND PIES	allspice, angelica, aniseed, basil, caraway, cardamom, coriander, fennel, ginger (dried), mace, vanilla
CHEESE	aniseed, caraway, curry powder, dill weed, garlic, lemon thyme, pepper, sage, thyme
FISH	aniseed, basil, bay leaves, bouquet garni, celery seed, chervil, chili powder, chives, dill weed, fennel, ginger, lemon thyme, nutmeg, paprika, parsley, pepper, saffron
FRUIT	allspice, anise, cinnamon, coriander, ginger, lemon balm, lemongrass, mint, mixed spice, nutmeg, rosemary, sweet cicely
LAMB	cayenne pepper, cumin, dill seed, garlic, lemon thyme, mustard, paprika, rosemary, thyme
PORK	allspice, caraway, dill, fennel, garlic, ginger, juniper berries, mace, mustard powder, paprika, pepper, rosemary, sage, savory
POULTRY	basil, bouquet garni, coriander, cumin, fennel, garlic, ginger, lemon balm, lemon thyme, mace, nutmeg, pepper, rosemary, sage, sorrel, thyme
SALADS	basil, chives, dill, garlic, marjoram, mustard powder, mint, oregano, pepper, rosemary, thyme
SOUPS	allspice, aniseed, basil, bay leaves, bouquet garni, cardamom, cayenne pepper, celery seed, chervil, chives, cumin, dill, fennel, fines herbes, lemon balm, marjoram, mustard powder, nutmeg, oregano, paprika, parsley, pepper, rosemary, saffron, sage, sorrel, thyme
VEGETABLES	allspice, aniseed, bouquet garni, cayenne pepper, chervil, coriander, cumin, dill, marjoram, mustard powder, pepper, rosemary, thyme

THE EVERYDAY PANTRY

For many of the recipes in this book and for general everyday cooking, we suggest keeping the following supplies on hand—in the cupboard, the refrigerator and the freezer.

THE CUPBOARD
Canned chicken broth
Canned beef broth
Bottled clam juice
Soy sauce: regular and low-sodium
Oils: vegetable, olive, peanut, sesame
Vinegar: red wine and apple cider
Canned tuna
Evaporated milk
Peanut butter, creamy and chunky
Prepared American mustard
Prepared horseradish
Dijon mustard
Worcestershire sauce
Hot pepper sauce (Tabasco)
Ketchup
Canned tomatoes, whole and crushed
Tomato puree
Tomato sauce
Tomato paste
Dried Beans and Grains
Chick-peas (canned)
Kidney beans (canned and dried)
Lentils
Lima beans
Split peas
Rice: long grain and brown
Bulgur
Cracked wheat
Quick-cooking oatmeal
Whole bran cereal

Pasta
Spaghetti
Fettuccine
Radiatore (wagon wheel)
Ziti
Small and medium shells
Cavatelli
Linguine
Penne

Nuts
Almonds
Walnuts

Sweeteners
Honey
Maple syrup
Light corn syrup
Dark and light molasses
Dark and light brown sugar
Confectioners' sugar
Superfine sugar

Baking supplies
Flour, all-purpose and whole wheat
Cornmeal, yellow and white
Bran, unprocessed
Cornstarch
Cream of tartar
Baking powder
Baking soda
Vanilla extract
Almond extract
Chocolate, semisweet or bittersweet
Chocolate syrup
Cocoa powder

Dried fruits and preserves
Dark raisins
Golden raisins (also called sultanas)
Fruit preserves
No sugar, all-fruit preserves
Marmalade, orange or lemon
Unsweetened applesauce

THE SPICE RACK
Allspice
Bay leaves
Black peppercorns
Cayenne pepper
Celery seed
Chili powder
Cloves, ground and whole
Curry powder
Dill
Garlic salt
Ground cinnamon
Ground ginger
Ground nutmeg
Marjoram
Oregano
Paprika
Red pepper flakes
Rosemary
Tarragon
Thyme

THE VEGETABLE BIN
(These vegetables do not require refrigeration)
Garlic
Onions
Shallots
Potatoes*

THE REFRIGERATOR
Eggs
Milk: regular, low-fat, skim
Half-and-half
Plain yogurt: regular and low-fat
Butter, salted and unsalted
Margarine, salted and unsalted

Cheese
Cheddar
Cottage cheese
Cream cheese
Low-fat ricotta
Mozzarella
Muenster
Neufchatel
Parmesan

Fruit
Apples
Lemons
Limes
Oranges

Vegetables
Carrots
Celery
Lettuce

THE FREEZER
Corn kernels
Peas
Orange juice concentrate
Frozen yogurt
Ice milk

* do not store potatoes and onions together

THE SPECIALTY PANTRY

The following list includes ingredients called for in some of the recipes in the book. Many of the foods listed here are available only in specialty stores; others are found in supermarkets, sometimes in the ethnic or gourmet sections. You may prefer to purchase these items only when you make a recipe requiring one or more of them, or you may want to keep a number on hand in the cupboard, refrigerator, or freezer.

THE CUPBOARD
Anchovy fillets
Anchovy paste
Balsamic vinegar
Capers
Canned artichoke hearts
Canned green chili peppers
Canned water chestnuts
Chili sauce
Coconut cream
Dates
Dried currants
Dried English mustard
Figs
Harissa
Hazelnuts
Hoisin sauce
Marinated artichoke hearts
Olives: green and ripe
Pine nuts
Prunes
Sesame oil
Sesame seeds
Raspberry vinegar

Rice vinegar
Tahini

Grains
Arborio rice
Basmati rice
Couscous
Millet
Pearl barley
Wild rice

THE SPICE RACK
Basil
Caraway seeds
Cinnamon sticks
Coriander seeds
Cumin seeds
Fennel seeds
Ground coriander
Ground cumin
Ground white pepper
Mint
Mustard seeds
Poppyseeds

Sage
Saffron threads
Turmeric
White peppercorns
Whole nutmeg

THE REFRIGERATOR
Buttermilk
Feta cheese
Gruyere cheese
Tortillas

THE FREEZER
Cranberries
Frozen artichoke hearts
Lima beans
Sweet cherries

THE LIQUOR CABINET
White wine
Red wine
Sherry
Dry vermouth
Kirsch

GUIDE TO BUYING FRUITS AND VEGETABLES

Gone are the days when fruits and vegetables were available for just one short season a year. Now, you can find strawberries in February without too much trouble and if you are willing to pay the price. But there is no doubt that most fruits and vegetables taste best (and cost less) in their own season. In compiling the following list, we have taken this into consideration and have indicated seasonal availability in cases where it makes a marked difference. We have not attempted a complete list of all fruits and vegetables but have concentrated largely on those used throughout the book.

YEAR-ROUND FRUITS
Apples
Bananas
Grapes
Lemons
Limes
Pears
Pineapple

YEAR-ROUND VEGETABLES
Avocados
Broccoli
Carrots
Celery
Chili peppers
Chard
Chinese cabbage
Chives
Eggplant
Iceberg lettuce
Jalapeno peppers
Mushrooms
Onions: white, red, pearl
Peppers: green, red, yellow
Parsley
Potatoes
Scallions (green onions)
Shallots

Spinach
Tomatoes: plum, cherry,
  hydroponic
White cabbage
Zucchini

SPRING FRUITS
Rhubarb
Strawberries

SPRING VEGETABLES
Asparagus
Bibb lettuce
Green and red leaf lettuce
Boston lettuce
Romaine lettuce
Snowpeas
Some herbs
Watercress

SUMMER FRUITS
Blueberries
Cherries
Melons
Nectarines
Peaches
Plums
Raspberries
Strawberries

SUMMER VEGETABLES
Corn
Green peas
Fennel bulb
Herbs including basil, dill, mint,
  rosemary, sage, tarragon, thyme
Leaf lettuce
Lima beans
Romaine lettuce
String beans
Summer squash
Vine-ripened tomatoes

FALL/WINTER FRUITS
Apples
Cranberries
Pears

FALL/WINTER VEGETABLES
Acorn squash
Broccoli rabe
Butternut squash
Leeks
Rutabaga
Sweet potatoes
Turnips
Turnip greens

MICROWAVE TIPS

• The recipes in this book developed specifically for the microwave oven are all designated by an @ symbol. They were developed for microwave ovens with 650 to 700 watts. If your oven has only 600 watts, or less, adjust the time accordingly: add a minute or so to the cooking time and rely on tests for doneness.

• In each microwave recipe, we have indicated the power setting to use. As a general rule, the high settings (between 70 and 100 percent) are for most cooking; medium settings (40 to 60 percent) are for reheating or gentle cooking or melting; low settings (10 to 30 percent) are for defrosting and warming food.

• You cannot use metal, most aluminum foil or dishes with metal trim, such as gold rimmed plates, in the microwave. In some of the newer ovens, lightweight aluminum foil can be used to shield the parts of the food that cook fastest, such as the bony parts of a piece of chicken.

• Heatproof glass dishes are terrific for microwave cooking. Also good are most plastics, ceramics, pottery and porcelain. Thin plastic tubs and bowls, not designed for the microwave, may become misshapen after long use. Test any questionable dish by placing it, empty, in the microwave. Put a glass cup measure filled with about a cup of water in the oven at the same time and microwave both on HIGH (100 percent) power for a minute. The water is necessary to absorb the microwaves. If the dish you are testing feels hot after the minute then it is absorbing microwaves and is therefore not suitable for microwave cooking. Round dishes are the best shape for success in the microwave oven.

• Keep in mind that food cooked in the microwave will get hot and transfer the heat to the dish. Often, you will need potholders to take the dishes from the microwave oven.

• Room temperature, uniformly sized pieces of food are best for microwave cooking.

• Stirring or rearranging food during cooking helps ensure even results. Rotating the dish in the oven does the same thing. Using the turntables built into the microwave oven or those bought as a microwave accessory are good ways to make sure the food cooks evenly.

• Microwave browning trays, available in housewares stores and wherever microwave ovens are sold, make it possible to brown meat in the microwave. Bottled sauces such as Worcestershire and Kitchen Bouquet also add color to microwaved foods.

• When using paper towels, it is best to use plain white towels without any dye in them. Paper towels prevent the food from splattering and absorb grease and moisture.

• To get the most juice from a lemon, warm it in the microwave oven for 30 to 35 seconds at 100 percent power.

• When baking potatoes in the microwave oven, pierce the potato in several places with a knife or fork to allow moisture to escape.

• Thinly sliced bacon cooks more rapidly than thickly sliced, and a few pieces cook faster than half a dozen or so.

• Frozen vegetables can be cooked right in their packages in the microwave oven. Pierce the package several times for venting and cook the vegetables for 5 to 8 minutes on 100 percent power.

● Dried beans that normally require overnight soaking before they can be cooked can be prepared for cooking in the microwave. Cover them with water, put a lid on the dish and microwave the beans at 100 percent power for 15 minutes. Take them from the oven and let them stand for an hour. They are now ready to cook.

● Chocolate sauce stored in a glass jar can be heated in the microwave oven anytime you want a smooth, fudgy topping for your favorite ice cream or bowl of berries.

● Melting chocolate chips in the microwave is a quick and convenient way to make chocolate sauce. The chips will not look completely melted until they are stirred.

● Whole fruits can be cooked in the microwave. For the best results, arrange them in a circle in a round dish.

● Plastic wrap is invaluable for microwave cooking. It holds in moisture and heat. It is a good idea to turn back the corner of the plastic wrap to allow steam to vent.

● Wax paper makes a good, loose covering when you simply want to hold in some heat.

● If a recipe requires standing time, be sure to follow the instructions. A lot of food cooked in the microwave oven completes its cooking cycle after it is taken from the oven and allowed to stand for a few minutes.

● Use visual tests for doneness provided by the recipes and your own cooking experience with conventional stoves to determine when the food is ready. Even microwave ovens with the same wattage will perform differently from each other and you cannot depend on the cooking time alone as the only guide.

● When reheating muffins, biscuits, slices of bread and so on, put the food in a plastic bag or container with a tight fitting lid and heat it for 20 to 30 seconds at 30 percent power. If you fail to use the plastic bag or container, the bread will turn hard.

● Food that splatters or boils over in the microwave oven will not bake on the sides of the cavity, as it will in a conventional oven. It is an easy chore to wipe the oven clean with a damp sponge and, if necessary, a mild cleanser.

● For long cooking foods that should be covered, glass lids are preferred to plastic wrap.

● To defrost chicken, allow about 6 minutes for each pound of bone-in poultry. Defrost it at 30 percent power.

● Vegetables wrapped in damp paper towels steam very well in the microwave at 100 percent power. A single serving takes less than 5 minutes.

● If your microwave oven is equipped with a probe, use it when cooking large cuts of meat. Make sure the meat is evenly shaped. Unlike in the conventional oven, meat without a bone will cook more rapidly in the microwave oven. Large cuts of meat should be cooked on a microwave-safe rack so that the meat sits above its juices and does not steam or stew in them.

● The microwave oven is not the place to hard cook eggs. Eggs still in the shells may explode in the microwave.

● It is a good idea to puncture egg yolks when cooking eggs in the microwave to ensure that they do not explode. Cook eggs only until they seem almost done — let them finish cooking as they stand for a minute or so.

FOOD SUBSTITUTIONS

INGREDIENT	SUBSTITUTION
baking powder (1¼ teaspoons)	½ teaspoon baking soda plus 2 tablespoons vinegar
baking powder (1 teaspoon)	¼ teaspoon baking soda plus ½ teaspoon cream of tartar
black pepper	white pepper or paprika
bouillon (1 cup)	1 bouillon cube dissolved in 1 cup hot water
bread crumbs (1 cup)	¾ cup cracker crumbs
butter	margarine *or* vegetable shortening *or* less cup lard
buttermilk or sour milk (1 cup)	1 cup yogurt *or* 1 cup whole milk with 1 tablespoon of lemon juice or vinegar for every cup of milk
carrots	parsnips or baby white turnips
chicken broth	vegetable or fish broth
chocolate:	
bittersweet	semisweet
semisweet (1⅔ ounces)	1 ounce unsweetened chocolate plus 4 teaspoons sugar
unsweetened (1 ounce — 1 square)	3 tablespoons cocoa powder plus 1 tablespoon shortening
cornichons	gherkins, bread and butter pickles
cottage cheese	pot cheese, farmers cheese
cream cheese	neufchatel cheese
cream, heavy (1 cup)	⅞ cup buttermilk or yogurt plus 3 tablespoons butter
croutons	crustless cubed white bread sautéed in butter
curry powder	turmeric with cardamom, ginger powder, and cumin
dry mustard	prepared mustard
egg, for thickening or baking	2 egg yolks
fish broth	diluted bottled clam juice, chicken broth or vegetable broth
flour:	
all-purpose, for thickening sauces	1½ teaspoons cornstarch *or* arrowroot *or* 1 tablespoon quick-cooking tapioca
all-purpose, for baking bread	up to ½ cup bran, whole-wheat flour, or cornmeal and enough all-purpose flour to fill cup
cake (1 cup sifted)	1 cup all-purpose flour minus 2 tablespoons
fresh herbs (1 tablespoon)	⅓ to ½ teaspoon dried herbs
hazel nuts	walnuts or pecans
honey (1 cup)	1¼ cups sugar plus ¼ cup liquid
jerusalem artichokes	water chestnuts
kidney beans	garbanzo beans; navy beans; pinto beans

leeks	mild scallions or shallots
lemon juice	vinegar, lime juice *or* white wine
mayonnaise, homemade (½ cup)	½ cup commercial mayonnaise plus ½ teaspoon lemon juice and ½ teaspoon prepared mustard
mushrooms	a 10-ounce jar of mushrooms, drained, can be substituted for 4 cups of sliced, fresh mushrooms
mustard, Dijon	spicy brown mustard
nectarines	peaches
olives, kalamata	oil-cured olives or Greek olives
olive oil	vegetable oil
onion, chopped (1 cup)	1 tablespoon minced onion, reconstituted
Parmesan cheese	romano cheese
parsley	chervil
peaches	nectarines
pecans	walnuts
pork tenderloin	rolled pork loin roast or any lean pork
prosciutto ham	Black Forest ham or any thinly sliced, smoked ham
raisins	currants
raspberries	blackberries and boysenberries
scallions	green or white onions, or onion powder to taste
shallots	2 parts onion plus 1 part garlic
sour cream	yogurt
spinach leaves	watercress leaves
sugar:	
granulated	
(1 tablespoon)	1 tablespoon maple sugar
(1 cup)	1¾ cups confectioners' sugar *or* 1 cup molasses plus ½ teaspoon baking soda
dark brown	light brown sugar
light brown	dark brown sugar
sweet potatoes	yams
Tabasco	hot pepper sauce
tomatoes	canned plum tomatoes; whole round canned tomatoes
tomato sauce (2 cups)	¾ cup tomato paste plus 1 cup water
tuna steak	swordfish steak
turnips	rutabaga
vinegar:	
balsamic	a little less red wine vinegar
wine	cider vinegar with a little red wine or white distilled vinegar with a little white wine
walnuts	pecans
water chestnuts	jerusalem artichokes
watercress	Italian parsley
yeast, active dry (1 tablespoon — 1 package)	1⅗ ounce cake yeast

SOUPS AND SANDWICHES

A bowl of soup, a quick sandwich with a glass of milk—these are the fast meals we prepare for our families when we are hungry but have little time for cooking. Admittedly, opening a can of soup and putting some cheese and cold meat between two slices of bread provides instant gratification but with a little more effort (and planning) it is also a great way to have an evening meal when everyone is busy—or feeling like having a nice lazy evening in front of the television.

All the soups in this chapter are easy to make. They keep well, too, and if you are really organized you may want to make them a day or two ahead. While the soup is heating, put a loaf of bread into the oven to crisp and perhaps make a salad. A pickle or two or some crisp carrot and celery sticks add a good crunch to the plate even though, in their heart, everyone would prefer a handful of potato chips!

All manner of ingredients may be used to garnish soup from a sprinking of freshly chopped herbs or a swirl of butter, to a touch of freshly ground pepper or dusting of paprika or cinnamon. Sour cream, yogurt or a spoonful of freshly grated Parmesan cheese can also be added at the last moment. Freshly chopped raw vegetables make a good contrasting texture for thick soups; chopped celery, sliced radishes, diced cucumber and grated carrots are particularly good used in this way. Diced ham, crumbled bacon and croutons are also good added to many soups.

MEATLOAF SANDWICH

A simple sandwich made with leftover meatloaf is far more enjoyable with mustard and horseradish added to bring out the flavor.

Serves 4
Preparation time: 10 minutes
Cooking time: 5 to 10 minutes

INGREDIENTS

Greek Meatloaf (page 170)
8 slices whole wheat bread, lightly toasted
Dijon mustard
Prepared horseradish
Tomato slices
Escarole lettuce

1. Heat the over to 350 degrees. Slice the meatloaf ½- to ¾-inch thick. Put the meatloaf sliccs in a baking dish, cover with aluminum foil and bake for 5 to 10 minutes until heated through.

2. Spread four of the slices of bread with mustard and horseradish. Add the warmed meatloaf and top with tomatoes and escarole. Spread the remaining slices of bread with mustard, if desired, and cover the sandwiches, mustard side down.

SHOPPING LIST

2 lbs. very lean ground beef
whole wheat bread
1 tomato
onions
escarole lettuce
garlic
oregano (fresh or dried)
parsley
2 11-oz. cans Italian plum tomatoes
red wine vinegar
honey
Dijon mustard
prepared horseradish
olive oil
eggs

CHICKEN AND AVOCADO SANDWICH

If you prefer, make these sandwiches with freshly grilled chicken or, as we suggest, with leftover cold chicken. Arizona Chicken (page 135), sliced from the bone, also makes a splendid sandwich.

Serves 4
Preparation time: 20 minutes

INGREDIENTS

2 cold Herb-Marinated Chicken Breasts
   (page 141)
8 slices rye bread, toasted
Herb Mayonnaise (page 63)
1 large tomato, sliced
1 medium-size avocado, halved, seeded,
   peeled and sliced
Freshly ground pepper
Arugula

1. Bone the chicken and cut it into large thin slices.

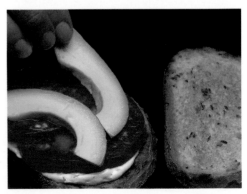

2. Spread the toasted bread slices with mayonnaise. Arrange the tomato slices and then the avocado slices over 4 of the pieces of toast. Top with chicken slices and season with pepper. Add arugula and then cover the sandwiches with the remaining slices of toast, mayonnaise side down.

SHOPPING LIST

2 chicken breast halves
rye bread
1 tomato
1 lemon
1 avocado
arugula
garlic
parsley
rosemary
bay leaves
mayonnaise
Dijon mustard
olive oil
balsamic vinegar

GRILLED TUNA SANDWICH WITH PESTO AND WATERCRESS

It is an art to make a good sandwich that turns into a fast supper, especially if you have some Coriander Pesto already made and waiting in the refrigerator. Buy the tuna and a loaf of bread on your way home from work— a chewy round loaf of peasant bread yields nice slices and you can cut the large center pieces in half. Serve the soup with sliced summer-ripe tomatoes tossed with a little oil and vinegar dressing.

Serves 4
Preparation time: 20 minutes
Cooking time: 20 minutes

INGREDIENTS

2 medium-size Vidalia or red onions
Olive oil
Salt and freshly ground pepper
4 $\frac{1}{2}$-inch-thick slices French or peasant-style
   bread
1 $\frac{1}{4}$ to 1 $\frac{1}{2}$ pounds tuna steak, cut into
   $\frac{3}{8}$- to $\frac{1}{2}$-inch-thick slices
Coriander Pesto (page 274)
Watercress

1. Heat the grill.

2. Slice the onions horizontally into $\frac{3}{8}$-inch-thick slices and skewer each slice with a toothpick to hold the rounds together. Drizzle the slices with 2 tablespoons of oil and sprinkle lightly with salt and pepper. Lightly brush the bread on both sides with oil.

3. Grill the onions for about 6 minutes on each side until they are golden brown. Move them to the side of the grill to keep warm. At the same time, grill the bread for about 5 minutes on each side until the slices are marked and slightly crisp. Move the bread to the side of the grill.

4. Drizzle the tuna with 4 teaspoons of oil and sprinkle lightly with salt and pepper. Grill the tuna for 2 to 3 minutes on each side.

5. Spread one side of each piece of bread with a generous amount of pesto. Arrange 3 or 4 branches of watercress over each piece. Cut the tuna if necessary so that it fits nicely on the bread and divide it between the sandwiches. Remove the toothpicks from the onions and separate each slice into rounds. Top the tuna with the onions.

SHOPPING LIST

$1 \frac{1}{4}$ to $1 \frac{1}{2}$ lbs. tuna steak, cut into $\frac{3}{8}$- to
$\frac{1}{2}$ in. thick slices
French or peasant-style bread
2 medium Vidalia or red onions
1 medium jalapeno pepper
garlic
1 lime or 1 lemon
coriander leaves
watercress
pine nuts
olive or vegetable oil

GRILLED TURKEY SANDWICH WITH BROCCOLI AND CHEDDAR

Cheddar cheese and a reduced-fat mozzarella combine to make a satisfying sandwich. The mixed cheese reduces both the fat and sodium without sacrificing taste. Turkey cutlets are readily available in most supermarkets but if you cannot find them, substitute chicken.

Serves 4
Preparation time: 15 minutes, plus 15 minutes for marinating
Cooking time: 10 minutes

INGREDIENTS

2 cups broccoli florets
1 pound turkey cutlets (4 to 5 cutlets, about 4 ounces each)
¼ cup olive oil
1 tablespoon lemon juice
Salt and freshly ground pepper
4 slices whole wheat bread, toasted
Dijon mustard
2 ounces cheddar cheese, coarsely grated
2 ounces low-fat mozzarella cheese, coarsely grated

1. Bring a large pot of salted water to the boil and cook the broccoli for 3 minutes until crisp-tender. Drain, rinse immediately under cold running water and drain again.

2. Position a broiling rack 5 to 6 inches from the heat source of a broiler. Heat the broiler to high.

3. Meanwhile, combine the turkey cutlets in a dish with the oil and lemon juice and set aside to marinate for 10 to 15 minutes. Remove the cutlets from the marinade and broil for 4 minutes, turning once. Set the cutlets aside and season with salt and pepper. Cut the cutlets in half.

4. Spread the toast with mustard and arrange the turkey pieces on top. Combine the cheeses. Place equal amounts of broccoli on the cutlets and sprinkle the cheese evenly over the sandwiches. Broil the sandwiches for about 1 minute until the cheese is melted. Serve immediately.

Bread
Store bread, well wrapped, in the freezer. It will not go stale and defrosts almost instantly.
Make stale bread into breadcrumbs in a blender or food processor, or cut it into croutons and store in a plastic bag in the freezer.

LAMB SANDWICH
WITH RAITA

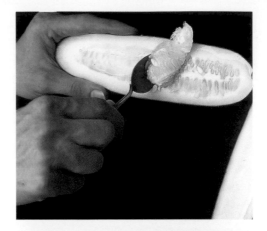

Raita is a traditional Indian salad made from cucumber slices that are marinated in yogurt. It is good on its own as a side dish and makes a marvelous contrast of taste and texture when added to a leftover roast lamb that is put into pita pockets. This is a good way to finish the last morsels of the Grilled Leg of Lamb with Cumin and Lemon (page 176).

Serves 4
Preparation time: 10 minutes

INGREDIENTS

¾ cup seeded diced cucumber (¼- to ⅜- inch dice)
¾ cup seeded diced tomato (¼- to ⅜-inch dice)
1 medium jalapeno, stemmed, seeded and finely chopped
1 tablespoon chopped fresh coriander
8 ounces plain low-fat yogurt
Salt
Grilled leg of lamb with cumin and lemon (page 176)
4 pita pockets
3 medium leaves romaine lettuce, shredded

1. Stir together the cucumber, tomato, jalapeno, coriander, yogurt and a pinch of salt. Thinly slice the lamb.

2. Stuff the pita pockets with lamb and lettuce. Spoon the raita over the top and serve.

22

Lamb

Approximately 300 million pounds of lamb are produced in the United States yearly, and around 40 million pounds more are imported from Australia and New Zealand. Besides being a delicious change from other red meats, lamb is more healthful for you. Only 6 g of fat are contained in a 3-oz serving.

Lamb is meat from sheep less than one year old. Because it is young, it is very tender. Even though it is available all year, meat labelled "Spring lamb" has been slaughtered between March and September. The color of lamb varies with the age of the animal. Light pink meat is from young, milk-fed lambs while the pinkish red meat comes from older animals.

As in microwaving other meats, the most tender cuts can be cooked on the faster power levels. Less tender cuts such as roasts and whole legs should be microwaved more slowly on a lower power level.

SHOPPING LIST

leftover leg of lamb
4 pita pockets
1 cucumber
1 tomato
1 medium jalapeno pepper
romaine lettuce
plain low-fat yogurt

HAM SALAD SANDWICH

One of the joys of baking a ham is the inevitable amount of leftovers that are available for making sandwiches. There is such an enormous variety of beautiful breads to choose from that every sandwich can have a different identity.

Serves 4
Preparation time: 20 minutes

INGREDIENTS

1 pound baked ham, cut into $\frac{1}{8}$-inch strips
6 cornichons, thinly sliced or chopped
1 stalk celery, thinly sliced
$\frac{1}{4}$ cup chopped fresh dill
$\frac{1}{4}$ cup chopped fresh chives
$\frac{1}{4}$ cup Lightened Mayonnaise (page 63) or store-bought mayonnaise
2 tablespoons Dijon mustard
$\frac{1}{8}$ teaspoon cayenne pepper
8 slices rye toast
2 hard-cooked eggs, sliced, optional

1. Combine the ham, cornichons, celery, dill, chives, mayonnaise, mustard and cayenne in a large bowl.

2. Spread the ham salad mixture over four of the rye toast slices. Top with egg slices, if desired, and then with the remaining slices of toast.

Drying Herbs

Fresh herbs (such as mint, dill, and parsley) will stay fresh in the refrigerator for only a few days. But by drying them in the microwave oven, you can preserve these herbs so that you have them to use months later.

While still fresh and bright, wash and blot them thoroughly with paper towels. Let them air-dry in the kitchen for several hours, because if any moisture remains on them when you dry them in the microwave, they will cook instead of dehydrating.

Put 3 paper towels on a glass pie plate. Arrange about 5 sprigs of herbs into a "wreath" on the towels. Do not remove the leaves from their stems. Cover herbs with another paper towel. Microwave on high for 1 minute.

Turn plate halfway around and look at herbs to see how dry they are becoming. Microwave on high for 1 minute and look at herbs again. If herbs are not dry, microwave on high for 1 minute.

It is possible for dry herbs to catch on fire if you microwave them too long, so take them out of the microwave when they no longer feel soft to the touch. Let dried herbs cool. Then crumble leaves from stems and store them in an airtight jar. Use in any recipe specifying the amount in dried form.

SHOPPING LIST

1 lb. baked ham
rye bread
celery
dill
chives
1 lemon
cornichons
mayonnaise
Dijon mustard
olive oil
cayenne pepper
eggs
plain low-fat yogurt

CUCUMBER AND RED PEPPER SANDWICHES

These little sandwiches are good to eat with a cup of hot soup. If you prefer, use Neufchatel cheese, which is lighter than cream cheese but very similar in taste and texture.

Serves 4
Preparation time: 10 minutes

INGREDIENTS

4 tablespoons cream cheese, softened
½ cup Lightened Mayonnaise (page 63) or store-bought mayonnaise
1 clove garlic
½ teaspoon Worcestershire sauce
½ teaspoon dried dill
16 slices white or whole wheat bread, crusts removed
1 seedless cucumber, cut into thin slices
2 red peppers, cut into thin rings

1. Mash the cream cheese with a fork and work in the mayonnaise to make a smooth spread. Press the garlic through a garlic press and add it to the spread with the Worcestershire sauce and the dill. Mix well.

2. Spread the cream cheese mixture thinly on the bread slices. Spread the cucumber slices and red pepper rings evenly over 8 of the bread slices. Top with the remaining 8 slices. Using a serrated knife, cut the sandwiches diagonally into triangles.

Menu Planning

If the main ingredient in the entree (the meat, poultry or fish) is served with a sauce, then the accompaniments should be kept simple and be served without a sauce.

If the main course requires last-minute attention, it is best to serve an appetizer and dessert that can be prepared completely in advance.

In order to balance the meal, try to visualize it in its entirety so that each food has a relationship to its surroundings. A good dinner should have a climax, though this supreme moment may come at the beginning, middle or end of the meal. Arrange the other dishes so that they do not compete for attention.

Neither ingredients nor cooking methods should be repeated in a single meal. For example, if you serve tomato soup, do not have a tomato salad or use tomatoes anywhere else in the meal. Do not serve a broiled appetizer followed by a broiled entree.

Textures are important. Contrast crisp foods with tender morsels. Serve a billowing cloud of soufflé with crusty bread.

Colors should contrast with each other, for part of the joy of eating lies in the visual presentation of the food.

Mashed potatoes, cauliflower and poached chicken breasts (even in a champagne sauce) pale when compared with poached chicken breasts served with a tomato sauce, saffron rice, and firm, freshly cooked green beans.

Menu planning is largely a matter of common sense. A hot pastrami sandwich, splendid after a football game, seems sadly out of place following a graceful evening at the ballet.

To be sure everything runs smoothly, make a timetable. Write everything down. Stick to it and do not try to turn your home into a three-star restaurant.

SHOPPING LIST

white or whole wheat bread
1 lemon
1 cucumber
2 red peppers
garlic
mayonnaise
Worcestershire sauce
Dijon mustard
olive oil
dried dill
cream cheese
plain low-fat yogurt

OYSTER ROLL

An oyster roll is one of the best ideas ever conceived. It is sometimes known as an Oyster Peacemaker, a name said to have been coined late in the last century by a philandering New Orleans husband who customarily brought home a freshly made oyster roll to calm the storms of his perpetually angry wife. In its original version the oysters were deep fried. In this recipe they are pan fried. Be careful not to overcook them and be sure the oil is nice and hot before adding the oysters to the pan in order to prevent it from seeping in. If the oysters are well chilled before frying, they remain plump and juicy.

Serves 4 to 6
Preparation time: 25 minutes plus chilling
Cooking time: 25 to 30 minutes

```
••••••••••••••••••••••••••••••
•                                    •
•          SHOPPING LIST             •
•                                    •
•        1 qt. shucked oysters       •
•    2 12-in. French or Italian bread •
•         2 large tomatoes           •
•            1 lemon                  •
•            lettuce                  •
•           cornmeal                  •
•          mayonnaise                 •
•         Dijon mustard               •
•         vegetable oil               •
•         Tabasco sauce               •
•           gherkins                  •
•       pitted green olives           •
•         anchovy paste               •
•          low-fat milk               •
•             eggs                    •
•       butter or margarine           •
•       plain low-fat yogurt          •
•                                    •
••••••••••••••••••••••••••••••
```

INGREDIENTS

Tartar Sauce:
1 cup Lightened Mayonnaise (page 63) or
   store-bought mayonnaise
1 tablespoon finely chopped scallions
2 tablespoons chopped gherkins
1 tablespoon chopped, pitted green olives
1 teaspoon anchovy paste
2 teaspoons lemon juice
Tabasco sauce

Sandwich:
2 12-inch loaves French or Italian bread
2 to 3 tablespoons melted butter or
   margarine, optional
4 eggs
1 cup low-fat milk
$\frac{1}{2}$ teaspoon Tabasco sauce
$\frac{1}{4}$ teaspoon freshly ground pepper
1 teaspoon salt
$1\frac{1}{2}$ cups very fine cornmeal
1 quart shucked oysters, drained
6 to 7 tablespoons vegetable oil
2 cups finely shredded lettuce
2 large, ripe tomatoes, sliced
Lemon wedges, for garnish

1. Combine the ingredients for the tartar sauce and mix well to combine.

2. Heat the broiler.

3. Half the loaves lengthwise and pull out the soft inside to leave a shell about $\frac{1}{4}$ inch thick. Process the removed bread in a food processor or blender to make bread crumbs, and set aside.

4. Brush the bread shells with the melted butter, if desired. Broil them 5 to 6 inches from the heat until golden brown.

5. Beat the eggs, milk, Tabasco, pepper and salt together in a shallow dish. Combine the cornmeal and bread crumbs in a wide shallow dish. Dip the oysters in the egg mixture and then roll them in the cornmeal and bread crumbs. Pat the crumbs on so they adhere well. Transfer the coated oysters to a plate or rack and refrigerate for at least 30 minutes.

6. Heat the oil in a heavy skillet. When the oil is hot, carefully put the prepared oysters in the hot oil, 6 at a time. Cook each batch for 2 to 3 minutes until they are golden brown. Drain on paper towels.

7. Spread the top and bottom halves of each loaf with tartar sauce. Scatter the shredded lettuce on the bottom half of each loaf and top with tomato slices. Put the oysters on top of the tomatoes and close the loaves together. Slice into serving portions and serve garnished with lemon wedges and with Tabasco sauce on the side.

Mayonnaise

Use half salad oil and half olive oil for making mayonnaise at home. If you use all olive oil, it has a dominant flavor that limits the mayonnaise's uses.

Homemade mayonnaise will curdle if the oil is added too quickly. Add the oil a little at a time. If it still separates, or fails to thicken, put an egg yolk and a teaspoon of prepared mustard in a small bowl. Use a wire whisk to beat in the curdled mayonnaise, a tablespoon at a time.

Stir mayonnaise into casseroles at the last minute to give flavor and body to a timid sauce. It will not curdle (surprisingly!).

Oysters

According to superstition, oysters should not be eaten in months lacking the letter r in their name (May through August). That's because before refrigeration, oysters would spoil rapidly during these warm months. The superstition has been disproved; now oysters can be eaten all year long, although they are at peak quality in winter and early spring.

When purchasing live oysters, make certain the shells are tightly closed. Closed shells mean the oysters are alive. Refrigerate oysters and make sure they can breathe (store in basket or open paper bag, for example). Use them within a week.

Shucked oysters (out of shell) are packed by the pint, quart, or gallon. Depending on size, a pint of shucked oysters may contain between 20 and 50 oysters. The oysters should be plump and cream colored, and the liquor should be clear. Refrigerate shucked oysters and use them within 2 days of purchase.

CHICKEN SALAD SANDWICH WITH ORANGES AND WATERCRESS

An elegant open-faced sandwich, this is a fast way to use leftover chicken and at the same time have a small evening meal after a seriously large lunch.

Serves 4
Preparation time: 20 minutes

INGREDIENTS

1 cup coarsely chopped cooked chicken
½ teaspoon dried tarragon
2 tablespoons chopped scallion, white part only
¼ cup lightened mayonnaise (page 63)
2 tablespoons plain yogurt
Salt and freshly ground pepper
1 navel orange
1 small loaf Italian or French bread
1 small bunch watercress

1. Combine the chicken, tarragon, scallion, mayonnaise and yogurt in a bowl. Toss thoroughly and season with salt and pepper to taste.

2. Cut the rind from the orange with a sharp knife. Remove all the white pith and membrane from the fruit. Cut the orange crosswise into ¼-inch slices.

3. Split the bread in half lengthwise. Spread the chicken salad on both halves of the bread. Lay the orange slices over the chicken salad and garnish with watercress. Slice into sections and serve.

SHOPPING LIST

cooked chicken
1 small Italian or French bread
scallions
1 navel orange
1 lemon
watercress
mayonnaise
Dijon mustard
olive oil
dried tarragon
plain low-fat yogurt

PISTOU

Here's a thoroughly American rendition of a soup borrowed from the sunny south of France where *pistou* is a thick, basil-based sauce rather like Italian pesto. For the best flavor, make the soup the night before you plan to serve it, adding the corn and rolled spinach leaves when you reheat it. If you do not have the time for such planning, replace about a quarter of the water with canned chicken broth to boost the flavor. For a slightly more sophisticated soup, substitute thin *haricots verts* for the green or wax beans. Toss these tender vegetables into the hot soup a couple of minutes before serving.

Serves 6 to 8
Preparation time: 35 minutes
Cooking time: 45 minutes

SHOPPING LIST

onion
garlic
celery
red potatoes
2 medium summer squash
carrots
1 lb. tomatoes
⅓ lb. green or yellow wax beans
1 ear fresh corn
leeks
basil leaves
chard, spinach, kale or broccoli rabe
pine nuts
canneloni or lima beans
olive oil
Parmesan cheese

INGREDIENTS

Pesto (page 275)
1 tablespoon olive oil
1 medium-size onion, chopped
1 small leek, including 2 inches of the
  green part, chopped (optional)
2 medium-size stalks celery, chopped
2 large red potatoes, chopped
2 medium-size summer squash, either
  crookneck, zucchini or a combination
2 medium-size carrots, peeled
1 pound tomatoes, cored
⅓ pound green or yellow wax beans or a
  combination
10 cups water
1 ear fresh corn, about 1 cup corn kernels
2 cups firmly packed leaves of a leafy green
  such as chard, spinach, kale or broccoli
  rabe
1 cup cooked cannelloni or lima beans

1. Make the pesto.

2. Heat the oil in a large pot over medium heat. Add the onion, leek (if using) and celery and cook for about 10 minutes until softened.

3. Meanwhile, cut the potatoes, squash, carrots, and tomatoes into ⅜- to ½-inch pieces. Stem the beans and cut them into 1- to 1½-inch lengths.

4. Add the potatoes, squash, carrots, tomatoes and beans to the pot along with the water. Bring the water to the boil, reduce the heat and cook gently for 25 minutes.

5. Meanwhile, cut the corn from the cob. Working with 5 or 6 leaves at a time, stack the leaves of the greens, roll the stacks loosely into cigar shapes and cut the rolls into ¼-inch-wide strips.

6. Add the corn and sliced greens to the pot and cook for 5 minutes longer. Add the cannelloni beans and cook for another 5 minutes. Ladle the soup into bowls and top each serving with a spoonful of pesto.

SUMMER VEGETABLE SOUP

Try this pretty green soup hot or cold, just made or leftover from the previous day. It bursts with the fresh flavors of a summer garden, and the pureed vegetables and rice give it so much body you will think it is laden with heavy cream. But there is not a drop!

Serves 4
Preparation time: 15 minutes
Cooking time: 35 minutes

INGREDIENTS

2 tablespoons olive oil
2 tablespoons butter or margarine
1 medium-size onion, chopped
2 medium-size cloves garlic, finely chopped
2 medium-size zucchini (about 12 ounces)
1 cup fresh shelled peas or defrosted frozen peas
$\frac{1}{4}$ pound trimmed green beans, coarsely chopped
$\frac{1}{3}$ cup uncooked white rice
4 cups chicken broth
$1\frac{1}{4}$ cups skim milk, plus additional skim milk if necessary for chilled soup
$\frac{1}{4}$ cup chopped fresh basil
Salt and freshly ground pepper
Plain low-fat yogurt for garnish (optional)

1. Heat the oil and butter in a large saucepan over medium heat. Add the onion and garlic and cook, stirring occasionally, for 5 minutes until softened. Add the zucchini, peas and beans and cook, covered, for 10 minutes. Add the rice and broth and bring to a simmer. Cook, uncovered, for about 20 minutes until the rice is tender.

2. Puree the mixture in batches with the skim milk in a food processor or blender. Return the puree to the saucepan and reheat until simmering. Add the basil and season to taste with salt and pepper. Serve hot or chilled with a spoonful of yogurt, if you like. The soup will thicken when it is chilled, add additional skim milk to get the desired consistency, and add a little more salt and pepper if it is needed.

CHINESE VEGETABLE SOUP WITH TOFU

This is a soup version of a Chinese stir fry. All the vegetables and good Oriental flavor are here, and it cooks in just a few minutes. For a more substantial soup, add two uncooked bonelesss, skinless chicken breasts to the soup with the tofu. If the chicken is sliced into thin slivers, it will take only three or four minutes to cook.

Serves 4
Preparation time: 20 minutes
Cooking time: 20 minutes

INGREDIENTS

1 pound firm block tofu
6 cups chicken broth
2¼-inch-thick slices fresh ginger
2 ounces mushrooms, thinly sliced
2 medium-size carrots, thinly sliced on the diagonal
3 ounces snowpeas, stemmed and halved on the diagonal
3 cups slivered Napa cabbage
8-ounce can water chestnuts, rinsed and sliced
2 scallions, chopped
2 teaspoons low-sodium soy sauce
1 egg, lightly beaten
Salt and freshly ground pepper

1. Cut the block of tofu into approximately ⅜-inch-thick slices. Stack the slices and cut them the short way into ⅜-inch lengths. Cut the lengths in half crosswise to get short, narrow pieces and then set aside.

2. Combine the broth and ginger in a soup pot. Bring to the boil, reduce the heat and simmer for about 10 minutes.

3. Add the mushrooms to the pot and simmer for 5 minutes. Add the tofu, carrots, snow peas and cabbage and simmer for another 5 minutes. Add the water chestnuts, scallions, and soy sauce, bring to the boil and remove from the heat. Slowly pour the egg into the soup in a steady stream, stirring constantly, so that it cooks into feathery wisps. Season to taste with salt and pepper.

TUSCAN TOMATO SOUP

Make this soup when the tomatoes are at their peak of flavor. If a hot soup in the summer does not appeal to you, serve it at room temperature, the way they do in Italy. You will notice that the last step of the recipe suggests that you drizzle extra virgin olive oil over the soup. This is entirely optional because it will add a few extra calories, albeit wonderfully-flavored ones, to the soup.

Serves 4 to 6
Preparation time: 20 minutes
Cooking time: 30 minutes

INGREDIENTS

¼ pound loaf Italian or French bread, thickly sliced
½ cup olive oil
2 medium-size cloves garlic, finely chopped
2½ pounds ripe tomatoes, peeled, seeded and chopped, or 4 cups drained canned Italian tomatoes
1 bay leaf
4 cups chicken broth
2 tablespoons chopped fresh basil or 2 teaspoons dried
Salt and pepper
Extra virgin olive oil, optional

1. Heat the broiler. Put the bread on a baking sheet and toast under the broiler on both sides. Tear the toast into 2-inch pieces.

2. Heat the olive oil in a large saucepan over very low heat. Add the garlic and cook, stirring often, for 5 minutes until the garlic is softened. Add the tomatoes and bay leaf, increase the heat to medium and cook, stirring often, for 5 minutes. Add the broth and bring the mixture to the boil. Reduce the heat and simmer for 10 minutes. Add the bread and cook, stirring, for 5 minutes until thick. Add the basil and season with salt and pepper to taste. Serve the soup hot or at room temperature, drizzled with extra virgin olive oil, if desired.

Olive Oil
Supermarkets and specialty food stores stock a fine array of olive oils. For the majority of cooking needs, a relatively inexpensive brand of olive oil, peanut or vegetable oil will suit most purposes. Expensive oils burn at a low temperature so they are not used for cooking but saved for making terrific salad dressings, for adding to a bowl a pasta or supplying an explosion of last minute flavor to other hot and cold dishes. The simple olive oils are made from the second or third pressing of the olives and lack the strong flavor and deep color of those made from the first pressing. First pressings produce the oils that are labeled virgin and extra virgin and you can certainly taste and see the differences between these and their humbler cousins. They taste strongly of olives and are a dark gold or even greenish color. Buy the extra virgins in small quantities because they do not keep very long and do be sure to store them in a cool, dark place.

SHOPPING LIST
¼ lb. loaf Italian or French bread
garlic
2 ½ lbs. ripe tomatoes (or drained canned Italian tomatoes)
bay leaves
basil (fresh or dried)
extra virgin olive oil
chicken broth

ROASTED VEGETABLE SOUP WITH POTATOES

For this soup, an assortment of vegetables is cooked, without liquid, over direct heat to accentuate their individual flavors. Once roasted, they are pureed and thinned with broth and milk.

Serves 4 to 6
Preparation time: 20 minutes
Cooking time: 40 minutes

INGREDIENTS

1 large onion, coarsely chopped
2 medium-size carrots, peeled and coarsely chopped
1 medium-size turnip, peeled and coarsely chopped
1 large leek, white and light green parts only, coarsely chopped
2 tablespoons unsalted butter or margarine
1 large potato, peeled and cut into $\frac{1}{2}$-inch pieces
1 stalk celery, thinly sliced
6 cups chicken broth
$\frac{1}{2}$ teaspoon dried thyme
Salt and freshly ground pepper
$\frac{3}{4}$ to 1 cup low-fat milk
2 tablespoons chopped parsley

1. In a medium-sized ovenproof casserole, combine the onion, carrots, turnip, leek and butter. Cook over moderate heat for about 5 minutes, stirring occasionally, until the butter is melted. Decrease the heat to low, cover and sweat the vegetables for about 5 minutes. Uncover the pan, increase the heat to medium and cook, stirring frequently, for 8 to 10 minutes until the vegetables are lightly browned.

2. Add the potato, celery, broth and thyme and season with salt and pepper to taste. Cover the pan and bring the mixture to the boil. Uncover the pan, reduce the heat to low and simmer for 20 minutes until the potato is soft.

3. Pour the soup through a wire strainer into another large pot, reserving the vegetables. In a blender or food processor fitted with the metal chopping blade, puree the vegetables in batches with some of the broth. Combine the puree with the remaining broth and place over low heat. Add sufficient milk to make the desired consistency. Stir in the parsley and serve immediately.

SHOPPING LIST

onion
carrots
1 medium turnip
leeks
potatoes
celery
parsley
chicken broth
butter or margarine
low-fat milk

MUSHROOM BARLEY SOUP

The ribs and veal bone give the soup a rich flavor while the barley adds nourishment. Though the cooking time is fairly long, it takes little time to assemble the ingredients. Cool and chill the completed soup and then skim off the thin layer of fat that will have risen to the surface before reheating it.

Serves 4 to 6
Preparation time: 20 minutes plus soaking
Cooking time: about 3 hours

INGREDIENTS

2 tablespoons vegetable oil
2 carrots, sliced
1 stalk celery, chopped
¼ cup chopped celery leaves
1 small turnip, chopped
1 small parsnip, chopped
1 medium-size onion, chopped
1 bay leaf
6 to 8 parsley stems
1 teaspoon dried thyme
1½ to 2 pounds short ribs
1 veal knuckle bone
Salt and freshly ground pepper
¼ ounce dried mushrooms, either Polish, Shiitake, cepes or porcini, or 1 cup sliced fresh mushrooms
¾ cup hot water
¼ cup medium pearl barley
1½ tablespoons finely chopped parsley

1. Heat the oil in a heavy saucepan or Dutch oven over medium heat. Add the carrots, celery, celery leaves, turnip, parsnip and onion. Cook, stirring frequently, for 7 minutes until the celery and onion are softened. Add the bay leaf, parsley stems and thyme.

2. Put the ribs and veal bone on top of the vegetables, add water to cover the meat and bring to the boil, skimming any fat that rises to the surface. Reduce the heat to low, add salt to taste and cook, covered, for 1 hour.

3. Meanwhile, soak the dried mushrooms in the hot water for 30 minutes. Strain the soaking liquid through a double thickness of cheesecloth and set it aside. Slice the mushrooms and set them aside.

4. After the soup has cooked for 1 hour, add the strained soaking liquid (or ¾ cup hot water if using fresh mushrooms) and the mushrooms. Cook the soup, covered, for 1 more hour.

5. Stir in the barley and cook, uncovered, for 30 to 60 minutes until the meat is very tender. Remove the ribs, veal bone, bay leaf and parsley stems from the soup. Cut the meat from the ribs and the veal bone and cut into bite-sized pieces. Discard the ribs and the veal bone. Skim the fat from the soup. Return the meat to the pan and season to taste with salt and pepper. Sprinkle with the chopped parsley before serving.

SHOPPING LIST

1 ½ to 2 lbs. short ribs
1 veal knuckle bone
medium pearl barley
carrots
celery
turnips
parsnips
onions
1 cup fresh mushrooms (or ¼ oz. dried)
bay leaves
parsley
dried thyme

FISH SOUP WITH PEPPERS

These ingredients make a pleasant light meal but if you want a more substantial soup, add some cooked rice or noodles just before it is served. If you do not have fish broth, use chicken broth or substitute three cups of bottled clam juice mixed with four cups of water.

Serves 6
Preparation time: 15 minutes
Cooking time: 10 minutes

INGREDIENTS

6 cups Fish Broth (page 48)
1 cup dry white wine
1 red pepper, seeded and finely sliced
1 yellow pepper, seeded and finely sliced
1 stalk celery, finely sliced
3 large tomatoes, skinned, seeded and chopped
1 clove garlic, finely chopped
¾ pound cod or haddock fillets, cut into strips
Salt and freshly ground pepper
1 tablespoon chopped chives

1. Combine the fish broth and the wine in a large saucepan and bring to the boil over moderate heat. Add the peppers, celery, tomatoes and garlic and simmer for 5 minutes.

2. Add the fish strips and cook for 5 more minutes. Season with salt and pepper to taste. Sprinkle with chives before serving.

Soup

If you make soup in advance, reheat only the quantity that you anticipate will be eaten. Those soups that contain meats, chicken, fish, vegetables and either rice or pasta will be overcooked if they are reheated two or three times.

Almost all homemade soups can be frozen. The only exceptions are those that contain either egg yolks and cream or tomatoes. Tomato soup has a tendency to separate if it is frozen.

Freeze the soup as soon as possible after it has been cooked to retain the freshness of the taste. It is useful to freeze individual portions of soup. Add additional salt, herbs or other flavorings as some of the taste is lost after freezing.

Store soup in the freezer in zip-lock bags and stack them like pages of a book so they do not take up too much space. Separate the bags with pieces of paper so they dot stick to each other.

SHOPPING LIST

¾ lb. cod or haddock fillets
2 lbs. bones, heads, trimmings from sole, haddock or flounder
1 red pepper
1 yellow pepper
3 large tomatoes
onions
garlic
carrots
leeks
celery
parsley
chives
bay leaves
dried thyme
white peppercorns
dry white wine

CARROT AND LEMON SOUP

T he carrots give this soup a pleasant sweetness which is offset by the tartness of the lemons. Slightly creamy and extremely satisfying, serve it with warm bread or rolls and a green salad.

Serves 4
Preparation time: 10 minutes
Cooking time: 15 minutes

INGREDIENTS

2 tablespoons butter or margarine
4 carrots, coarsely grated
2 onions, finely chopped
3½ cups Vegetable Broth (page 49) or
    chicken broth
Grated rind and juice of 1 lemon
½ teaspoon sugar
1 egg yolk
¼ cup light cream or half-and-half
Salt and freshly ground pepper
½ tablespoon finely chopped parsley or fresh
    dill

1. Heat the butter in a large saucepan over low heat. Add the carrots and onions and cook gently for 3 minutes.

2. Pour in the broth. Add the lemon rind and juice and stir in the sugar. Bring the soup to the boil, reduce the heat to low and simmer for 10 minutes until the carrots are tender.

3. Blend the egg yolk and cream together in a bowl. Slowly stir 3 tablespoons of hot soup into the cream mixture and then return it to the pan. Cook for 2 minutes, stirring constantly, until the soup is thickened. Do not let the soup boil. Season with salt and pepper to taste.

4. Serve the soup garnished with the parsley or dill.

Parsley
Store parsley and other fresh herbs in a covered glass jar in the refrigerator.
It is easier to chop parsley when it is dry. After chopping, wrap it into a ball in the corner of a kitchen towel and run cold water through it to remove sand and grit.
Keep a supply of chopped parsley in a covered jar in the refrigerator to use as a last-minute garnish.

SHOPPING LIST

carrots
onions
turnips
parsnips
leeks
celery
lemon
parsley
bay leaves
thyme (fresh or dried)
cayenne pepper
butter or margarine
light cream or half-and-half
chicken broth (optional)

CELERY YOGURT SOUP

Serve this soup warm or cold. It is pleasant and undemanding and a makes a fast healthful first course.

Serves 2
Preparation time: 5 minutes plus chilling
Cooking time: 25 minutes

INGREDIENTS

1 tablespoon butter or margarine
4 to 5 celery stalks with leaves, cut into small pieces
2 tablespoons finely chopped onion
1¾ cups chicken broth
Salt and freshly ground pepper
¼ cup plain yogurt
1 tablespoon finely chopped fresh dill or parsley

1. Heat the butter or margarine in a saucepan over moderate heat. Add the celery and onions and cook, stirring, for about 2 minutes until softened.

2. Add 1 cup of broth to the pan and bring the mixture to a boil. Reduce the heat to low, cover the pan and simmer for about 10 minutes until the vegetables are very soft. Puree the mixture in a food processor or blender. If using a blender, you may have to puree it in several batches and add a little broth to make pureeing easier.

3. Return the pureed vegetables to the saucepan. Whisk in the remaining broth. Increase the heat to medium and bring the mixture to the boil. Return the heat to low and simmer the soup for about 5 minutes until it is thickened and smooth. Season with salt and pepper to taste.

4. To serve warm, stir in the yogurt just before serving and sprinkle with the chopped dill. To serve cold, first let the soup cool. Stir in the yogurt and dill and chill the soup in the refrigerator for at least 2 hours.

Yogurt
Regular, low-fat or nonfat, yogurt is a marvellous cooking aid that has gained in popularity over the last five or six years. And it is very high in calcium and comparatively low in fat and calories. A cup of plain low-fat yogurt contains about 140 calories as opposed to a cup of regular, which is about 190 calories. Nonfat yogurt has about 115 calories per cup. Use yogurt as you would sour cream—in dips, salad dressings and cold soups or spooned onto baked potatoes. It is a little tangier and not as dense. When combining it with other ingredients, fold rather than whisk. Whisking or stirring tends to thin yogurt.

SHOPPING LIST

celery
onion
fresh dill or parsley
chicken broth
butter or margarine
plain yogurt

OLD-FASHIONED FISH CHOWDER

Small pieces of potato and firm-fleshed fish make this into a soup that generations have enjoyed. If you are lucky enough to have a fish shop in your neighborhood, the fish will be fresher than at any but the most conscientious of supermarkets.

Serves 4
Preparation time: 15 minutes
Cooking time: 25 minutes

INGREDIENTS

1 tablespoon olive oil
1 tablespoon butter or margarine
1 large onion, chopped
2 medium stalks celery, chopped
1 medium clove garlic, chopped
Salt and freshly ground pepper
1 large baking potato, peeled and cut into
    ½-inch dice
1 tablespoon flour
1 tablespoon chopped parsley
2 teaspoons chopped fresh tarragon
1 quart whole milk
1 bay leaf
1½ pounds skinned firm-fleshed white fish,
    such as cod, haddock or tilefish, cut into
    1½-inch chunks
¾ cup frozen corn kernels or from 1 ear of
    fresh corn
2 tablespoons lemon juice

1. In a soup pot, heat the oil and butter over moderate heat. Add the onion, celery and garlic and season with salt. Cook for about 5 minutes until the vegetables are soft. Add the potato and stir in the flour, parsley and 2 teaspoons of tarragon.

2. Slowly stir in the milk, add the bay leaf and bring to the boil. Reduce the heat and cook gently for 15 minutes. Add the fish and the corn and cook for about 5 minutes until the fish has cooked through. Stir in the lemon juice and season to taste with salt and pepper.

SHOPPING LIST
1 ½ lbs. cod, haddock or tilefish
onion
celery
garlic
1 baking potato
1 lemon
parsley
fresh tarragon
bay leaves
1 ear of fresh corn (or frozen kernels)
olive oil
flour
butter or margarine
whole milk

CLAM CHOWDER

Creamy clam chowder, full of tender clams and small pieces of potato, has long been an American favorite. It is as good in the winter as on a summer day served with a tomato salad and a glass of iced tea. It is easy to shuck the clams yourself—pry the shells open all the way and cut out the meat with a small, sharp knife—and buying them in the shells generally assures freshness.

Serves 4
Preparation time: 15 minutes
Cooking time: 30 to 40 minutes

INGREDIENTS

2 pounds clams
1 cup white wine
2 tablespoons butter or margarine
1 small onion, chopped
1 cup bottled clam juice
1½ cups half-and-half
1 pound potatoes, peeled and cut into
   ¾-inch cubes
Salt and freshly ground pepper

1. Wash and scrub the clams under cold running water. Discard any that are not closed.

2. Put the clams in a large pot with the white wine. Cover the pot tightly and put over medium heat. Steam for 4 or 5 minutes, just until the clams have opened. Drain the clams, reserving the liquid, and discard any that have not opened.

Shuck the clams and strain the liquid through 2 layers of cheesecloth.

3. Heat the butter in a saucepan over medium heat. Add the onion and cook for about 5 minutes, until softened. Add the strained clam liquid and the bottled clam juice and bring to the boil. Add the half-and-half and the potatoes and bring back to the boil. Lower the heat and simmer for 20 to 25 minutes until the potatoes are tender. Add the clams and season with salt and pepper taste. Cook just long enough to warm the clams through. Serve at once.

Clams
To open clams, slip the clam knife through the shell on the side opposite the hinge. Release the clam from its moorings so that it will be easier to eat.
If clams are very muddy, soak them for an hour in a bowl of cold salted water. Add 1 tablespoon of salt to each quart of water.

SHOPPING LIST

2 lbs. clams
onion
1 lb. potatoes
bottled clam juice
butter or margarine
half-and-half
white wine

CREAM OF BROCCOLI SOUP

Potatoes

Maine and Long Island potatoes are used primarily for mashing and frying. Use Idaho potatoes for baking and small new potatoes for making potato salad.

If potatoes are peeled in advance, put them in a bowl of lightly salted water in the refrigerator to prevent them from discoloring.

Peel old potatoes and cook in boiling salted water. New potatoes are cooked unpeeled and started in cold water.

An economical soup, this recipe can be used as a pattern for making cauliflower, pea, spinach and other vegetable soups.

Serves 4
Preparation time: 5 minutes
Cooking time: 20 minutes

INGREDIENTS

1 tablespoon butter or margarine
1 onion, finely chopped
4 cups chicken broth
2 medium-size potatoes, peeled and diced
1 pound cooked frozen or fresh broccoli florets
½ cup half-and-half
Salt and freshly ground pepper

Broccoli Flowerets and Stems

To make broccoli "flowerets," place a bunch of broccoli on your cutting board. Using a chef's knife, cut across broccoli, leaving about 2 in. of stems attached to flowered tops. Cut tops into small bunches of bite-size "flowerets."

Save the broccoli stems for other uses. They can be sliced crosswise into coins, to be used raw in tossed salads or on a tray with other vegetables for dips. Broccoli coins can also be microwaved on high for 6 minutes per lb. and served as a hot vegetable.

Another way to prepare stems is to grate them, using the shredding blade in a food processor or the large side of a hand grater. They can be used raw this way in salads, or microwaved in combination with other vegetables.

Broccoli stems can also be cut into pieces and microwaved to serve as a hot, green vegetable. For 2 cups broccoli pieces, place in a 1-qt. casserole dish with 2 Tbsp water. Cover with lid or plastic wrap and microwave on high for 4 to 5 minutes, or until tender. Broccoli pieces are also good in soup.

1. Heat the butter and cook the onion over low heat for 5 minutes until softened. Add the broth and potatoes. Cover and simmer for 15 minutes until the potatoes are tender. Add the broccoli florets and continue cooking for 5 to 8 minutes until just tender, if fresh, or for 3 to 4 minutes until softened, if frozen.

2. Puree the soup in a food processor or blender and return to the saucepan. If using a blender, you may have to puree the mixture in several batches. Add the half and half. Season with salt and pepper and continue cooking gently until the soup is hot. Do not allow the soup to boil.

SHOPPING LIST

onion
potatoes
broccoli (fresh or frozen)
chicken broth
butter or margarine
half-and-half

GAZPACHO

2. Stir in the ground almonds and the chicken broth and transfer to a serving bowl or tureen. Cover the bowl and chill the soup for at least 2 hours.

3. Season the soup with salt and pepper to taste. Sprinkle with chopped parsley before serving.

In its native Spain, gazpacho is often served with small bowls of chopped salad vegetables and hard-cooked eggs as a garnish. Sometimes cubes of bread are added instead of bread crumbs. The soup requires no cooking and it is good to keep a crock of it in the refrigerator throughout the summer. Each batch will last about three days.

Serves 4
Preparation time: 15 minutes plus chilling

INGREDIENTS

2 tablespoons bread crumbs
1 clove garlic, peeled
1 tablespoon red wine vinegar
4 tablespoons olive oil
1 green pepper, seeded, ribs removed and
    quartered
1 small onion, quartered
2 large tomatoes, peeled and seeded
½ cucumber, peeled and quartered
1 tablespoon ground almonds
1 cup chicken broth
Salt and freshly ground pepper
2 tablespoons finely chopped parsley

1. Put the bread crumbs, garlic, vinegar, olive oil, green pepper, onion, tomatoes and cucumber in a food processor or blender and process until smooth.

Tomatoes
The best tomatoes are the vine-ripened garden fruits available in much of the country only in the late summer. These are characteristically a deep red, although some strains are golden colored. As far as flavor, no other tomatoes compare. Hydroponic tomatoes are usually a good choice in the off-season although they can be pretty pricey, and small cherry tomatoes are often flavorful and juicy during those months when other tomatoes are not. Otherwise, buy Italian plum tomatoes if you want fresh tomatoes. Canned tomatoes, particularly canned plum tomatoes, are a good substitute and we suggest buying these rather than the sorry, taste-less "fresh" tomatoes sold during the winter, which most likely were picked green and left to turn red in chemically treated cold rooms.

When you get tomatoes home, do not refrigerate them. If necessary, leave them out on the kitchen counter or window sill to deepen in color and ripen even further. Most tomatoes, with the exception of the ones you pick from the garden in August, benefit from a few days on the counter.

SHOPPING LIST

1 green pepper
onion
2 large tomatoes
1 cucumber
parsley
garlic
red wine vinegar
olive oil
chicken broth
almonds
bread crumbs

MINTED PEA SOUP

The combination of mint and peas makes a lovely fresh taste. This soup is especially good in the spring when the first young peas and fresh mint appear in the garden and the stores.

Serves 6
Preparation time: 10 minutes
Cooking time: 15 to 20 minutes

INGREDIENTS

2 tablespoons butter or margarine
1 small head Boston lettuce, shredded
1 medium-size onion, chopped
2 teaspoons finely chopped parsley
2 stalks celery with leaves, chopped
4 cups chicken broth
2 teaspoons dried mint
2 10-ounce packages frozen peas
1 cup plain yogurt
Salt and freshly ground pepper
1 tablespoon chopped fresh mint

1. Heat the butter in a large skillet. Add the shredded lettuce, onion, parsley and celery and cook gently for 5 to 7 minutes until tender but not browned. Remove from the heat and gradually stir in 2½ cups of the chicken broth and the dried mint.

2. Reserve 1 cup of frozen peas and stir the rest into the broth. Cover and simmer until the peas are very soft. Puree in a food processor or blender until smooth. You may have to puree the soup in several batches if using a blender.

3. Cook the reserved cup of peas in the remaining broth until just tender. Add the peas and broth to the puree. Stir in the yogurt.

4. Return the soup to the pan and reheat gently but do not allow to boil. Season with salt and pepper to taste. Serve warm or chilled, garnished with the chopped fresh mint.

Using Fresh Parsley
You may not be able to locate other fresh herbs, but you can always find bright green parsley in the produce section of the supermarket, either curly or flat-leaved. By itself, parsley has many uses, but it can also be used as a stand-in for other fresh herbs which may not be in season. Combine it with nearly any dried herb to make a passable substitute for the fresh variety. It will not replace the fresh flavor, but will add color and texture to a dish. Combine one tablespoon of chopped parsley and one teaspoon of a dried herb for every tablespoon of fresh herbs called for in the recipe.

SHOPPING LIST

Boston lettuce
onion
parsley
celery
fresh mint
dried mint
2 10-oz. pkgs. frozen peas
chicken broth
butter or margarine
plain yogurt

RED AND GREEN PEPPER SOUP WITH SCALLOPS

A light, delicate soup, this should be made at the very last minute to retain the bright color and crisp texture of the peppers. If you cannot find bay scallops, substitute the larger sea scallops and cut them into small pieces.

Serves 4
Preparation time: 10 minutes
Cooking time: 15 minutes

INGREDIENTS

4 cups chicken broth
6 shallots or 12 scallions, thinly sliced
1 red pepper, seeds and ribs removed, diced
1 green pepper, seeds and ribs removed, diced
$\frac{1}{2}$ pound bay scallops
$\frac{1}{4}$ cup chopped fresh chives or 2 tablespoons finely chopped parsley

1. Heat the broth in a large saucepan. Add the shallots and peppers and simmer for 10 minutes until almost tender.

2. Add the scallops and poach gently for 3 minutes. Garnish with chives or parsley before serving.

Scallops
The most readily available scallops are sea scallops, which are brawnier and slightly less tender than their cousins from the bay. Atlantic sea scallops have a longer season and a larger spawning ground than do bay scallops and therefore find their way to more markets. If you come across sweet-tasting bay scallops—and the best come from the cold waters off Long Island—please try them. They are tiny, no bigger than the top joint of a finger, will look pearly white and smell fresh and sweet. Sea scallops, too, should gleam white and both ought to glisten with moisture. Buy scallops on the day you plan to cook them, keep them in the refrigerator until suppertime and then be very careful not to overcook.

SHOPPING LIST

$\frac{1}{2}$ lb. bay scallops
shallots or scallions
1 red pepper
1 green pepper
fresh chives or parsley
chicken broth

FRENCH ONION SOUP

If you have forgotten how absolutely delicious hot onion soup tastes with its succulent strings of partially melted cheese, make this recipe as soon as you can. Toss a green salad and set it with the soup before your family. You will immediately be transported to a tiny cafe on a back street in Paris. *Bon appetit!*

Serves 4
Preparation time: 5 minutes
Cooking time: 6 minutes

INGREDIENTS

3 tablespoons butter or margarine
2 cups sliced onions
2 14½-ounce cans beef broth
3 beef bouillon cubes
4 slices melba toast
4 tablespoons freshly grated Parmesan
   cheese

1. Put the butter in a 2-quart microwave-safe casserole. Microwave on High (100 percent) for 30 seconds until the butter is melted.

2. Add the onions to the casserole and stir to coat them with the melted butter. Cover and microwave on High (100 percent) for 5 to 6 minutes until the onions are soft. Add the beef broth and the bouillon cubes. Cover again and microwave on High (100 percent) for 5 to 7 minutes, stirring after 2½ to 3 minutes, until the soup is heated through.

3. Pour the soup into 4 microwave-safe soup bowls. Lay 1 slice of melba toast on top of each serving and sprinkle with 1 tablespoon of Parmesan. Microwave on High (100 percent) for 2½ to 3 minutes, until the cheese melts.

Melba Toast
To make Melba toast, toast sliced bread and cut each slice in half vertically. Arrange the halves with the soft sides facing the broiler and broil until lightly browned.

Onions
Cut a cross in the root end of whole onions so that they will cook evenly and the center will not fall from the outer part.
To glaze onions and carrots, sauté them in hot butter and sprinkle them with a teaspoon or two of granulated sugar.

Canned Bouillon
To remove excessive sweetness from canned bouillon and beef broth, simmer it for 5 minutes with a little chopped onion, garlic and celery. Do not add carrots

---

SHOPPING LIST

onions
2 14 ½-oz. cans beef broth
beef bouillon cubes
melba toast
butter or margarine
Parmesan cheese

FISH BROTH

Homemade fish broth is easily prepared and adds a good flavor to fish soups. Any leftover broth may be stored in a covered container in the refrigerator for up to two days, or in the freezer for up to a month. Ask your fish store for the fish bones, heads and trimmings you need. They are free for the asking.

Makes about 1½ quarts
Preparation time: 15 minutes
Cooking time: 35 minutes

INGREDIENTS

2 pounds bones, heads and trimmings from
    non-oily white fish such as sole, haddock
    or flounder, rinsed
1 medium-size onion, sliced
1 carrot, sliced
1 leek, sliced, or 1 medium-size onion
1 celery stalk, sliced
6 parsley stems
½ teaspoon dried thyme
1 bay leaf
6 white peppercorns
1 cup white wine
Water

1. Break up the fish bones, chop the trimmings, if necessary, and put them in a large saucepan. Add the remaining ingredients and enough cold water to cover. Bring to the boil over high heat and skim any foam that rises to the surface. Reduce the heat to low and simmer, partially covered, for 30 minutes.

2. Pour through a fine strainer and use the broth as required.

> *Flatfish*
> Flounder is the flatfish sold in the U.S. The term "flounder" encompasses the fishes we know as sole, fluke, halibut, plaice, sand dab and turbot, as well as what we actually call flounder. For most uses, these fish can be substituted for each other in recipes calling for any of them. Flatfish swim near the floor of the ocean along our coastlines and are among the most familiar and widely available fish in the markets. They are rarely sold whole—you most likely will purchase them as practically boneless fillets. Their mild flavor and flaky texture suit them for a number of preparations, often those involving sauces, fillings and/or gentle, quick cooking.

> **SHOPPING LIST**
> *2 lbs. bones, heads and trimmings from sole,*
> *haddock or flounder*
> *onions*
> *carrots*
> *celery*
> *leeks*
> *parsley*
> *white peppercorns*
> *dried thyme*
> *bay leaves*
> *white wine*

VEGETABLE BROTH

Keep some of this broth on hand; it freezes very well and will last for a month or more. Have the broth instead of tea or coffee or use it as the base for other soups.

Makes 5 to 6 cups
Preparation time: 10 minutes
Cooking time: 1 to 1½ hours

INGREDIENTS

2 tablespoons butter or margarine
2 onions, finely chopped
2 to 3 carrots, finely chopped
1 turnip, finely chopped
1 parsnip, finely chopped
1 leek, finely chopped
2½ cups finely chopped celery, stalks and
  leaves
⅛ teaspoon cayenne pepper
Salt and freshly ground pepper
6 cups water
1 bouquet garni consisting of 3–4 sprigs
  parsley, ½ bay leaf and 2 sprigs fresh
  thyme or 1 teaspoon dried thyme, tied in
  cheesecloth

1. Heat the butter in a large saucepan or stock pot over low heat. Add the onions and cook, stirring, for 2 to 3 minutes until softened.

2. Add the chopped carrots, turnip, parsnip, leek and celery. Stir in the cayenne and season with salt and pepper to taste. Add the water and the bouquet garni. Bring to the boil, partially cover the pan and reduce the heat to low. Simmer the broth for 1 to 1½ hours until the vegetables are very tender.

3. Pour the broth through a strainer, pressing the cooked vegetables to extract as much liquid as possible. Chill the broth and skim off any fat before using.

Leeks
When washing leeks, cut off the root and the upper two-thirds of the green stem. Make a cut about 3 inches from the root and draw the knife to the top of the leaves. Bisect the leaves in the opposite direction. By separating the leaves you will be able to wash away the sand more easily.

SHOPPING LIST

onions
carrots
turnips
parsnips
leeks
celery
bay leaves
fresh thyme
parsley
cayenne pepper
butter or margarine

POTATO APPLE SOUP

Potatoes and dill, enlivened with a tart apple, seem made for each other in this delicately flavored soup, which may be served hot on a cold, autumn evening, or refreshingly chilled on a summer afternoon.

Serves 4
Preparation time: 15 minutes
Cooking time: 20 to 25 minutes

INGREDIENTS

1 cup chopped onions
¼ cup sliced celery
1 pound potatoes, peeled and cut into
　½-inch slices
1½ cups chicken broth
1 tart apple, finely chopped
¼ cup finely chopped fresh dill
1 cup light cream or half-and-half
Salt and freshly ground pepper

1. Combine the onion and celery in a large casserole. Cover and microwave on High (100 percent) for 4 to 5 minutes or until the onion is soft.

2. Add the potatoes and broth and microwave, covered, on High (100 percent) for 14 to 15 minutes or until the potatoes are tender, stirring once. Add the chopped apple and let the mixture stand, covered, for 5 minutes.

3. Puree the mixture in a blender or food processor until smooth. Stir in the dill and cream and season with salt and pepper to taste.

4. Microwave for 2 to 3 minutes on High (100 percent). Serve the soup immediately or let it chill.

Hearty Homemade Soups
　The best utensil for microwaving soup is either a 2-qt. glass batter bowl or a 4-qt. microwave-safe simmer pot.
　Since soups microwave from all sides (instead of from the bottom only, as in stovetop cooking), it is rarely necessary to stir except to redistribute ingredients midway through cooking to promote even heating.
　If you are thickening a soup base with flour, however, you will need to use a wire whisk to blend the ingredients once or twice.
　If you do not need the soup immediately, flavors will have more time to blend and develop if you make the soup the day before. When soup has been refrigerated, it is also very easy to skim any fat which rises to the surface.
　When reheating soup, stir it first. (Liquids which have been standing for a time may erupt due to a lack of air within.) Outer edges of the soup will reheat more quickly than the center, so you should also stir once or twice during reheating.
　Cover soup to speed reheating. A cup of broth will reheat in about 2 minutes on high. For the same amount of a cream-based soup, reheat on 70% (medium-high) for 2½ minutes.

SHOPPING LIST

onions
celery
1 lb. potatoes
1 tart apple
fresh dill
chicken broth
light cream or half-and-half

CREAM OF SPINACH SOUP

Fresh spinach, easy to find in the markets all year long, is often quite sandy and gritty. To wash it, fill the sink or a large bowl with cold water and soak the leaves for 5 or 10 minutes. Lift them out and cut or snap off the tough stems. Put the trimmed leaves in a colander, rinse them again with cold water, and let them drain in a colander. For this recipe, do not worry if the leaves are not completely dry when you add them to the pan. The water clinging to the spinach will help steam it.

Serves 4
Preparation time: 5 minutes
Cooking time: 20 minutes

INGREDIENTS

1 pound fresh spinach
2 tablespoons butter or margarine
1 quart hot chicken broth
Freshly grated nutmeg
Salt and freshly ground pepper
½ cup light cream
2 tablespoons finely chopped parsley

1. Wash the spinach thoroughly. Remove and discard the stems and roughly chop the leaves.

2. Heat the butter in a large saucepan and add the spinach. Cover the pan and cook over low heat for 7 to 8 minutes, stirring frequently, until wilted.

3. Slowly stir in the hot broth. Season with nutmeg, salt and pepper to taste and cook, stirring constantly, until the soup starts to thicken. Simmer for 3 minutes.

4. Pour the soup into a food processor or blender and process until smooth. Return the soup to the pan. Stir in the cream and heat through. Do not allow the soup to boil. Sprinkle the soup with the chopped parsley before serving.

Freezing

When freezing foods in jars or rigid containers, allow ½ inch headspace to permit expansion.

Freeze liquid preparations such as soups and sauces in plastic freezer bags and stack them in the freezer like the pages of a book; they will take up less space than when packed in boxes.

Make sauces that will be frozen slightly thinner than usual as there will be some loss of liquid in the freezer.

Keep a current list of all the foods in the freezer—or some may get lost and forgotten.

Defrost meats and poultry in the refrigerator to allow them to thaw slowly. If time does not permit this, rub the meat's surface with oil to prevent excess loss of moisture and leave it to defrost in a colander placed in the kitchen sink.

SHOPPING LIST

1 lb. fresh spinach
parsley
freshly grated nutmeg
chicken broth
butter or margarine
light cream

SALADS AND SALAD DRESSINGS

During the last decade, the humble salad has been elevated to a glorious culinary height. A lighter, leaner style of cooking swept through restaurant and home kitchens alike, stirring up the salad bowl with delicious whimsy. All at once, the options for main course salads went far beyond chef's salads and tuna salad platters; side salads became small masterpieces of taste, texture and color. Unfamiliar lettuces with exotic sounding names began appearing in specialty stores and then in supermarkets, and while red leaf, bibb, mache and raddichio had been around for years, they finally were available to more than a few avid gardeners.

In this chapter we have assembled a bright jumble of salads. Some could be main courses, others are clearly side dishes. We also have recipes for salad dressings you could try with your favorite mixture of fresh greens. These, we hope, will be particularly useful as throughout the book we frequently suggest serving a lightly dressed green salad to accompany a main course. As a rule, we suggest light vinaigrettes, such as the Balsamic Vinaigrette or Mustardy Red Wine Vinaigrette

and soft-leaved lettuces such as Boston, bibb and red leaf. Creamy dressings such as the Curried Yogurt Dressing stand up better to firmer greens such as romaine and spinach. But let your inclinations be your guide.

Beyond traditional green salads, we offer recipes such as an Orange and Avocado Salad—light and refreshing when the weather is warm—a hearty Bulgur and Lentil Salad that will hit the spot when you want something filling, and two cheerful beet salads to add strong color to your table. We have dressed up an old favorite, potato salad, by adding some marinated artichoke hearts, and when you see what we have done to coleslaw, you will have new respect for the cabbage. Many of these salads take well to advance preparation and in fact do well when left to marinate for a day or so in the refrigerator. Others can be put together with foods you have just bought or with leftovers from last night's meal. As you turn the following pages you will surely want to open your kitchen to all incarnations of this new kind of salad tailored for the way we live now.

CHINESE CABBAGE SLAW

Made in a food processor, this slaw is as easy as one, two, three. Chinese cabbage is sometimes called Napa cabbage, but its elongated shape and light green color make it easy to spot, regardless of nomenclature.

Serves 4 to 6
Preparation time: 20 minutes

INGREDIENTS

2 large carrots, trimmed and peeled
½ head Chinese cabbage, cored
3 tablespoons rice vinegar
1 teaspoon sugar
Salt and freshly ground pepper
½ cup vegetable oil
2 tablespoons sesame oil
2 scallions, trimmed and chopped
2 tablespoons sesame seed (optional)

1. Grate the carrots in a food processor fitted with the shredding blade. Leave the carrots in the workbowl. Replace the shredding blade with the medium slicing blade and process the cabbage.

2. In a large bowl, combine the rice vinegar with the sugar. Season with salt and pepper and whisk to combine. Gradually whisk in the vegetable and sesame oils.

3. Add the carrots, cabbage and chopped scallions to the bowl and toss to mix. Chill, covered, until serving time. Sprinkle the slaw with sesame seeds before serving, if desired.

Vinegar

Although considered a staple item to be stored on a pantry shelf, vinegar can spoil. Maximum storage time for cider and distilled vinegars is about 6 months. Since wine and herbal vinegars are less acid, they will last at room temperature only about 2 to 3 months. We recommend storing wine vinegars in the refrigerator to retain optimum quality.

Vinegars should be stored in their own bottles, tightly capped, on a cool, dark, dry shelf. An unopened bottle will last almost indefinitely, but once opened, it is exposed to airborne yeasts and molds. Vinegar may cloud, mold, leave a sediment in the bottom, or grow a jellylike layer on top known as a "mother." The mother is harmless and can be removed by pouring the vinegar through a paper towel-lined tea strainer into a clean jar.

Once a vinegar clouds or shows sediment, use it promptly. Discard it if badly clouded.

SHOPPING LIST

Chinese cabbage
carrots
scallions
sesame seeds
sugar
rice vinegar
vegetable oil

LEMONY CUCUMBER SALAD

Mix this up and keep a bowl of it in the refrigerator for a day or two. Served with lettuce, as directed in the recipe, it makes a great salad at supper but also is a nice accompaniment with a quick sandwich. Be sure to let the cucumbers drain for at least 15 minutes; otherwise they will be too watery and will dilute the good flavor of the salad.

Serves 4
Preparation time: 15 minutes, plus 15 to 30 minutes standing time

INGREDIENTS

3 medium-size cucumbers, peeled
Salt and freshly ground pepper
1 medium-size lemon
$\frac{1}{2}$ teaspoon sugar
$\frac{1}{2}$ cup vegetable oil
3 tablespoons chopped fresh dill
Fresh salad greens, washed and dried

1. Cut the cucumbers in half lengthwise. Using a dessert spoon, scoop out the seeds in the center of each cucumber. Slice the cucumbers $\frac{1}{4}$-inch thick. Put the cucumbers in a colander and sprinkle lightly with salt. Let stand 15 to 30 minutes.

2. While the cucumbers are standing, make the dressing. Grate the rind from the lemon. Cut the lemon in half and squeeze out the juice. You should have $1\frac{1}{2}$ teaspoons of grated rind and 3 tablespoons of juice. In a medium-sized bowl, whisk together the lemon juice, rind, sugar and salt and pepper to taste. Gradually whisk in the oil. Stir in the dill.

3. Rinse the cucumbers briefly under cold running water, drain well and pat dry with paper towels. Add to the dressing in the bowl and toss well to combine. Serve the salad on a bed of salad greens.

Lettuce

If you cut lettuce with a knife, the edges will turn brown. If you tear lettuce leaves, you will bruise them. Whichever method you use, do not prepare salad greens more than 24 hours before they are to be eaten and no harm will come to them.

To remove the core from a lettuce cut a V-shaped notch in the base.

Store washed lettuce leaves in a plastic bag and add two or three wet paper towels. They will keep longer with the towel for company.

SHOPPING LIST

3 medium cucumbers
1 lemon
fresh dill
salad greens
sugar
vegetable oil

POTATO AND ARTICHOKE SALAD

The whole family will love this chunky potato salad. It is so easy to dress up a dish that so often is ordinary fare by using the jar of marinated artichoke hearts in the cupboard and varying the herbs. Basil, rosemary, tarragon, oregano or dill would be great.

Serves 4 to 6
Preparation time: 15 minutes
Cooking time: 20 minutes, plus cooling time if desired

INGREDIENTS

1½ pounds small new potatoes, scrubbed
⅓ cup plain low-fat yogurt, chilled
⅓ cup mayonnaise
2 scallions, trimmed and chopped
¼ cup chopped fresh basil, rosemary, tarragon, oregano or dill, or ¼ cup chopped parsley with 1 tablespoon desired dried herb
2 6-ounce jars marinated artichoke hearts, drained, marinade reserved
Salt and freshly ground pepper

1. Put the potatoes in a medium saucepan, cover with salted water, cover and bring to the boil over high heat. Remove the cover and cook for 15 to 20 minutes until just tender.

2. Meanwhile, fold together the yogurt, mayonnaise, scallions and herbs in a large bowl. Set aside in the refrigerator.

3. Drain the potatoes in a colander and rinse well with cold running water. Drain again and place in a large bowl of iced water for 5 to 10 minutes to cool quickly. Drain again, peel if desired, and slice thickly into the bowl of dressing. Add the drained artichoke hearts and sprinkle with the reserved artichoke marinade. Toss gently and season with salt and pepper to taste. Chill the salad in the freezer for 10 minutes if desired, or serve immediately.

> *Microwaving Potatoes*
> *The best way to determine microwaving time is to weigh your potatoes and multiply by 6 to 7 minutes per pound on high power.*
> *One curious thing about microwaving potatoes is that whole potatoes take less time to microwave than sliced ones. This is because the skin holds in the heat and steam, which speeds cooking. When slicing potatoes for a casserole, don't peel them. Leaving the skin on takes less preparation time and is more nutritious.*

> **SHOPPING LIST**
> *1 ½ lbs. small new potatoes*
> *scallions*
> *fresh basil, rosemary, tarragon, oregano or dill*
> *parsley*
> *2 6-oz. jars marinated artichoke hearts*
> *mayonnaise*
> *plain low-fat yogurt*

BEET, CARROT AND WALNUT SALAD

Food processors make grating raw vegetables a simple task, while in days gone by it was a tedious chore. This colorful, crunchy salad benefits from advance preparation—store the dressed, grated vegetables separately in covered bowls or plastic bags. When it is time to serve, mound the beets on individual serving plates or one large platter and then nestle the carrots in the middle of them. If you have time, roast the nuts in a 350 degree oven for about 10 minutes to heighten their flavor. Spread them out on a baking sheet and stir once or twice during roasting. Let them cool completely before you chop them.

Serves 4 to 6
Preparation time: 15 minutes

INGREDIENTS

3 large carrots (about 12 ounces), trimmed
    and scrubbed
4 medium-size beets without tops (about 14
    ounces), scrubbed
½ cup coarsely chopped walnuts
2 scallions, trimmed and chopped
¼ cup red wine vinegar
1 teaspoon dried tarragon
Salt and freshly ground pepper
¾ cup walnut, olive or vegetable oil

1. Grate the carrots in a food processor fitted with the shredding blade. Put the grated carrots in a bowl or plastic bag and set aside. Rinse the workbowl and grate the unpeeled beets, putting them in another bowl or bag. (Grate the carrots first. If you grate the beets first, the juice could stain the carrots.) Put half of the walnuts and scallions in each bowl and mix.

2. Put the vinegar, tarragon and salt and pepper to taste in a medium-sized bowl and whisk together. Gradually whisk in the oil. Add half the dressing to each bowl holding the vegetables and mix. Cover and chill until serving time.

3. When ready to serve, put the beets on a serving plate. Make a space in the center, mound the carrots in the space and serve at once.

```
SHOPPING LIST

carrots
beets
scallions
walnut, olive or vegetable oil
red wine vinegar
chopped walnuts
dried tarragon
```

SPINACH SALAD WITH CHERRY TOMATOES AND CROUTONS

You make the dressing for this spinach salad right in the serving bowl. What could be easier? The anchovies add subtle richness but their flavor is not overwhelming—your kids probably will never detect them. For stronger anchovy flavor, use three or four fillets. The salad is a filling side dish with soup, simple broiled chicken or fish.

Serves 4
Preparation time: 20 minutes
Cooking time: 25 minutes

INGREDIENTS

1 bunch spinach, about ¾ pound
2 cups cubed, peasant-style white bread,
    ½- to ¾-inch cubes
½ cup olive oil
Salt and freshly ground pepper
2 anchovy fillets, rinsed
1 medium-size clove garlic, finely chopped
Grated rind of 1 lemon
2 teaspoons lemon juice
1 tablespoon red wine vinegar
⅓ to ½ pound cherry tomatoes
1 tablespoon grated Parmesan cheese

1. Stem and rinse the spinach carefully. Drain in a colander and spin dry.

2. Heat the oven to 425 degrees. Toss the bread cubes with 2 tablespoons of the oil on a baking sheet. Sprinkle lightly with salt and pepper.

Bake the croutons for 20 to 25 minutes, tossing occasionally, until golden brown and crisp.

3. Meanwhile, mash the anchovies into a paste on a plate. Add a pinch of salt and the garlic and mash until blended. Transfer mixture to a salad bowl. Add the lemon rind. Whisk in the lemon juice and the vinegar. Slowly whisk in the remaining 6 tablespoons oil until emulsified.

4. Add the spinach to the bowl along with the tomatoes and croutons. Sprinkle with the Parmesan cheese and pepper to taste. Toss before serving.

SHOPPING LIST

peasant-style white bread
spinach
garlic
1 lemon
⅓ to ½ lb. cherry tomatoes
anchovy filets
olive oil
red wine vinegar
Parmesan cheese

ORANGE AND AVOCADO SALAD WITH CITRUS VINAIGRETTE

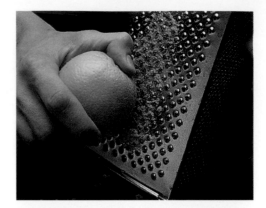

Oranges and avocados team up for a cool refreshing salad which is especially good in the summer.

Serves 4
Preparation time: 20 minutes

INGREDIENTS

2 medium-size juice oranges
1 tablespoon red wine vinegar
Salt and freshly ground pepper
$\frac{1}{3}$ cup olive oil
1 tablespoon chopped fresh basil
5 to 6 cups trimmed and torn greens such
    as arugula, watercress or romaine
1 medium-size avocado, halved, pitted,
    peeled and sliced lengthwise

1. Grate $\frac{1}{2}$ teaspoon orange rind. Cut the remaining rind and all the white pith from the oranges. Working over a bowl to catch the juice, cut the orange segments away from the membrane with a small sharp knife. Squeeze the juice from the remaining membrane into the bowl.

2. In a small bowl, combine the grated rind, 3 tablespoons orange juice, the vinegar and salt and pepper to taste. Whisk in the oil and then the basil.

3. Toss the greens with the orange sections and dressing. Garnish with the avocado.

Watercress
Immerse watercress, leaves down, in a bowl of cold water until you are ready to use them.

Knives

Slice citrus fruits, onions and avocadoes with a stainless steel knife. Carbon steel will cause discoloration.

Use a knife with a serrated edge for cutting bread, cake and tomatoes.

Use a knife with a thin, flexible blade for filleting fish. It is more sensitive than a firm blade and you will be able to reach closer to the bone.

Keep knives on a rack. It is not only dangerous to keep them in kitchen drawers, but sharp blades can be damaged if they are jostled against other utensils.

Avocado

To ripen an avocado, keep it in a brown paper bag at room temperature.

Cut avocados with a stainless steel knife; carbon steel will cause discoloration.

SHOPPING LIST

2 medium oranges
fresh basil
arugula, watercress or romaine
1 medium avocado
red wine vinegar
olive oil

BULGUR AND LENTIL SALAD

2. Put the lentils in a saucepan. Add water to cover by 2 inches and ¼ teaspoon salt. Bring to the boil, lower the heat and cook gently for 25 to 30 minutes until tender. Drain in a colander.

3. Combine the bulgur and lentils in a bowl. Stir in the remaining ingredients and season with salt and pepper to taste.

A satisfying salad and one that is easy to make, this keeps well in the refrigerator for a couple of days. What is more, it is terribly economical. Serve it as a main course on a bed of greens or as an accompaniment to meat or chicken. For a fast and healthy supper or lunchbox meal, stuff it into pita halves and top it with chopped tomatoes and shredded lettuce. The lentils, which are dried when you begin, may take as long as 40 minutes to cook. Just keep checking them for tenderness.

Serves 4
Preparation time: 15 minutes
Cooking time: 30 minutes

INGREDIENTS

¾ cup bulgur
Salt and freshly ground pepper
¾ cup lentils
2 scallions, chopped
1 small clove garlic, finely chopped
1 red pepper, cut into ¼-inch pieces
½ cup loosely packed parsley leaves, coarsely chopped
½ cup loosely packed mint leaves, coarsely chopped
⅓ cup olive oil
3 to 4 tablespoons lemon juice

1. Bring 1½ cups of water to the boil and remove from the heat. Add ¼ teaspoon salt and the bulgur, cover and let stand for ½ hour. Strain in a fine sieve, pressing with the back of a spoon to remove excess water.

Lentils
Dried beans, a category among which lentils figure prominently, are full of protein and nutrients. Cultivated and cooked with since Roman times, they turn up in nearly every cuisine in a variety of guises. Because they are so nutritious (and low in cost), you will surely want to include them in your family's diet as often as possible. Lentils and other dried beans such as navy beans, fava beans and kidney beans, are easy to find in supermarkets and health food stores and once bought keep well in the cupboard.

Before cooking lentils and other dried beans, sift through them to rid them of stones and other harmless debris and rinse them under cold running water. Cover lentils with cold water in a good, deep pot and let the water come to the boil before reducing the heat and completing the cooking. Lentils are fast-cooking dried beans, but other sorts need to be soaked to insure tenderness. To do so, cover them with cold water and leave them on the countertop for several hours or overnight before cooking. Drain and cook in fresh water.

SHOPPING LIST

scallions
garlic
1 red pepper
parsley
mint
1 lemon
lentils
bulgur
olive oil

LIGHTENED MAYONNAISE

1. Lemon Mayonnaise: Add an additional $\frac{1}{2}$ teaspoon of lemon juice and 1 teaspoon of grated lemon rind.
2. Herb Mayonnaise: Add $\frac{1}{4}$ cup of loosely packed fresh herbs (such as sage, parsely or basil), chopped.
3. Lime and Coriander Mayonnaise: Add 1 teaspoon of grated lime rind and $\frac{1}{4}$ cup loosely packed coriander leaves, chopped. A small amount of finely chopped, seeded jalapeno pepper adds zing. Try a quarter of a jalapeno and add to taste; remember that the pepper will get hotter as it sits.
4. Curry or Cumin Mayonnaise: Add 1 teaspoon of curry powder or ground cumin.
5. Garlic Mayonnaise: Add 1 clove of garlic, chopped.

This lightened version of mayonnaise combines yogurt with regular mayonnaise and can be used as you would the "real" thing—on sandwiches, salads and so on. Remember that yogurt may become liquid if stirred, so blend all the ingredients with the mayonnaise before carefully folding in the yogurt. If you have time, drain the yogurt in a fine-meshed sieve or in cheesecloth overnight in the refrigerator. This will thicken it. We have lots of suggestions for flavoring the mayonnaise following the master recipe. These taste good with fish and chicken and mixed into salads.

Makes about $\frac{1}{2}$ cup
Preparation time: 5 to 10 minutes, depending on variation.

INGREDIENTS

$\frac{1}{4}$ cup mayonnaise
2 teaspoons olive oil
1 teaspoon Dijon mustard
$\frac{1}{2}$ teaspoon lemon juice
Freshly ground pepper
$\frac{1}{4}$ cup plain low-fat yogurt

1. Put the mayonnaise in a bowl and stir in the oil, mustard, lemon juice and pepper to taste. Gently fold in the yogurt.

> *Lemon Juice*
> To obtain a small amount of lemon juice, make a hole at one end of the lemon. Insert your thumb to enlarge the hole and squeeze out the required amount of juice. Seal the opening with butter.

SHOPPING LIST

1 lemon
mayonnaise
Dijon mustard
olive oil
plain low-fat yogurt

MUSTARDY RED WINE VINAIGRETTE

A classic dressing, use this on any tossed green salad or spooned over sliced tomatoes and onion.

Makes about ⅔ cup
Preparation time: 5 to 10 minutes, depending on variation.

INGREDIENTS

2 teaspoons Dijon mustard
2 tablespoons red wine vinegar
Pinch of salt and freshly-ground pepper
½ cup olive or vegetable oil

In a small bowl, whisk together the mustard and vinegar and season with salt and pepper to taste. Gradually whisk in the oil—the vinaigrette should be thick and emulsified.

VARIATIONS

1. Substitute lemon juice for the vinegar or use 1 tablespoon of vinegar and 1 tablespoon of lemon juice.
2. Whisk 1 small clove of garlic, finely chopped, into the vinegar mixture, then add the oil.
3. Add 1 tablespoon of finely chopped fresh herbs such as basil, parsley, chives, tarragon or mint.
4. Add 1 teaspoon of finely chopped scallion.
5. Add 1 teaspoon of chopped capers.
6. Add 1 peeled, seeded, and chopped plum tomato.
7. Substitute white wine vinegar for the red wine vinegar.

SHOPPING LIST
Dijon mustard
red wine vinegar
olive or vegetable oil
(for Variations)
1 lemon
garlic
fresh basil, parsley, chives, tarragon or mint
scallions
plum tomato
capers
white wine vinegar

BALSAMIC VINAIGRETTE

Balsamic vinegar is slightly sweet and not as sharp as apple cider or red or white wine vinegars. If you like a vinaigrette with more of a bite, replace one tablespoon of balsamic vinegar with the same amout of red wine vinegar. Vary the flavor of this vinaigrette as you would the Mustardy Red Wine vinaigrette with capers, garlic, scallion, tomato or herbs.

Makes about ⅔ cup
Preparation time: 5 to 10 minutes, depending on variation.

INGREDIENTS

2 tablespoons balsamic vinegar
Pinch of salt and freshly ground pepper
7 to 8 tablespoons olive oil

In a small bowl, whisk together the vinegar and salt and pepper to taste. Gradually whisk in the oil. The vinaigrette should be emulsified although it will not be as thick as the mustard vinaigrette.

SHOPPING LIST
balsamic vinegar
olive oil

ORANGE POPPYSEED AND HONEY VINAIGRETTE

Once you start making this dressing—with orange juice rather than the more expected lemon juice as its base—it surely will become a family favorite. Use it to dress a simple salad of soft lettuce (Boston, red leaf or bibb), orange slices and red onion, or toss it with cold chicken, celery and radishes. For a more intense orange flavor, use two tablespoons of frozen orange juice concentrate instead of the orange rind and fresh juice.

Makes about ¾ cup
Preparation time: 5 minutes

INGREDIENTS

1 medium-size orange
3 tablespoons red wine or cider vinegar
1 tablespoon poppyseeds
1 tablespoon honey
1 teaspoon paprika
Salt and freshly ground pepper
⅔ cup vegetable oil

1. Finely grate the rind from the orange. You should have about 2 teaspoons. Cut the orange in half and squeeze out the juice. You should have about ¼ cup. Reserve 3 tablespoons of the orange juice.

2. In a medium-sized bowl, combine the orange rind, orange juice, vinegar, poppyseeds, honey, paprika and salt and pepper to taste. Gradually whisk in the oil until smooth.

SHOPPING LIST

1 medium orange
poppyseeds
honey
paprika
red wine or cider vinegar
vegetable oil

CURRIED YOGURT DRESSING

Toss this mildly-flavored dressing with cold chicken, tart apples and celery for a crunchy chicken salad. It is terrific with sliced tomatoes or shredded carrots, too, and makes a tasty dip for raw vegetables.

Makes about 1 cup
Preparation time: 10 minutes

INGREDIENTS

2 tablespoons apple cider vinegar
Salt and freshly ground pepper
6 tablespoons vegetable or olive oil
6 tablespoons plain low-fat yogurt
1 teaspoon curry powder
1 tablespoon chopped fresh basil or parsley

1. In a small bowl, combine the vinegar and a pinch of salt and pepper. Whisk in the oil, then the yogurt. Whisk in the curry powder and basil. Taste and adjust the seasonings.

SHOPPING LIST

fresh basil or parsley
curry powder
vegetable or olive oil
apple cider vinegar
plain low-fat yogurt

TANGY CALICO SLAW WITH YOGURT DRESSING

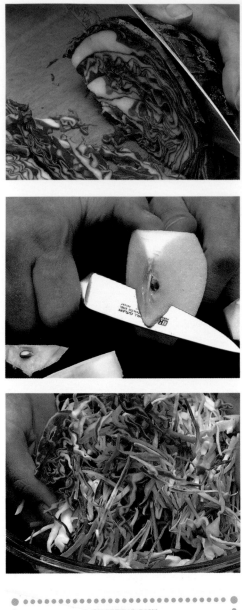

A new twist on a favorite recipe, this coleslaw is made with red and green cabbage as well as tart apples and sweet carrots. And you can mix it up in minutes.

Serves 6 to 8
Preparation time: 20 minutes

INGREDIENTS

½ medium head red cabbage, shredded
   (about 3 cups)
½ medium head green cabbage; shredded
   (about 3 cups)
3 large carrots, peeled, trimmed and
   coarsely grated
2 medium green apples, peeled, cored and
   coarsely grated
⅓ cup chopped fresh chives or 2
   tablespoons freeze-dried chives
¼ cup apple cider vinegar
½ cup plain low-fat yogurt
½ cup mayonnaise
2 teaspoons celery seed
Salt and freshly ground pepper

1. In a large bowl, combine the red and green cabbage with the carrots, apples, chives and vinegar. Toss well to combine.

2. In a medium bowl, fold together the yogurt, mayonnaise and celery seed. Add to the vegetables and toss well. Season to taste with salt and pepper. Serve immediately or cover and refrigerate until ready to use.

SHOPPING LIST

red cabbage
green cabbage
carrots
2 medium green apples
fresh chives (or freeze-dried)
mayonnaise
apple cider vinegar
celery seeds
plain low-fat yogurt

BEET AND ORANGE SALAD WITH BALSAMIC VINAIGRETTE

You may be able to cut back a little on the cooking time if you choose small beets for this recipe. Opting to cook them in the microwave is a good plan, particularly if the day is warm and you do not fancy heating up the kitchen with the conventional oven, or if you need it for another cooking task. However you decide to cook the beets, the final result is a bright, pretty salad bursting with sweet flavor.

Makes 4 to 6 servings
Preparation time: 20 minutes
Cooking time: 45 minutes, conventional; 15 minutes, microwave

INGREDIENTS

2 bunches small beets, tops included
2 medium navel oranges, rind and pith
    removed, cut into rounds
¼ cup balsamic vinegar
¼ cup extra-virgin olive oil
1 tablespoon chopped fresh tarragon or 1
    teaspoon dried
Salt and freshly ground pepper

1. Heat the oven to 400 degrees. Cut off the beet greens, leaving about ½ inch of the stem. Scrub the beets well; wash the greens in several changes of cold water. Cut the stems off the greens, reserving the stems and leafy parts in separate piles.

2. Bake the beets, uncovered, for 30 to 45 minutes until a sharp knife can pierce through to the center. In a microwave, arrange the beets in a circle on a plate and bake at medium-high (70 percent) power for 2 minutes. Turn the beets over and cook for 2 to 3 minutes longer until they are barely tender. Let the beets stand for 5 minutes before proceeding.

3. Rinse the beets under cold water and drain well. Slip off their skins, if desired, and slice the beets into rounds.

4. While the beets are baking, in a large pan of salted water, boil the stems for 5 minutes. Add the leaves and boil for an additional 5 minutes until the leaves and stems are tender. Drain, rinse and drain again.

5. In a medium bowl, whisk together the balsamic vinegar, olive oil, tarragon, salt and pepper until well combined.

6. Arrange the cooked greens around the edge of a medium platter. Arrange the sliced beets and oranges, alternating the overlapping, in a circle on the platter. Sprinkle with the balsamic vinaigrette and serve immediately.

Beets
Do not cut off the stems of beets too closely. Leave at least 1 inch of stem and the root intact or the beets will "bleed" into the cooking water.

SHOPPING LIST

2 bunches beets
2 medium navel oranges
fresh tarragon (or dried)
balsamic vinegar
extra-virgin olive oil

EGGS AND CHEESE

Eggs and cheese are two of the world's most magical ingredients. Alone, they contribute to endless cooking preparations. The egg in particular shows up in recipe after recipe, acting as an emulsifier, binding agent, rising agent, flavorer and colorer. Whole shops are dedicated to cheese and there is hardly a corner of the western world that does not boast of a special local cheese. When the two are brought together in fast, simple recipes, they triumph.

Neither eggs nor cheese are especially healthy foods. Both are high in fat and cholesterol, although new studies reveal that egg yolks contain less cholesterol than originally believed: about 213 milligrams as compared to the 274 milligrams that has been the quoted figure since 1976. Egg whites, by the way, are cholesterol-free. The American Heart Association gives the green flag to three or four eggs a week for the healthy adult and suggests that we substitute low-fat cheeses whenever possible for those with higher fat contents. With this in mind, we have assembled a group of recipes that will, we hope, make your life simpler and provide your family with some truly delicious dishes.

On the following pages are recipes for omelettes, a frittata, a piperade and several cheese dishes. All can be made in a flash. All use easily found ingredients such as peppers, mushrooms, potatoes and fresh herbs—foods that marry so well with eggs and cheese you know how good the dish will taste even before you make it. Keep a good supply of fresh eggs in the refrigerator and stock up on low-fat cheeses as well as a good, hard block of Parmesan for grating. With these ingredients on hand, you will never be at a loss for a quick, last-minute meal that will nourish your family with protein, vitamins and lots of great taste.

Buying and Storing Eggs

Buy the freshest eggs you can find. Some supermarkets stock organic or locally produced eggs and while they may cost a bit more, buy them if you can. Mass produced eggs most likely have already been stored for a week or so before they reach the market, while these other eggs are probably only a few days old. If you know of a local supplier, use it as your source for fresh eggs. You will not be disappointed; fresh eggs really do taste better. Otherwise, check the date on the carton of supermarket eggs and buy those with the latest date.

Do not remove the eggs from the cardboard carton when you get home. Your refrigerator may be equipped with a handy little tray for holding eggs but using it is counterproductive. The carton forms a second shield—the egg shell being the first—which protects the eggs from too much air and accelerated spoiling. Yet the porous cardboard allows the eggs to breathe, which is why it is preferable to styrofoam. Eggs will keep in the refrigerator for three to four weeks, depending on how fresh they were to begin with. You can determine an egg's freshness by checking the white membrane inside the narrower ends of the shell. If it is puffy and firm, the egg is fresh but if it is deflated and shriveled, the egg has been separated from the chicken for quite awhile. Use older eggs for cooking and baking, fresher ones for eating "straight."

FRITTATA WITH PEPPERS AND ARTICHOKES

3. Press the edges of the eggs with a fork so that they are evenly distributed over the bottom of the pan. Spread the artichokes, peppers and parsley over the eggs. Sprinkle with the Parmesan cheese.

4. Put the frittata in the oven for 5 to 8 minutes or until the edges are lightly browned and the cheese has melted. Cut into wedges to serve.

A frittata, an Italian omelette, is simpler to make then a classic French omelette, but like it, is a dressy way to serve what essentially amounts to scrambled eggs. Be sure you have an oven-proof frying pan before attempting this recipe.

Serves 6
Preparation time: 10 minutes
Cooking time: 15 minutes

INGREDIENTS

12 eggs, lightly beaten
Salt and freshly ground pepper
2 tablespoons butter or margarine
3 tablespoons olive oil
8 canned artichoke hearts, drained and
   sliced
2 canned roasted red peppers, sliced
2 tablespoons finely chopped Italian parsley
$\frac{1}{2}$ cup grated Parmesan cheese

1. Heat the oven to 450 degrees.

2. Season the eggs with salt and pepper to taste. Heat the butter and oil in a 12-inch skillet with an ovenproof handle. When the butter foams, add the eggs and stir until they resemble loosely scrambled eggs. Remove from the heat.

SHOPPING LIST

Italian parsley
canned artichoke hearts
canned roasted red peppers
olive oil
12 eggs
butter or margarine
Parmesan cheese

THREE-CHEESE OMELETTE

The three different sorts of cheese give this omelette rich body and a creamy, smooth texture that is apparent when you cut into the folded egg.

Serves 2 to 3
Preparation time: 15 minutes
Cooking time: 5 minutes

INGREDIENTS

4 tablespoons grated mozzarella cheese
4 tablespoons grated Gruyere cheese
2 tablespoons grated Parmesan cheese
4 eggs
3 tablespoons milk
Freshly ground pepper
Freshly grated nutmeg
2 tablespoons butter or margarine
1 tablespoon chopped parsley

1. Heat the oven to 200 degrees. Combine the cheeses and set aside.

2. Lightly beat 2 of the eggs with half the milk. Season with freshly-ground pepper and nutmeg to taste.

3. Heat 1 tablespoon of butter in an 8-inch omelette pan or skillet over high heat. When the butter stops foaming, pour in the beaten eggs. With the flat side of a fork, stir the eggs lightly while shaking the pan gently back and forth.

4. When the eggs have set to the desired consistency, add the cheese. Tilt the pan to fold or roll the omelette over and tip it out onto a warmed plate. Put the omelette in the oven to keep warm while you cook the second omelette with the remaining ingredients.

5. Garnish both omelettes with chopped parsley before serving.

Omelettes
Fillings for omelettes may be hot or cold, cooked or uncooked, but if you decide to have a hot filling, heat it in a separate pan. The cooking time within the folded omelette is so brief that the filling will not be heated through before the omelette is ready to be served.
To improve an omelette's final appearance, brush it with melted butter just before serving.

Cheese
Always rewrap cut cheeses in fresh transparent wrap to exclude the air as completely as possible.
Unless it is a gala occasion, serve only the quantity of cheese you estimate will be eaten. If cheese is left at room temperature for too long it "sweats" butterfat and deteriorates rapidly.
Wrap blue cheeses in cheesecloth drizzled with vinegar or port wine to extend their life. Overwrap them in aluminum foil.
Turn boxed cheeses over onto the reverse side each day or they will sink in the center.
Store Parmesan and other hard cheeses in the vegetable drawer of the refrigerator covered tightly with transparent wrap. The humidity will prevent them from drying and cracking.

SHOPPING LIST

parsley
nutmeg
mozzarella cheese
Gruyere cheese
Parmesan cheese
eggs
milk
butter or margarine

POTATO AND BACON OMELETTE

This hearty supper omelette would taste just right any time of day. If you prefer, wipe the pan clean of bacon fat after the bacon is cooked and add a touch of vegetable oil to the pan to cook the onions and potatoes. Or, you may opt to cook the bacon in the microwave and the vegetables in a pan lightly brushed with oil.

Serves 2
Preparation time: 10 minutes
Cooking time: 15 minutes

INGREDIENTS

4 to 6 slices bacon, cut into small pieces
$\frac{1}{4}$ cup thinly sliced onions or scallions
$\frac{1}{2}$ cup chopped cooked potatoes
1 tablespoon chopped parsley
4 eggs
3 tablespoons milk
Salt and freshly ground pepper
2 tablespoons butter or margarine
1 tablespoon chopped fresh chives

1. Heat the oven to 200 degrees.

2. Cook the bacon over medium-high heat until the fat has rendered. Add the onions and cook until softened. Reduce the heat to medium and add the potatoes and parsley. Cook until the potatoes are lightly browned. Pour off the excess fat.

3. Beat 2 of the eggs lightly with half the milk. Season with salt and pepper to taste.

4. Heat 1 tablespoon of the butter in an 8-inch omelette pan or skillet over high heat. When the butter stops foaming, pour in the beaten eggs. With the flat side of a fork, stir the eggs lightly while shaking the pan gently back and forth. When the eggs have set to the desired consistency, add half the filling. Tilt the pan to fold or roll the omelette. Tip it onto a warmed plate and put in the oven to keep warm while you prepare the second omelette, using the remaining ingredients.

5. Sprinkle the chopped chives over the omelettes before serving.

To Make an Omelette
When making omelettes, be sure the eggs are at room temperature—cold eggs will not cook fast enough at first and the results will be disappointing. Beat the eggs very lightly—just enough to incorporate the yolks and whites. If you overbeat the eggs, the omelette will be heavy. Let the pan and the butter get hot, but not so hot that the butter turns brown. Stir the eggs in a circular motion with a fork, tilting the pan so that they cover the bottom completely. You may want to lift the pan above the burner a little during cooking to keep the eggs from cooking too quickly. When the eggs begin to set, sprinkle or spoon any filling over the surface and cook for a few minutes more. Lift the pan from the heat and tilt it so that the omelette slides right out onto a waiting plate and folds in half as it does so, or fold it in the pan with a gentle push from the fork. If you're making more than one omelette at a time, wipe the pan clean after each one with a paper towel slightly dampened with vegetable oil. While there is no need to have a special omelette pan for good success, make sure the pan you use heats evenly and has a smooth surface so the egg mixture can slide over the surface.

SHOPPING LIST
bacon
onions or scallions
potatoes
parsley
fresh chives
eggs
milk
butter or margarine

73

FRESH HERB OMELETTE

Any fresh herbs are very good in this recipe. Try thyme, tarragon, oregano or sage, for example, rather than parsley and basil. Whatever you select, the marriage of herbs and eggs is always a happy one.

Serves 3
Preparation time: 10 minutes
Cooking time: 10 minutes

INGREDIENTS

6 eggs
1 tablespoon chopped fresh chives
2 tablespoons finely chopped Italian parsley
2 tablespoons finely chopped fresh basil
Salt and freshly ground pepper
3 tablespoons butter or margarine

1. Heat the oven to 200 degrees.

2. Lightly beat 2 of the eggs with half the chives, parsley and basil. Season with salt and pepper to taste.

3. Heat 1 tablespoon of the butter in an 8-inch omelette pan or skillet over high heat. When the butter stops foaming, pour in the beaten eggs. With the flat side of a fork, stir the eggs lightly while shaking the pan gently back and forth. When the eggs have set to the desired consistency, tilt the pan to fold or roll the omelette. Tip it onto a warmed plate and put in the oven to keep warm while you prepare the second and third omelettes, using the remaining ingredients.

SHOPPING LIST

Italian parsley
basil
chives
eggs
butter or margarine

Herbs

Smell herbs and spices to determine their freshness. If there is no aroma, throw them out and buy a new supply. Suppliers claim that herbs and spices should be replaced every six months.

To keep fresh herbs, put them in ice cube trays, cover them with cold water and freeze. When ready to use, melt the cube and you will have "fresh" herbs.

To dry fresh herbs, spread them on a flat surface and leave them overnight in the oven. The heat from the pilot light will be sufficient to dry them. Crumble the leaves, discard the stems and pack in small containers.

To keep the flavor and color of herbs and spices as long as possible, store them in a cool, dark place.

When substituting fresh herbs for dried, triple the quantity.

Iron Pans

To season an iron pan, half fill it with vegetable oil and heat the oil until tiny bubbles appear. Remove the pan from the heat and leave it to stand for 12 hours. Do not wash the pan after use but wipe it clean with paper towels. If there is a particle of food sticking to the pan, use salt as a scouring powder. Omelette and crêpe pans are seasoned in the same way.

MUSHROOM OMELETTE

Here is a classic everybody loves.

Serves 2
Preparation time: 15 minutes
Cooking time: 10 minutes

INGREDIENTS

2 tablespoons butter or margarine
$\frac{1}{4}$ cup thinly sliced onions or scallions
1 cup sliced fresh mushrooms
2 tablespoons chopped fresh chives
Salt and freshly ground pepper
4 eggs
3 tablespoons milk

1. Heat the oven to 200 degrees.

2. Heat 1 tablespoon of butter in a skillet over medium heat. Add the onions and cook until softened. Add the mushrooms and cook until softened. Remove from the heat, add the chives and season with salt and pepper to taste.

3. Beat two of the eggs with half the milk. Season with salt and pepper to taste.

4. Heat 1 tablespoon of butter in an 8-inch omelette pan or skillet over high heat. When the butter stops foaming, pour in the eggs. With the flat side of a fork, stir the eggs lightly while shaking the pan gently back and forth.

5. When the eggs have set to the desired consistency, spread half the filling over them. Tilt the pan to roll or fold the omelette and tip it onto a warmed plate. Put it in the oven to keep warm while you prepare the second omelette, using the remaining ingredients.

6. Sprinkle each omelette with the remaining chopped chives before serving.

Mushrooms
Do not soak mushrooms in cold water or they will become waterlogged. Wipe them clean with a damp cloth.
Save mushroom stems for use in making stocks and broths.
Buy a whole box of mushrooms and sauté them in butter. Freeze them in small batches.

SHOPPING LIST

onions or scallions
mushrooms
chives
eggs
milk
butter or margarine

APPLE AND SPICE OMELETTE

Now, here is a simple way to make an omelette. No fussing with an omelette pan—you make the entire dish in the microwave and fold the eggs, once set, over a slightly sweetened apple filling. As good as this tastes at breakfast, try it, too, for lunch or supper.

Serves 2
Preparation time: 10 minutes
Cooking time: 9 minutes

INGREDIENTS

2 to 3 slices bacon, cut into small pieces
1 small, tart apple, thinly sliced
1 tablespoon honey
Pinch of cinnamon
Pinch of ground nutmeg
1 tablespoon melted butter or margarine
4 eggs, separated
Salt and freshly ground pepper

1. Put the bacon in a small glass bowl and microwave on High (100 percent) for 3 to 4 minutes or until the bacon is crisp. Drain the bacon, discarding the drippings.

2. Combine the apple, honey, cinnamon and nutmeg in a bowl and set aside. Pour 1 tablespoon of melted butter onto a 9-inch glass plate, turning the plate to coat it.

3. Beat the egg whites with a whisk until stiff but not dry. Lightly beat the egg yolks with salt and pepper to taste. Fold the egg whites into the yolks and spoon the mixture onto the glass plate. Microwave on Medium (50 percent) for 4 to 5 minutes until the eggs are set.

4. Loosen the eggs from the plate with a spatula. Spoon the apple mixture over half the omelette and fold over the remaining side. Cover and let stand for 2 minutes before serving.

Eggs
One of the easiest ways to separate an egg is to break it into your (clean) hand and let the white drip between your fingers.

If a speck of egg yolk drops into the egg white, lift it out with an empty egg shell.

To store unbroken egg yolks, cover them with cold water and keep them in the refrigerator. Store leftover egg whites in a covered jar, or freeze them. One egg white weighs 1 ounce.

SHOPPING LIST
bacon
1 small, tart apple
nutmeg
cinnamon
honey
eggs
butter or margarine

PIPERADE

Full of lightly cooked vegetables, a piperade is one of the easiest egg dishes to cook—which is saying something, since most are quite simple. Beware of cooking the eggs too long or too hot once they have been added to the pan holding the vegetables. The piperade looks pretty on a large platter surrounded by sliced tomatoes and roasted peppers, which echo the ingredients cooked with the eggs.

Serves 4 to 6
Preparation time: 20 minutes
Cooking time: 25 to 30 minutes

INGREDIENTS

2 tablespoons olive oil
2 red or green bell peppers, cored, seeded
   and cut into strips.
1 medium-size onion, finely chopped
3 tomatoes, peeled, seeded and chopped
1 teaspoon salt
Freshly ground pepper
1 tablespoon chopped fresh chives
6 eggs, lightly beaten

1. Heat the oil in a 10-inch frying pan or omelette pan. Add the peppers and onion and cook gently, without browning, for 10 minutes. Add the tomatoes, season with $\frac{1}{2}$ teaspoon of salt and pepper and cook for 5 to 10 minutes, stirring occasionally, until the liquid has evaporated.

2. Stir the chives and the remaining salt into the eggs.

3. Set the vegetables over medium heat. When they are hot, pour in the eggs. Stir gently as they begin to cook and then allow to set for about 2 minutes. Transfer the piperade to a warmed serving platter.

SHOPPING LIST
2 red or green bell peppers
onion
3 tomatoes
chives
olive oil
eggs

CHEESE BLINTZES

These crepes, stuffed with a slightly sweet mixture of low-fat cheese, are a good choice when you want to serve a meal that is a little different from the usual meat and potatoes. We suggest them for those evenings you might otherwise consider French toast or scrambled eggs for dinner. Since they freeze very well, you might decide to make some on a rainy day to have on hand for quick suppers, lunches or even breakfasts. Traditionally, blintzes are served with a spoonful of sour cream but you may substitute plain yogurt or dispense with a topping altogether.

Serves 6 to 8
Preparation time: 45 minutes
Cooking time: 15 minutes

INGREDIENTS

Batter:
¾ cup all-purpose flour
¼ teaspoon salt
2 eggs, lightly beaten
⅔ cup low-fat milk
⅓ cup water
Cheese filling:
2 cups dry cottage cheese, farmer cheese or
   pot cheese
1 egg
1 tablespoon sugar
1 teaspoon vanilla extract
¼ teaspoon cinnamon
2 tablespoons butter or margarine
2 tablespoons vegetable oil
Sour cream

1. Combine the flour and salt.

2. Combine the eggs, milk and water, mixing well. Gradually add the flour, beating well after each addition. The mixture should be the consistency of heavy cream. Let the batter sit for about 15 minutes before cooking.

3. Lightly oil a small skillet or crepe pan and heat over medium heat. Pour a thin film of batter into the pan and cook over moderate heat until the edges are lightly browned and crisp-looking. Turn the crepe out onto a clean towel or plate. Repeat the procedure until the batter is used up. You will probably have 14 to 16 pancakes.

4. In a bowl, combine the cheese, egg, sugar, vanilla and cinnamon and mix well. Place about 2 tablespoons of the filling in the center of each crepe. Fold the edges up and over from either side to form small rectangular packets.

5. Place the filled blintzes seam side down in a baking dish and chill until ready to use. (The blintzes may be frozen at this point and kept for several weeks.)

6. Heat half the butter and oil in a frying pan over medium heat. Add 3 or 4 blintzes to the pan, seam side down, and cook until golden brown. Turn and cook the second side. Remove from the pan and keep warm in the oven while you cook the remaining blintzes. Add the remaining butter and oil to the pan as necessary.

7. Serve the blintzes warm, with sour cream.

SHOPPING LIST

flour
sugar
vanilla extract
cinnamon
vegetable oil
eggs
low-fat milk
dry cottage cheese, farmer cheese or pot cheese
sour cream
butter or margarine

MELTED CHEESE AND HAM TOASTS

This toasted cheese open-face sandwich is a far cry from processed cheese on white bread. The ham turns it into a substantial meal, needing only a tangy green salad or cold vegetable salad for accompaniment.

Serves 4 to 8
Preparation time: 10 minutes
Cooking time: 10 minutes

INGREDIENTS

$\frac{1}{2}$ cup grated Emmentaler or Gruyere
  cheese
$\frac{1}{2}$ cup grated Parmesan cheese
3 tablespoons milk
1 egg, separated
1 tablespoon brandy (optional)
8 slices French bread, $\frac{1}{2}$- to $\frac{3}{4}$-inch thick,
  crusts removed
4 thin slices ham, preferably prosciutto, cut
  in half
Parsley or watercress sprigs, for garnish

1. Heat the broiler.

2. Combine the cheese in a bowl. Add the milk, egg yolk and brandy, if desired, and mix well.

3. Place the bread slices under the broiler and toast on one side.

4. Beat the egg white until stiff but not dry, and fold it carefully into the cheese mixture.

5. Place a piece of ham on the untoasted side of each bread slice. Top with the cheese mixture, spread to within $\frac{1}{2}$ inch of the edge.

6. Broil the toasts until the cheese is melted and golden brown. Serve immediately, garnished with the parsley or watercress.

SHOPPING LIST

4 slices ham (preferably prosciutto)
French bread
watercress or parsley
grated Emmentaler or Gruyere cheese
grated Parmesan cheese
milk
eggs
brandy

SCRAMBLED EGGS WITH FRESH HERBS AND PARMESAN

2. Melt the butter in a large skillet over moderate heat. Add the eggs. Fold the eggs over and over with a fork until soft, moist curds are formed.

3. Fold in the cheese and serve immediately. (The heat of the eggs will melt the cheese.)

Simply by adding a handful of fresh herbs and a sprinkling of freshly grated Parmesan cheese, you can turn ordinary scrambled eggs into a super dish fit for lunch or supper. Of course, it is wonderful for breakfast or brunch, too.

Serves 4 to 6
Preparation time: 5 minutes
Cooking time: 5 minutes

INGREDIENTS

8 eggs
Salt and freshly ground pepper
3 tablespoons low-fat milk
1 tablespoon parsley, finely chopped
1 tablespoon chives, finely chopped
1 teaspoon fresh thyme, tarragon or chervil, or
    ¼ teaspoon dried
2 tablespoons butter or margarine
¼ cup grated Parmesan cheese

SHOPPING LIST

1 bunch fresh parsley
1 bunch fresh chives
1 bunch fresh thyme,
tarragon or chervil,
or 1 package dried thyme,
tarragon or chervil
1 stick butter or margarine
1 oz. Parmesan cheese
low-fat milk
8 eggs

1. Combine the eggs with the remaining ingredients except the butter and cheese.

CHEESE FONDUE

Because fondue is prepared in and eaten from a communal pot, it creates an instant camaraderie, and even the most grumpy children (and let's face it, they are sometimes grumpy!) will settle down and enjoy themselves when faced with some bread cubes and melted cheese. Keep the fondue warm at the table on a burner or hot tray and serve it with a bright, fresh salad. The alcohol in the wine cooks off while the fondue heats, leaving behind nothing more than good flavor.

Serves 4
Preparation time: 10 minutes
Cooking time: 10 minutes

INGREDIENTS

1 medium-size clove garlic, halved
1 tablespoon cornstarch
2 cups dry white wine
2 cups (½ pound) coarsely grated Swiss cheese, preferably Emmentaler
2 cups (½ pound) coarsely grated Gruyere cheese
⅛ teaspoon ground nutmeg
¼ teaspoon salt
⅛ teaspoon white pepper
3 tablespoons kirsch
1 loaf French bread, cut into 1-inch cubes

1. Rub the inside of the fondue pot with the garlic and discard.

2. Blend the cornstarch with 2 tablespoons of the wine in a small bowl.

3. Bring the remaining wine to a boil in the fondue pot. Gradually add the cheese, stirring continuously until melted. When the cheese is bubbling, add the cornstarch mixture and cook for 2 to 3 minutes until the fondue has thickened.

4. Season with the nutmeg, salt and pepper. Stir in the kirsch. Serve with a basket of the bread cubes and a fondue fork for each person.

CHEESE, BACON AND EGG PIE

This crustless pie works any time of day, although we especially like it for a weekend breakfast when the whole family lingers over the meal, drinking an extra glass of juice and perhaps a second cup of coffee.

Serves 6
Preparation time: 10 minutes
Cooking time: 30 minutes

INGREDIENTS

2 to 3 slices bacon
$\frac{1}{4}$ cup chopped onion
2 cups plain croutons
1 cup grated cheddar cheese
4 eggs
2 cups half-and-half
$\frac{1}{2}$ teaspoon salt
$\frac{1}{2}$ teaspoon Dijon mustard
$\frac{1}{8}$ teaspoon freshly ground pepper

1. Put the bacon on a double thickness of paper towel on a microwave-safe rack or a paper plate and cover with a paper towel. Microwave on High (100 percent) for $2\frac{1}{2}$ to 3 minutes, until the bacon is crisp.

2. Put the onion in a small microwave-safe dish. Cover and microwave on High (100 percent) for 45 seconds to 1 minute, until soft. Combine the croutons and the cheese in an $8\frac{1}{4}$-inch round microwave-safe dish.

3. Whisk together the eggs, half-and-half, salt, mustard and pepper. Stir in the onion. Pour the mixture over the croutons and cheese. Crumble the bacon and sprinkle it over the top. Microwave on Medium (50 percent) for 20 to 25 minutes, until a knife inserted in the center comes out clean.

Measuring
To obtain accurate measurements, use a glass measure for liquid ingredients and metal or plastic cups to measure dry ingredients such as flour and sugar. Level dry ingredients with a spatula or the edge of a straight-bladed knife.

SHOPPING LIST
bacon
onions
Dijon mustard
croutons
grated cheddar cheese
eggs
half-and-half

SPANISH EGGS

If you have leftover chicken and ham, cook them with eggs for a quick microwave dish that makes a very satisfying supper indeed. A mere half cup of each is all you need to fill up your kids and leave everybody at the table smiling.

Serves 4
Preparation time: 15 minutes
Cooking time: 11 minutes

INGREDIENTS

1 tablespoon vegetable oil
$\frac{1}{4}$ small onion, finely chopped
1 clove garlic, finely chopped
$\frac{1}{2}$ green pepper, stemmed, seeded and finely chopped
$\frac{1}{2}$ cup cooked chicken diced
$\frac{1}{2}$ cup cooked ham, diced
2 tablespoons all-purpose flour
$\frac{3}{4}$ cup chicken broth
$1\frac{1}{2}$ teaspoons chopped fresh basil or $\frac{1}{2}$ teaspoon dried
1 tomato, peeled, seeded and chopped
Salt and freshly ground pepper
2 tablespoons butter or margarine
4 eggs
Parsley, for garnish

1. Combine the oil, onion, garlic and green pepper in an 8-inch glass pie plate. Microwave on High (100 percent) for 1 minute until the onion is softened.

2. Add the chicken and ham. Stir in the flour and add the chicken broth and basil. Microwave on High (100 percent) for 3 minutes. Add the tomato and microwave on High (100 percent) for 1 minute. Season with salt and pepper to taste and set aside.

3. Put the butter in a shallow, microwave-safe dish and microwave on High (100 percent) for 1 minute or until melted. Break the eggs onto the dish and pierce the yolks with a fork. Microwave on Medium (50 percent) for 3 to 5 minutes or until set. Slide the eggs onto the meat and vegetables and garnish with parsley.

SHOPPING LIST

cooked chicken
cooked ham
onion
garlic
1 green pepper
1 tomato
basil (fresh or dried)
parsley
vegetable oil
chicken broth
eggs

POACHED EGGS WITH AVOCADO AND TOMATO

Poached eggs get a Southwestern flavor in this recipe. Warm tortillas would make a terrific accompaniment.

Serves 4
Preparation time: 15 minutes
Cooking time: 15 to 20 minutes

INGREDIENTS

2 tablespoons olive oil
½ small onion, finely chopped
2 cloves garlic, finely chopped
1 jalapeno pepper, seeds and stem removed, finely chopped
3 large ripe tomatoes, peeled, seeded and roughly chopped
¼ cup chopped coriander leaves
1 quart water
2 teaspoons salt
2 tablespoons white vinegar
8 large eggs
2 ripe avocados, peeled and cut into wedges

1. To make the sauce, heat the olive oil in a medium-sized saucepan. Add the onion and cook, stirring occasionally, for about 5 minutes or until softened. Add the garlic and jalapeno and continue cooking for another minute. Add the tomatoes and, when the mixture is very hot, add the chopped coriander. Cook rapidly for 5 minutes. Remove from the heat and keep warm.

2. Bring the water to the boil in a large saucepan or deep frying pan. Add the salt and vinegar. Lower the heat until the water is simmering gently. Stir the water with a spoon so that it forms a slowly swirling whirlpool. Break one egg at a time into a small bowl and slide it into the moving water, creating a new whirlpool for each egg. Lower the heat until there is barely a bubble appearing on the surface. Cook the eggs, uncovered, for about 4 minutes until set.

3. While the eggs poach, arrange the avocado slices on four plates so that they form nests for the poached eggs.

4. Remove the eggs from the pan with a slotted spoon. Place two eggs in the center of each nest and cover with the sauce.

SHOPPING LIST

onion
garlic
1 jalapeno pepper
3 tomatoes
coriander leaves
2 avocados
olive oil
white vinegar
eggs

PIZZAS AND HAMBURGERS

Ask nearly any child what his or her favorite food is and chances are the answer will be pizza and/or hamburgers. Fast food restaurants from coast to coast sell both in astonishing numbers and astounding guises. The Beef Industry Council estimates that every American averages about three hamburgers a week! Surely when you, as the cook in the family, try to make a list of fast and easy meals for the family both pizza and hamburgers are near the top. You might think of ordering out for pizza and tossing a salad to accompany it. When it comes to hamburgers, you will cook them on the grill but stop by the deli and buy potato salad. Either way, you have a simple meal, put together in minutes and always enjoyed.

In this chapter, we take you into the kitchen and away from the take-out store. This does not mean a take-out pizza is not the best solution some evenings, nor do we rule out supplementing a meal of burgers with salads from the deli, but you may want more choices. And here they are.

Once you begin making your own pizza, you will want to continue. The dough is easy to put together and keeps nicely in the freezer. Or, you may opt to buy the pre-made pizza dough sold in the refrigerator section of the supermarket—a fine alternative to homemade. Our pizzas could seem a little dressy, perhaps, if you are not used to the stylish pizzas being made in America's bistros. We are not trying to be clever or fancy. We have discovered that a simple pizza dough is a perfect canvas for any number of marvellous ingredients. The baked pizza pie is fun and easy to eat and the possibilities for experimenting are endless (pizza is a good way to use up leftovers, for instance). But do not worry—we have included a traditional tomato and cheese pizza, calling it Pizza Joint Pizza. The only thing missing is the cardboard box. Our recipes are for two pies each. We figure your family will be hungry enough to finish two off, but if you think one will suffice, cut the ingredients in half or freeze the other pie for later in the month. Heat it, still frozen, in the same hot oven until the ingredients are hot and the cheese, if any, bubbles.

Hamburgers are another story. We offer a couple of traditional renditions and then move on to more adventurous ideas. The Mexican Burger, Oriental Burger and L.A. Burger will please young and old alike and turn an ordinary cookout into something kind of special—with very little effort. What is more, we have four recipes that use ground turkey meat rather than beef. Since it has less fat than beef to melt away during cooking, you need less turkey for the same number of burgers. All our recipes can be made with turkey or lean beef—which, by the way, is allowed by law to contain just over 22 percent fat by weight, even when labeled "lean." The choice is yours. So fire up the grill and tell the kids they're having burgers tonight.

PIZZA PRIMAVERA WITH ZUCCHINI, RED ONION AND FONTINA

This is a robust, thick-crusted pizza laden with vegetables and mild cheese. Delicious.

Makes two 10-inch thick-crusted pizzas or two
   12-inch pizzas
Preparation time: 45 minutes
Cooking time: 10 minutes

INGREDIENTS

Pizza Dough (page 94)
1 pound asparagus
Olive oil
1 pound mixed zucchini and yellow
   summer squash, sliced $\frac{1}{4}$-inch thick
Salt and freshly ground pepper
Cornmeal
1 medium-size red onion, thinly sliced
1 cup grated Fontina cheese
2 tablespoons mixed fresh herbs such as
   parsley, chervil, thyme, chives or
   tarragon

1. Snap off the tough asparagus ends and discard. Bring a large saucepan of water to the boil. Add the asparagus and simmer for 7 to 10 minutes until tender. Drain and cut into 2-inch pieces.

2. Heat 1 tablespoon oil in a large frying pan over medium-high heat. Working in batches, add the squash in a single layer and cook for 3 to 4 minutes per batch until tender and lightly browned on both sides. Add more oil as needed. Sprinkle the squash lightly with salt and pepper.

3. Heat the oven to 500 degrees. Oil 2 baking sheets and sprinkle lightly with cornmeal. Divide the dough into 2 pieces on a lightly floured work surface. Shape each into a ball and flatten each ball into a 10-inch round. Transfer the rounds to the baking sheets. Sprinkle each with half of the onion and $\frac{1}{2}$ cup cheese. Spread the squash and asparagus over the cheese and bake the pizzas for about 10 minutes until the crusts are golden brown. Sprinkle with the herbs.

SHOPPING LIST

1 lb. asparagus
1 lb. mixed zucchini and yellow summer squash
1 red onion
parsley, chervil, thyme, chives or tarragon
olive oil
unbleached all-purpose flour
cornmeal
1 pkg. active dry yeast
sugar
Fontina cheese

PIZZA WITH ONIONS, OLIVES AND ROSEMARY

The olives and anchovies do well on a pizza with a thick crust, as its mild flavor balances their saltiness. The same amount of dough as called for in the recipe for Pizza Dough makes thick-crusted 10-inch pizzas. However, you might prefer the thinner crusts of the 12-inch pies, which is just fine.

Makes two 10-inch thick-crusted pizzas or two
    12-inch pizzas
Preparation time: 45 minutes
Cooking time: 10 minutes

INGREDIENTS

2-ounce can anchovy fillets, drained and
    rinsed
3 tablespoons olive oil
2 pounds onions, thinly sliced
1 teaspoon dried rosemary
Salt and freshly ground pepper
Cornmeal
Pizza Dough (page 94)
½ cup pitted and halved Kalamata olives
2 tablespoons chopped basil

1. Combine the anchovies with the oil in a large frying pan over low heat and mash to a paste. Add the onions and rosemary, increase the heat to medium and cook for about 25 minutes, stirring occasionally, until the onions are very tender. Increase the heat to high and cook for 5 to 10 minutes, stirring often, until the liquid evaporates and the onions are golden brown. Stir in salt and pepper to taste.

2. Heat the oven to 500 degrees. Oil 2 baking sheets and sprinkle lightly with cornmeal. Divide the dough into 2 equal pieces on a lightly floured work surface. Shape each piece into a ball and flatten each ball into a 10-inch round. Transfer the rounds to the baking sheets and spread each with half of the onions. Sprinkle the olives over the onions and bake the pizzas for about 10 minutes until the crusts are golden brown. Sprinkle with basil before serving.

Olives
Cover olives with water or oil to prevent them from drying out in the refrigerator.

Pizza-Making Tips
The order in which the ingredients are put on the dough make a difference. The cheese sprinkled over more fragile ingredients such as tomatoes and mushrooms acts as a barrier, holding in the moisture. It is important to give the oven plenty of time to heat up. A hot oven is essential to a good crust. Pizza stones, which are unglazed pottery tiles sold in kitchenware shops, insure that the crust will be crispy. The pizza is cooked directly on the stones, which turn your oven into a suitable replica of a pizza parlour oven. If you think you might make pizza often, consider buying the stones as well as a long-handled wooden pizza paddle to slide the pies in and out of the hot oven.

SHOPPING LIST

onions
basil
dried rosemary
Kalamata olives
2-oz. can anchovy filets
olive oil
cornmeal
unbleached all-purpose flour
1 pkg. active dry yeast
sugar

PIZZA WITH EGGPLANT, PEPPERS AND FETA CHEESE

Your children will think it's fun to have their own mini pizzas rather than the usual slices of a large pie. If the children are young, one of these will probably feed two or three of them. Vary the topping on these little pizzas, following our instructions for cooking times.

Serves 4 (makes 4 individual pizzas)
Preparation time: 45 minutes
Cooking time: 10 minutes

INGREDIENTS

7-ounce jar roasted red peppers
Olive oil
$\frac{1}{4}$ pound tomatoes, cored, seeded and chopped
1 medium-size clove garlic, chopped
$\frac{3}{4}$ teaspoon fresh thyme or $\frac{1}{4}$ teaspoon dried
Salt and freshly ground pepper
1 large eggplant, $1\frac{1}{2}$ to $1\frac{3}{4}$ pounds, cut lengthwise into $\frac{1}{2}$-inch-thick slices
Cornmeal
Pizza Dough (page 94)
1 small red onion, thinly sliced
$\frac{1}{2}$ cup crumbled feta cheese
2 tablespoons chopped parsley

1. Drain and rinse the peppers. Cut into wide strips and toss with 1 teaspoon oil.

2. Combine the tomatoes, garlic and thyme with 2 teaspoons oil. Add salt and pepper to taste.

3. Heat the broiler. Oil a baking sheet with 1 tablespoon oil. Brush the eggplant slices on both sides with 5 to 6 tablespoons oil and sprinkle lightly with salt and pepper. Broil for 10 to 15 minutes until lightly browned and tender, turning the slices often so that they brown evenly and brushing with oil if they dry out. Drain on paper towels.

4. Heat the oven to 500 degrees. Oil 2 baking sheets and sprinkle lightly with cornmeal. Divide the dough into 4 pieces on a lightly floured work surface. Shape each into a ball and flatten each ball into a 7- to 8-inch round. Transfer the rounds to the baking sheets. Brush 1 round lightly with olive oil and sprinkle with one quarter of the onion slices. Spread a quarter of both the eggplant slices and the peppers over the onion, cutting the eggplant as necessary. Sprinkle with one quarter of the tomato mixture and 2 tablespoons of the cheese. Repeat to make 3 more pizzas. Bake for about 10 minutes until the crusts are golden brown. Sprinkle with parsley before serving.

SHOPPING LIST

$\frac{1}{4}$ lb. tomatoes
1 large eggplant (1 $\frac{1}{2}$ to 1 $\frac{3}{4}$ lbs.)
1 small red onion
thyme (fresh or dried)
garlic
parsley
7-oz. jar roasted red peppers
olive oil
cornmeal
unbleached all-purpose flour
1 pkg. active dry yeast
sugar
feta cheese

91

SPINACH-MUSHROOM CALZONE

Calzone are folded pockets of pizza dough filled with a variety of ingredients. One of these makes a hearty meal for anyone.

Serves 4
Preparation time: 45 minutes
Cooking time: 10 minutes

INGREDIENTS

1 bunch spinach, about ¾ pound
¼ cup olive oil
1 pound mushrooms, thinly sliced
½ medium-size red onion, chopped
2 medium-size cloves garlic
¾ cup part-skim ricotta cheese
2 tablespoons grated Parmesan cheese
3 tablespoons chopped parsley
¼ teaspoon dried thyme
⅛ teaspoon ground nutmeg
Salt and freshly ground pepper
Cornmeal
Pizza Dough (page 94)

1. Stem and rinse the spinach. Drain in a colander but do not spin dry.

2. Heat 2 tablespoons oil in a large frying pan over high heat. Add half of the mushrooms and cook, stirring, for 3 to 4 minutes until lightly browned and tender. Add half of the onion and cook for 1 minute. Lower the heat if the vegetables begin to burn but don't let any liquid accumulate in the pan. Add half of the garlic and stir for 30 seconds. Transfer the mixture to a bowl. Repeat with the remaining oil, mushrooms, onion and garlic.

3. Decrease the heat to medium. Add the spinach with just the water that clings to the leaves. (If the spinach is very dry, add 2 to 3 tablespoons water.) Cover and cook for about 5 minutes until wilted. Drain the spinach in a colander and squeeze out the water. Chop the spinach and add it to the bowl with the other vegetables. Add the cheeses, parsley, thyme, nutmeg and salt and pepper to taste. Stir to combine.

4. Heat the oven to 500 degrees. Oil 2 baking sheets and sprinkle lightly with cornmeal. Divide the dough into 4 equal pieces on a lightly floured work surface. Shape each into a ball and flatten each ball into a 7- to 8-inch round. Spread a quarter of the filling over one half of one dough round. Fold the remaining half over the filling to form a semicircle and fold the bottom edges over the top to seal. Transfer to a baking sheet. Repeat with the remaining dough rounds and filling. Bake the calzone for about 10 minutes until the crusts are golden brown.

SHOPPING LIST

spinach
1 lb. mushrooms
1 medium red onion
garlic
parsley
ground nutmeg
thyme (dried)
unbleached all-purpose flour
1 pkg. active dry yeast
sugar
cornmeal
olive oil
Parmesan cheese
part-skim ricotta cheese

PIZZA DOUGH

Once you have mastered this simple pizza dough, you will want to experiment with all sorts of toppings. No doubt your children will have lots of ideas, too. The dough—quickly mixed in the food processor—requires only a short rising and so can be ready to pop in the oven in less than half an hour. However, you may prefer to make up a few batches and freeze them for those times when you want a really fast meal. Wrap the finished dough in plastic and foil for freezing. Take the packet from the freezer a half-hour or so before you will need it and let it thaw in a warm kitchen or, if you remember, remove it early in the morning before you go to work and let it thaw in the refrigerator. If it seems puffy when it comes time to bake, just punch it down.

Makes two 12-inch pizzas or four 8-inch pizzas
Preparation time: 10 minutes, plus 20 minutes for the dough to rise

INGREDIENTS

$3\frac{1}{2}$ cups unbleached all-purpose flour
1 teaspoon salt
1 package ($2\frac{1}{2}$ teaspoons) active dry yeast
$\frac{1}{2}$ teaspoon sugar
$1\frac{1}{4}$ cups warm (105 to 115 degrees) water
2 tablespoons olive oil

1. In a food processor fitted with the metal chopping blade, pulse the flour and salt briefly to combine. In a glass measuring cup, dissolve the yeast and sugar in the warm water. Let stand 5 minutes until foamy. Add the olive oil to the yeast mixture.

2. With the food processor running, add the liquid to the dry ingredients in a steady stream, processing until the dough forms a ball on top of the blade. (If the dough doesn't form a ball, it is too dry. Add more cold water, a tablespoon at a time, while processing, until a ball forms. If the dough seems sticky, it is too wet. Add more flour, a tablespoon at a time, while processing, until the dough is moist but not sticky.)

3. Process the dough for 45 seconds to knead it. Transfer it to a lightly oiled bowl and cover tightly with plastic wrap. Let the dough rise in a warm, draft-free place until it is doubled in volume. A finger inserted in the dough will leave an imprint when it is ready. Punch the dough down and use as directed in the recipes.

Yeast
Active dry yeast, sold across the country in pre-measured packages, should be kept in the refrigerator. Yeast is a living organism that remains dormant when kept cool and will die if too hot. Proofing yeast in warm water lets you know if it is active (alive). If the water does not foam the yeast is either no longer active or the water is too hot and has killed the yeast. In either case, start again with another package.

SHOPPING LIST

unbleached all-purpose flour
1 pkg. active dry yeast
sugar
olive oil

PIZZA MARGHERITA WITH TOMATOES, MOZZARELLA AND HERBS

The story behind this forerunner of the classic tomato and cheese pizza dates back to 1889 when a special pizza was made for Queen Margherita of Italy. Italians had been putting their beloved tomatoes on pizza dough for a while, but the addition of cheese was a new idea. The white cheese, the red tomato and the green basil were selected to represent the colors of the Italian flag. For this recipe, tomatoes are not cooked into a sauce but are left in thick slices, as they were for the Italian Queen.

Makes two 12-inch pizzas
Preparation time: 15 minutes
Cooking time: 15 minutes

INGREDIENTS

Pizza Dough (page 94)
2 cups grated part-skim mozzarella cheese
½ cup grated Parmesan cheese
12 fresh plum tomatoes, sliced ½-inch thick
¼ cup chopped fresh basil
Salt and freshly ground pepper
Olive oil

1. Position two racks in the oven, one in the bottom third and the other in the center. Heat the oven to 500 degrees.

2. On a floured surface, roll out half the dough into a 12-inch circle. Transfer the dough to a pizza pan or large baking sheet. Pinch up a ½-inch rim around the outside edge of the dough. Repeat with the remaining dough to form another pizza.

3. Prepare the first pizza in the following sequence: Sprinkle the dough with one-quarter of both the mozzarella and the Parmesan. Arrange half of the tomatoes in concentric circles on top of the cheeses. Sprinkle the tomatoes with another quarter of the cheeses. Repeat the procedure with the second pizza and the remaining cheese and tomatoes.

4. Bake the pizza for 15 minutes, switching shelves halfway through the baking time, until the crusts are golden brown. Sprinkle the pizzas with the basil and season with salt and pepper to taste. Brush the crusts with olive oil, cut into wedges and serve immediately.

SHOPPING LIST

12 plum tomatoes
basil
unbleached all-purpose flour
1 pkg. active dry yeast
sugar
olive oil
part-skim mozzarella cheese
Parmesan cheese

PIZZA WITH SHRIMP AND ARTICHOKE HEARTS

With some frozen artichoke hearts and a pound of fresh shrimp, you can make a very special pizza. To butterfly the shrimp, first shell them and pull out the black intestine. With the tip of a sharp knife, cut each shrimp up the inside curve, about halfway through the body, and flatten it out. This way the shrimp will lie flat on the pizza.

Makes 4 individual pizzas
Preparation time: 45 minutes
Cooking time: 10 minutes

INGREDIENTS

1 pound medium-size shrimp, unshelled
Olive oil
2 teaspoons chopped fresh oregano or sage, or ½ teaspoon dried
Salt and freshly ground pepper
9-ounce package frozen artichoke hearts, thawed and cut in half if large
1 small onion, thinly sliced
2 teaspoons chopped fresh thyme or ½ teaspoon dried
Cornmeal
Pizza Dough (page 94)
1 medium-size lemon

1. Shell, devein and butterfly the shrimp. Rinse and pat them dry. Toss the shrimp in a small bowl with 1 tablespoon of oil, the oregano and salt and pepper.

2. In a medium frying pan, heat 2 tablespoons of oil over medium-high heat. Add the artichoke hearts, sprinkle lightly with salt and pepper and cook, stirring occasionally, for about 5 minutes until lightly browned. Remove from the pan.

3. Lower the heat to medium. Add another tablespoon of oil to the pan. Add the onion and thyme and cook, stirring occasionally, for 4 to 5 minutes until the onion is softened. Season to taste with salt and pepper and remove from the pan.

4. Heat the oven to 500 degrees. Oil 2 baking sheets and sprinkle lightly with cornmeal. Divide the dough into 4 pieces on a lightly floured work surface. Shape each into a ball and flatten each ball into a 7- to 8-inch round. Transfer the rounds to the baking sheets. Brush 1 round lightly with olive oil and spread with one-quarter of the onion. Arrange one-quarter of the artichoke hearts over the onions, and then one-quarter of the shrimp. Repeat to make three more pizzas. Bake the pizzas for 8 to 10 minutes until the crusts are golden. Squeeze a little lemon juice over the top of each one and serve.

SHOPPING LIST

1 lb. medium shrimp
onion
oregano or sage (fresh or dried)
thyme (fresh or dried)
1 lemon
9-oz. pkg. frozen artichoke hearts
olive oil
unbleached all-purpose flour
1 pkg. active dry yeast
sugar

PIZZA-JOINT PIZZA

As much as the over-21 set in residence may enjoy experimenting with eggplant, anchovies, shrimp and herbs on their pizzas, the kids will no doubt clamor for a good old American tomato and cheese pie. Look no further.

Makes two 12-inch pizzas
Preparation time: 20 minutes
Cooking time: 15 minutes

INGREDIENTS

Pizza Dough (page 94)
1½ to 2 cups Quick Marinara Sauce (page 121) or commercially prepared marinara sauce
1 cup chopped peppers, optional
¼ pound hard salami or pepperoni, sliced, optional
¼ pound fresh mushrooms, sliced, optional
2 cups grated part-skim mozzarella cheese
½ cup grated Parmesan cheese

1. Position two racks in the bottom third and center of the oven. Heat the oven to 500 degrees.

2. On a floured surface, roll out half the pizza dough into a 12-inch circle. Transfer the dough to a pizza pan or a large baking sheet. Pinch up ½ inch of the outside edge of the dough to form a rim. Repeat the procedure with the remaining dough to make the second pizza.

3. Spoon the sauce over the pizzas, spreading it out so that it covers the entire surface. Sprinkle both pizzas with mozzarella cheese and then with Parmesan. Top with peppers, salami or mushrooms, or a combination of two or three, if desired.

4. Bake the pizzas for about 10 minutes until the crusts are golden brown and the cheese is melted.

SHOPPING LIST

¼ lb. hard salami or pepperoni
¼ lb. mushrooms
1 green pepper
1 jar marinara sauce
unbleached all-purpose flour
1 pkg. active dry yeast
sugar
olive oil
part-skim mozzarella cheese
Parmesan cheese

PIZZA NICOISE WITH GREEN BEANS, TOMATOES AND TUNA

Here is a "pizza play" on the salad made famous in the south of France. Since nearly everyone has canned tuna in the cupboard, we have made the pizza with it, but for a fancier pizza, try fresh tuna. Slice a half pound of raw fresh tuna into 2-by-¼-inch strips. Toss the strips in olive oil and proceed as with canned tuna. The tuna will cook to a turn in the hot pizza oven.

Makes two 12-inch pizzas
Preparation time: 15 minutes
Cooking time: 15 minutes

INGREDIENTS

Pizza Dough (page 94)
1 cup grated part-skim mozzarella cheese
½ cup grated Parmesan cheese
6 fresh plum tomatoes, sliced ½-inch thick
½ pound fresh green beans, trimmed and
    cut into 1-inch pieces
1 small red onion, thinly sliced
1 medium-size clove garlic, finely chopped
2 6½-ounce cans tuna, preferably packed in
    olive oil, drained
20 green or black olives, pitted and chopped
    (optional)
3 tablespoons drained and rinsed capers
    (optional)
2 tablespoons fresh rosemary, basil, oregano
    or parsley
Salt and freshly ground pepper
Olive oil

1. Position two racks in the oven, one in the bottom third and the other in the center. Heat the oven to 500 degrees.

2. On a floured surface, roll out half the dough into a 12-inch circle. Transfer the dough to a pizza pan or large baking sheet. Pinch up a ½-inch rim around the outside edge of the dough. Repeat with the remaining dough to make another pizza.

3. Prepare the first pizza in the following sequence: Sprinkle the dough with one-quarter of both the mozzarella and the Parmesan. Arrange half the tomatoes in concentric circles on top of the cheeses. Sprinkle the green beans, onion and garlic on the tomatoes. Sprinkle the vegetables with another quarter of the cheeses. Repeat the procedure with the second pizza and the remaining cheese and vegetables.

4. Bake the pizzas for 10 minutes. Switch the positions of the pizzas. Quickly sprinkle the top of each with half the tuna and, if desired, the olives and capers. Bake the pizzas for 5 to 8 minutes more until the crusts are golden brown. Sprinkle each pizza with rosemary and season with salt and pepper to taste. Brush the crusts with olive oil, cut into wedges and serve at once.

> **SHOPPING LIST**
>
> *6 plum tomatoes*
> *½ lb. green beans*
> *1 small red onion*
> *garlic*
> *capers*
> *rosemary, basil, oregano or parsley*
> *unbleached all-purpose flour*
> *1 pkg. active dry yeast*
> *sugar*
> *olive oil*
> *2 6 ½ oz.-cans tuna*
> *green olives*
> *black olives*
> *Parmesan cheese*
> *part-skim mozzarella cheese*

BROCCOLI AND RICOTTA PIZZA

Normally, your children may object to eating broccoli ("we don't eat trees," they might say), but presented with a broccoli pizza they will quickly change their minds. But maybe not . . . which is fine, since that leaves all the more for the grown-ups in the family, who will adore this pie.

Makes two 12-inch pizzas
Preparation time: 20 minutes
Cooking time: 15 minutes

INGREDIENTS

Pizza Dough (page 94)
3 cups broccoli florets
2 cups part-skim ricotta cheese
½ cup grated Parmesan cheese
3 medium-size cloves garlic, finely chopped
20 black olives, pitted and halved
2 tablespoons olive oil, plus additional for
　brushing crust
2 tablespoons chopped fresh rosemary or
　dried
Salt and dried red pepper flakes

1. Position two racks in the bottom third and center of the oven. Heat the oven to 500 degrees.

2. On a floured surface, roll out half the pizza dough into a 12-inch circle. Transfer the dough to a pizza pan or a large baking sheet. Pinch up ½ inch of the outside edge of the dough to form a rim. Repeat the procedure with the remaining dough to make the second pizza.

3. Cook the broccoli in salted boiling water for 2 minutes until it is just crisp-tender. Drain, rinse under cold running water and drain well.

4. In a medium bowl, combine the ricotta, Parmesan and garlic.

5. Prepare one of the pizza rounds in the following sequence: Drop half of the ricotta mixture in tablespoons on top of the round of dough. Arrange half the broccoli on top of the ricotta mixture. Sprinkle half the olives over the broccoli. Drizzle the top of the pizza with 1 tablespoon of olive oil. Repeat the procedure with the remaining dough, ricotta, broccoli, olives and olive oil.

6. Bake the pizzas for 15 to 18 minutes, switching positions halfway through the baking time. Sprinkle the pizzas with the rosemary and season with salt and dried red pepper flakes to taste. Brush the crusts with olive oil, cut into wedges and serve immediately.

SHOPPING LIST

1 bunch broccoli
garlic
rosemary (fresh or dried)
red pepper flakes (dried)
black olives
olive oil
unbleached all-purpose flour
1 pkg. active dry yeast
sugar
part-skim ricotta cheese
Parmesan cheese

NEAPOLITAN PIZZA

3. Combine the tomatoes with the garlic and spread over the pizzas. Arrange the anchovies, olives and basil leaves on top of the tomatoes. Sprinkle with salt and pepper and olive oil.

4. Bake the pizzas for 15 to 20 minutes, switching shelves halfway through, until the crusts are golden brown.

Here is a classic pizza from the south of Italy where they like bold, full flavors, lots of tomatoes and garlic and a chewy crust.

Makes two 10-inch pizzas
Preparation time: 10 minutes
Cooking time: 15 to 20 minutes

INGREDIENTS

Pizza Dough (page 94)
2 cups coarsely chopped canned plum tomatoes
2 cloves garlic, finely chopped
2-ounce can anchovies, drained
8 to 10 thinly sliced black olives
6 to 8 basil leaves
Salt and freshly ground pepper
2 tablespoons olive oil

1. Position two racks in the oven, one in the bottom third and the other in the center. Heat the oven to 450 degrees.

2. On a floured surface, roll out half the dough into a 10-inch circle. Transfer the dough to a pizza pan or large baking sheet. Pinch up a ½-inch rim around the outside edge of the dough. Repeat with the remaining dough to form another pizza.

SHOPPING LIST

1 head garlic
1 bunch fresh basil leaves
2 1-lb. cans plum tomatoes
1 2-oz. can anchovies
1 small can black olives (pitted if possible)
olive oil

CALIFORNIA HAMBURGER

I t's the pesto, avocado and sprouts that turn this ordinary burger into one named for the Golden State.

Serves 4
Preparation time: 30 minutes
Cooking time: 15 minutes

INGREDIENTS

1½ pounds very lean ground beef
2 small scallions, chopped
1½ tablespoons olive oil
Salt and freshly ground pepper
8 slices whole wheat bread
Pesto (page 275)
1 large tomato, sliced
1 medium-size avocado, halved, seeded,
   peeled and sliced
Alfalfa sprouts or leaf lettuce

1. Light the charcoal grill or heat the broiler. Let the coals get medium hot.

2. In a large bowl, combine the beef, scallions, oil, salt and pepper and mix gently to avoid mashing the beef. Form into 4 patties. Grill or broil the hamburgers for 6 to 7 minutes on each side for medium-rare. At the same time, grill the bread lightly, about 5 minutes on each side, or toast it in the toaster.

3. Spread each slice of bread with pesto. Arrange tomato and avocado slices over 4 pieces of the bread and top each with a hamburger. Top the hamburgers with sprouts or lettuce and then with the remaining bread slices, pesto side down.

Grilling Over Charcoal
Outdoor grilling adds wonderful flavor to so many foods and, being so easy, has mushroomed in popularity during recent years. Today it is as much a part of how we cook as is boiling water or stir frying. There is no reason to reserve grilling for the summer months only; except in the most severe weather, you can always fire up the grill. You may have to don a warm jacket over your apron in order to tend the food, but the results are well worth it—including the benefit of easy cleanup. To maintain the correct degree of heat, remember to add more coals than usual to a cold weather fire.

For most grilling needs you will need enough coals to form a single layer beneath the food and extending about two inches beyond it. If you are grilling for longer than 40 or 50 minutes you will have to add six or seven raw coals to the fire after half an hour or so to maintain the temperature. When starting the fire, let the coals turn ashy grey before testing the temperature. Hold the palm of your hand about five inches above the hot coals. If you can keep it there for five or six seconds the coals are medium hot. If you have to pull it away after two or three seconds, the coals are very hot and good for searing.

SHOPPING LIST

1 ½ lbs. lean ground beef
whole wheat bread
scallions
garlic
1 large tomato
1 medium avocado
basil
alfalfa sprouts or leaf lettuce
pine nuts
olive oil
Parmesan cheese

ORIENTAL TURKEY BURGERS

Here we have combined ground turkey with Asian cooking ingredients for snappy-tasting burgers. This and the following three recipes offer variations on turkey burgers, easily transformed into flavorful incarnations by the simple addition of a few ingredients. Elementary—but so good!

Serves 4
Preparation time: 10 minutes
Cooking time: 10 minutes

INGREDIENTS

1¼ pounds ground turkey
1 tablespoon grated fresh ginger
1 tablespoon hoisin sauce, plus additional
   for garnish
1 tablespoon low-sodium soy sauce
1 tablespoon dry sherry
1 medium scallion, finely chopped
Freshly ground black pepper
4 sesame hamburger buns, toasted
Chinese mustard
Chinese Cabbage Slaw (page 53)

1. In a large mixing bowl combine the turkey, ginger, hoisin sauce, soy sauce, sherry, scallion and pepper to taste. Mix well to combine. Divide the mixture into four equal parts and shape each into patties. Cover and refrigerate until ready to cook.

2. Heat the broiler. Broil the patties about 5 inches from the heat source for about 8 minutes, turning once halfway through the cooking time, until the burgers are well done. Serve immediately on toasted hamburger buns with additional hoisin sauce and Chinese mustard, topped with Chinese Cabbage Slaw.

Ground Turkey
Take advantage of the ground turkey being sold nowadays (alongside the turkey breasts and turkey parts) in the meat section of the supermarket. It is leaner (approximately 93 percent fat free) and lower in cholesterol than beef and has a mild flavor that blends wonderfully with other ingredients. Because of turkey's leanness, some people complain that their cooked turkey burgers are dry. To assure moistness, stir a tablespoon of vegetable or olive oil into the raw ground turkey—if you feel you can afford the extra calories. Cooking turkey burgers just until they are well-done with medium, not hot, heat also helps.

SHOPPING LIST

1 ¼ lbs. ground turkey
sesame hamburger buns
fresh ginger
Chinese cabbage
carrots
scallions
sesame seeds
hoisin sauce
low-sodium soy sauce
dry sherry
rice vinegar
Chinese mustard
sugar

ITALIAN TURKEY BURGERS

These rate the nomenclature because of the addition of cheese, marinara sauce and Italian bread.

Serves 4
Preparation time: 20 minutes
Cooking time: 10 minutes

INGREDIENTS

1¼ pounds ground turkey
1 tablespoon olive or vegetable oil, optional
2 teaspoons Italian seasoning
Salt and freshly ground pepper
4 slices low-fat mozzarella cheese
8 slices French or Italian bread
Olive oil, for brushing bread
Quick Marinara Sauce (page 121)

1. Heat the broiler or light the charcoal grill. Let the coals get medium hot.

2. In a medium bowl, combine the turkey, the tablespoon of olive oil, Italian seasoning, salt and pepper. Shape the mixture into 4 patties, about ¾-inch thick.

3. Cook the turkey burgers in the broiler or on a lightly oiled grill, about 5 inches from the heat, if possible, turning once, for 4 to 5 minutes. Top each burger with a slice of cheese and continue cooking for another 4 to 5 minutes until the cheese is melted and the burgers are done but still juicy.

4. While the turkey burgers are cooking, grill or toast the bread slices, turning once, until lightly toasted. Brush one side of each grilled slice with olive oil.

5. Serve the turkey burgers immediately with some of the warm Quick Marinara Sauce on the toasted bread slices.

Cans
Never buy dented cans even at supermarket bargain prices. The contents may have been contaminated through hairline cracks in the tin that permit bacteria to enter. Even perfect cans do not keep forever.

SHOPPING LIST

1 ¼ lbs. ground turkey
French or Italian bread
olive oil
Italian seasoning
onion
garlic
35-oz. can plum tomatoes
low-fat mozzarella cheese

L.A. TURKEY BURGERS

3. Serve the turkey burgers immediately on whole wheat toast, spread with Guacamole to taste and garnished with alfalfa sprouts.

The difference between these and the California burgers (page 103) is the use of Guacamole as well as the call for ground turkey rather than beef. You could apply this treatment to the California burgers, and vice versa.

> *Guacamole*
> *To prevent guacamole from darkening, leave the avocado pit in the mixture and cover the surface with a thin layer of mayonnaise to exclude the air. Immediately before serving, discard the pit and stir the mayonnaise into the guacamole.*

Serves 4
Preparation time: 20 minutes
Cooking time: 15 minutes

INGREDIENTS

$1\frac{1}{4}$ pounds ground turkey
1 tablespoon olive or vegetable oil
  (optional)
Salt and freshly ground pepper
8 slices whole wheat bread, toasted
Guacamole (page 273)
Alfalfa sprouts

SHOPPING LIST

1 ¼ lbs. ground turkey
whole wheat bread
alfalfa sprouts
3 medium avocados
onions
garlic
1 medium tomato
1 lime
coriander
1 chili pepper (fresh or canned)
olive or vegetable oil

1. Heat the boiler or light the charcoal grill. Let the coals get medium hot.

2. In a medium bowl, combine the turkey, oil, salt and pepper. Shape the mixture into 4 patties, each about ¾-inch thick. Cook the burgers in the broiler or on a lightly oiled grill, about 5 inches from the heat, turning once, for 8 to 10 minutes until the burgers are well done but still juicy.

MEXICAN BURGERS

And now for some burgers with a difference. Sometimes you need a change from the usual, and this juicy beef burger livened up with chili powder and served with salsa does the trick. It is served inside a corn tortilla for another switch from the everyday.

Serves 4
Preparation time: 20 minutes
Cooking time: 15 minutes

INGREDIENTS

1½ pounds very lean ground beef
1 tablespoon chili powder
Salt and freshly ground pepper
4 corn tortillas
Vegetable oil, for frying
Chopped lettuce, for garnish
Five-Alarm Salsa (page 273)
Plain low-fat yogurt, for garnish

1. In a large skillet, heat the vegetable oil over medium-high heat until very hot. One at a time, fry the tortillas for about 30 seconds on each side until they are golden and crispy. Drain the tortillas on paper towels.

2. Heat the broiler or light the charcoal grill. Let the coals get medium hot. In a medium bowl, combine the beef, chili powder, salt and pepper. Shape the mixture into 4 patties, each about ¾-inch thick.

3. Cook the hamburgers in the broiler or on a lightly oiled grill, about 5 inches from the source of heat, turning once, for 8 to 10 minutes until well done but still juicy.

4. Spread the tortillas on individual plates. On each tortilla, put a mound of chopped lettuce, one burger and salsa to taste. Top with a dollop of yogurt, fold the tortilla over and serve immediately.

SHOPPING LIST
1 ½ lbs. lean ground beef
4 corn tortillas
lettuce
2 medium tomatoes
onions
garlic
1 green chili pepper (fresh or canned)
1 lime
chili powder
plain low-fat yogurt

TURKEY BURGERS WITH CRANBERRY KETCHUP

Did you know that ketchup isn't always made from tomatoes? Walnuts, mushrooms, plums or, as we have done here, cranberries, can be blended with other ingredients to make a delicious tangy-sweet condiment. Keep this wonderful relish in mind for grilled chicken and pork dishes as well.

Serves 4
Preparation time: 15 minutes
Cooking time: 30 minutes

INGREDIENTS

Ketchup:
12-ounce bag fresh or frozen cranberries
⅓ cup maple syrup
⅓ cup sugar, plus more, if desired
2 tablespoons cider vinegar
2 tablespoon finely chopped onion
1 teaspoon dried red pepper flakes
½ teaspoon salt
⅛ teaspoon ground allspice
⅛ teaspoon ground cloves
⅛ teaspoon pepper
⅛ teaspoon celery seed
⅛ teaspoon crushed mustard seeds
½ bay leaf
Turkey burgers:
1¼ pounds ground turkey
1 tablespoon vegetable or olive oil
   (optional)
½ teaspoon poultry seasoning
Salt and freshly ground pepper
6 hamburger buns

1. Make the ketchup by putting all of the ingredients in a medium-sized heavy-bottomed saucepan over medium-low heat. Simmer, stirring frequently, for 10 to 15 minutes until all the cranberries have burst and the mixture is thickened. Cool completely, cover and chill. Leftover ketchup will keep, chilled, for up to 2 weeks. (To quick-chill ketchup, transfer the mixture to a medium-sized bowl set in a larger bowl of ice water and stir often until cooled.)

2. Heat the broiler or light the charcoal grill. Let the coals get medium hot. Make the turkey burgers by placing the meat, oil, seasoning, salt and pepper is a medium-sized bowl. Shape the mixture into 4 patties, each about ¾-inch thick.

3. Cook the burgers in the broiler or on a lightly oiled grill, about 5 inches from the heat, turning once, for 8 to 10 minutes until the burgers are well done but still juicy.

4. Serve the turkey burgers immediately on the hamburger buns with the Cranberry Ketchup on the side.

SHOPPING LIST

1 ¼ lbs. ground turkey
hamburger buns
onion
bay leaf
12-oz. bag fresh or frozen cranberries
dried red pepper flakes
ground allspice
ground cloves
celery seeds
mustard seeds
poultry seasoning
maple syrup
cider vinegar
sugar
olive oil

BARBECUED HAMBURGERS

1. Heat the oil in a heavy skillet over medium heat. Add the onion and garlic and cook for 10 minutes until softened but not browned. Stir in the tomatoes, tomato paste, Worcestershire sauce, mustard and paprika and simmer for 30 minutes. Season with salt and pepper to taste.

2. Meanwhile, heat the broiler or light the charcoal grill. Let the coals get medium hot.

3. Divide the meat into 4 patties. Brush with the sauce and broil or grill for 6 to 7 minutes on each side for medium-rare, brushing frequently with the sauce. Serve immediately on the hamburger buns and pass the extra sauce on the side.

Tired of "designer" hamburger recipes? Does your family yearn for an all-American burger tucked into a traditional bun? Here you are: a burger made with good, lean beef and flavored with a simple basting sauce of tomatoes and onions. A *sauce*, you say?! Well, yes . . . we had to do something to make a technique (broiling or grilling a burger) into a recipe. And this easy sauce is good. If you prefer, of course, simply cook the burgers and set sliced onions, sliced tomatoes, pickle chips and ketchup on the table. Who can blame you?

Serves 4
Preparation time: 45 minutes
Cooking time: 15 minutes

Tomato Paste
Transfer tomato paste from an opened can to a covered glass jar to prevent it from discoloring. Add a tablespoon of tomato paste to homemade tomato soup to give it extra strength and body.

INGREDIENTS

1 tablespoon vegetable oil
1 small onion, finely chopped
4 ounces canned tomatoes, crushed
1 tablespoon tomato paste
1 teaspoon Worcestershire sauce
1 teaspoon Dijon mustard
$\frac{1}{2}$ teaspoon paprika
Salt and freshly ground pepper
$1\frac{1}{2}$ pounds lean ground beef
4 hamburger buns, toasted

SHOPPING LIST

1 $\frac{1}{2}$ lbs. lean ground beef
hamburger buns
onion
canned tomatoes
tomato paste
Dijon mustard
Worcestershire sauce
paprika
vegetable oil

PASTA

Most Americans would agree that one of the most successful culinary revolutions of the past 10 or 15 years was the pasta invasion. Long gone are the days when "spaghetti" was synonymous with pasta, and the word "pasta" was giggled over and considered pretentious. Today, we revel in the scores of pasta shapes available to the everyday shopper. We may still spoon rich red sauces over cooked noodles (who doesn't love spaghetti and a simple marinara sauce?) but we are just as apt to toss the pasta with crisp-cooked vegetables, creamy cheese, grilled poultry or fish and fragrant fresh herbs.

Our love affair with pasta is sure to be a lasting one. Endlessly adaptable, always economical and fast and easy to cook, it might be considered the perfect food. But there is more. Like the potato, pasta by itself is not high in calories; there are just over 200 in a cup of cooked pasta (which is about two ounces, dry)—and nearly all of those calories are from complex carbohydrates, which we all need. Pasta contains only traces of cholesterol and a cup, cooked, has about 10 percent of our daily allowance of protein as well as a fair share of niacin, thiamin, riboflavin and iron. (These last are present if the pasta is enriched, as nearly all domestic brands are.)

We have far to go to catch up with the Italians as far as pasta consumption goes. Americans eat only about a third as much pasta: Italians average 55 pounds per person per year. But we down a good amount, and once you browse through the following recipes, your family most likely will consume more than ever before. Here we have recipes for classics such as Pasta Primavera and Pasta with White Clam Sauce as well as the familiar and beloved Baked Macaroni and Cheese. We invite you also to try other pasta dishes. Serve your family Cavatelli with Spinach and Feta Cheese or Lamb and Caponata with Pasta for exciting new taste sensations. Try Spaghetti with Chicken and Peanut-Sesame Sauce for a hint of Asia, or Ziti with Turkey Meatballs for a new twist on an old theme. Put the pasta water on to boil. Good things are in store for your family.

CAVATELLI WITH SPINACH AND FETA CHEESE

By the time the pasta is cooked, the spinach sauce is ready. We have made the sauce with butter, which gives it good flavor and a silky consistency, but if you are concerned about cholesterol, substitute olive oil for the butter.

Serves 4
Preparation time: 15 minutes
Cooking time: 30 minutes

INGREDIENTS

2 tablespoons olive oil
2 tablespoons butter (or margarine)
2 medium-size onions, thinly sliced
Salt and freshly ground pepper
$\frac{1}{3}$ cup water
2 bunches spinach (about 1 pound each),
    stemmed and cut into wide strips
$\frac{3}{4}$ pound cavatelli or small shells
$\frac{1}{2}$ cup crumbled feta cheese
2 tablespoons chopped fresh basil or parsley

1. Heat water for the pasta in a large saucepan.

2. Heat the oil and butter in a large, heavy frying pan over medium heat. Add the onions and cook for about 20 minutes, stirring occasionally, until very soft. Increase the heat to high and cook, stirring often, for about 5 minutes until the liquid has evaporated and the onions are golden. Add salt to taste. Add the water and the spinach. Cover and steam over medium heat for 4 to 5 minutes until the spinach is just cooked. (There will be some liquid in the pan as well, which will be the sauce for the pasta.)

3. Meanwhile, cook the pasta in boiling salted water for 12 to 15 minutes until tender. Drain in a colander and return to the pan. Pour the contents of the frying pan over the pasta and toss to coat the pasta with the sauce. If the sauce is too liquid, toss the pasta for 1 to 2 minutes over high heat to reduce. Add the cheese, herbs and plenty of pepper, and stir gently to combine.

SHOPPING LIST
$\frac{3}{4}$ lb. cavatelli or small shells
spinach
onions
basil or parsley
olive oil
butter or margarine
feta cheese

Cooking Pasta

A pound of pasta needs a lot of water when it cooks. Some experts recommend as much as seven quarts while others say that four quarts is adequate. In any event, use a large pot and do not economize with the water. Add about a tablespoon of salt for every three or four quarts of water and as soon as the water boils, plunge the pasta into it. Be sure the heat is high so that the water will quickly return to the boil. We have estimated cooking times based on dry pasta, but if you prefer fresh pasta, adjust the times accordingly. Fresh pasta, which is very moist, takes far less time to cook—usually only a couple of minutes.

FETTUCCINE WITH ASPARAGUS AND WALNUTS

Pureed asparagus, crunchy walnuts and a sprinkling of fresh basil make this bright, fresh pasta dish a winner.

Serves 4
Preparation time: 10 minutes
Cooking time: 20 minutes

INGREDIENTS

$\frac{1}{3}$ cup chopped walnuts
$1\frac{1}{4}$ pounds thin asparagus
2 tablespoons olive oil
4 scallions, chopped
2 medium-size cloves garlic, crushed
Salt and freshly ground pepper
$\frac{3}{4}$ cup chicken broth or water
1 cup part-skim ricotta cheese
$\frac{3}{4}$ pound dried fettuccine
$\frac{1}{4}$ cup chopped fresh basil
$\frac{1}{4}$ cup grated Parmesan cheese (optional)

1. Heat water for the pasta in a large saucepan.

2. Heat the oven to 425 degrees. Spread the walnuts on a baking sheet and toast for about 7 minutes until fragrant.

3. Meanwhile, snap off the tough ends of the asparagus and discard. Cut off the tips, leaving them about 2 inches long, and reserve. Cut the stalks into 1-inch pieces.

4. Heat the oil in a saucepan over medium heat. Add the scallions and garlic and cook for about 5 minutes until softened. Add $1\frac{1}{2}$ cups of the asparagus stalks and cook for 1 minute. Add $\frac{1}{2}$ teaspoon salt and the broth, cover and simmer for 5 to 10 minutes until the asparagus is tender. Puree the asparagus and cooking liquid with the ricotta cheese in a food processor. If the mixture is very thick, stir in enough of the pasta cooking water to give it the consistency of thickened cream.

5. Meanwhile, cook the pasta for 9 minutes in boiling salted water. Add the reserved asparagus tops and stalks and continue cooking for about 3 more minutes until both the pasta and asparagus are tender. Drain in a colander and return to the pan. Add the pureed asparagus mixture and toss to coat with the sauce. Sprinkle with the chopped basil and toasted walnuts and season with pepper. Serve with Parmesan cheese, if desired.

SHOPPING LIST

$\frac{3}{4}$ lb. dried fettucine
scallions
garlic
basil
1 $\frac{1}{4}$ lbs. thin asparagus
chopped walnuts
chicken broth
part-skim ricotta cheese
Parmesan cheese

PASTA PRIMAVERA

Pasta Primavera, which traditionally celebrates springtime and the fresh vegetables that arrive with the season, is a marvelously versatile dish that can be made with nearly any assortment of vegetables. We have used squashes, asparagus and carrots for a colorful, tasty primavera, but you might also try mushrooms, snow peas, green peas, spinach and peppers.

Serves 4
Preparation time: 20 minutes
Cooking time: 20 minutes

INGREDIENTS

2 tablespoons butter or margarine
2 tablespoons olive oil
6 scallions, chopped
2 medium-size carrots, cut into thin rounds
1 medium-size zucchini, cut into thin rounds
1 medium-size yellow squash, cut into thin rounds
½ pound thin asparagus, trimmed and cut into 2-inch lengths
1 cup water
Salt and freshly ground pepper
¼ cup chopped fresh herbs such as parsley, basil, chives, chervil and tarragon
¾ pound dried radiatore or wagon wheel pasta
½ cup grated Parmesan cheese

1. Heat water for the pasta in a large pot.

2. Heat the butter and 1 tablespoon of oil in a large frying pan over low heat. Add the scallions and carrots and cook for 5 minutes, stirring occasionally. Add both the squashes and the asparagus and cook for about 5 minutes until the squash wilts. Add the water and ½ teaspoon of salt, cover the pan and cook for 7 to 8 minutes until the vegetables are tender. (There should be some lightly thickened liquid in the pan—this will be the sauce for the pasta.) Stir in the herbs.

3. Meanwhile, cook the pasta in boiling salted water for 12 to 15 minutes until tender. Drain in a colander and return to the pot. Toss with the remaining tablespoon of oil. Pour the contents of the frying pan over the pasta and toss to coat the pasta with sauce. If the sauce is too liquid, toss the pasta over high heat until the sauce is reduced. Season with pepper and serve with Parmesan cheese.

Asparagus
Peel asparagus with a cheese slicer; it is easier than using a potato peeler or a paring knife.
To keep asparagus fresh, wrap it in wet paper towels and keep it in the refrigerator.

SHOPPING LIST

¾ lb. radiatore or wagon wheel pasta
scallions
carrots
1 medium zucchini
1 medium yellow squash
½ lb. thin asparagus
parsley, basil, chives, chervil and tarragon
olive oil
butter or margarine
Parmesan cheese

SPAGHETTI WITH CHICKEN AND PEANUT-SESAME SAUCE

This is a dish inspired by the cooking of China—the country where pasta was invented. Marco Polo may have brought the technique of making pasta back to Italy, but you can be sure he did not teach his countrymen to cook a dish resembling this one. A pity- —pasta and sesame sauce is one of the most delicious preparations we know. Since it is best served at room temperature, we recommend that you rinse the cooked pasta in cold water to lower its temperature quickly.

Serves 4
Preparation time: 10 minutes
Cooking time: 15 minutes

INGREDIENTS

3 tablespoons vegetable oil
12 ounces boneless, skinless chicken breast,
    cut crosswise into thin slices
Salt and freshly ground pepper
$\frac{1}{3}$ cup chunky peanut butter
2 medium cloves garlic, chopped
1 tablespoon Oriental sesame oil
2 teaspoons low-sodium soy sauce
$\frac{1}{2}$ teaspoon dry sherry
$\frac{1}{8}$ teaspoon cayenne pepper
1 teaspoon honey
12 ounces spaghetti
2 scallions, chopped
2 tablespoons chopped fresh coriander or
    parsley

1. In a large frying pan, heat 1 tablespoon of oil over medium-high heat. Sprinkle the chicken with salt and pepper and add it to the pan. Cook, stirring, for about 3 minutes until the chicken is cooked through. Remove the chicken to a large serving bowl.

2. In the bowl of a food processor or blender, combine the peanut butter, garlic, 2 tablespoons of vegetable oil, sesame oil, soy sauce, sherry and cayenne. Process to a paste and add more cayenne if desired. Stir in the honey and add the mixture to the bowl with the chicken.

3. Bring a large pot of water to the boil for the pasta. Add salt and the spaghetti and cook for 8 to 10 minutes until the pasta is tender. Drain in a colander and rinse under cold running water. Add the spaghetti, scallions and coriander to the bowl with the chicken and peanut sauce and toss to coat the pasta with the sauce. Season with pepper and serve.

Pasta
Always add pasta to boiling water a little at a time so that the water remains at a rolling boil.
Always cook pasta in a large quantity of vigorously boiling salted water. Add a tablespoon of vegetable oil to the water to prevent the pasta from sticking to itself.
At the end of the cooking time, add a cup of cold water to the pot to check the cooking. Drain the pasta and serve on hot plates.

SHOPPING LIST

12 oz. boneless, skinless chicken breast
spaghetti
garlic
scallions
coriander or parsley
chunky peanut butter
Oriental sesame oil
low-sodium soy sauce
dry sherry
honey
cayenne pepper
olive oil

LAMB AND CAPONATA
WITH PASTA

Try this if you are fortunate enough to have some leftover lamb. If not, buy some chops to cook—this is a dish that allows a little lamb to go a long way. As simple as it is to make the caponata while the pasta water boils, if you already have some made, the cooking time will only be 40 minutes.

Serves 4
Preparation time: 35 minutes
Cooking time: 50 minutes
    (including Caponata)

INGREDIENTS

Salt
12 ounces fettuccine
Caponata (page 218)
1 cup boneless cooked lamb, cut into
    chunks
1 tablespoon olive oil
2 tablespoons chopped parsley

1. Bring a large pot of water to the boil for the pasta. Add salt and the fettuccine and cook for about 10 minutes until the pasta is tender. Drain in a colander.

2. Heat 2 cups of caponata with the lamb in a saucepan over medium-low heat until heated through.

3. Return the pasta to the pot and toss with the oil. Add the caponata mixture and the parsley and toss to combine.

118

Lamb
When buying a leg of lamb, approximately one-third of the weight will be bone. So a 6-pound leg of lamb will yield approximately 4 pounds of meat. Allow ⅓ to ½ pound of lamb for each person for lamb cooked without the bone. With the bone in, allow ½ to ¾ pound of meat per person.

SHOPPING LIST

boneless cooked lamb
fettucine
parsley
capers
1 large eggplant
celery
1 medium red onion
raisins
tomato paste
pitted green olives
red wine vinegar
sugar
coarse salt
olive oil

CHICKEN, BROCCOLI AND GARLIC PASTA CASSEROLE

Casseroles are a boon to most family cooks. They are easy to put together and once in the oven, require no tending. What is more, if it takes some doing to get the entire family assembled for the evening meal, the casserole will wait. This dish is so tasty, you may decide to double the ingredients and make a large casserole which will feed the family two nights running. Or, make two casseroles and freeze one for later in the month.

Serves 4
Preparation time: 45 minutes
Cooking time: 20 minutes

INGREDIENTS

8 ounces penne or other small tube-shaped pasta
Salt and freshly ground pepper
3 cups broccoli florets and thinly sliced peeled stems
$2\frac{1}{2}$ tablespoons butter or margarine
1 cup chopped onion
2 medium cloves garlic, chopped
3 tablespoons flour
1 teaspoon dried thyme
$1\frac{1}{2}$ cups chicken broth or water
$1\frac{1}{2}$ cups whole milk
1 bay leaf
$\frac{3}{4}$ pound boneless, skinless chicken breast, cut crosswise into thin strips
Pinch ground nutmeg
2 tablespoons chopped parsley
$\frac{1}{2}$ cup low-fat ricotta cheese
3 tablespoons grated Parmesan cheese

1. Bring a large pot of water to the boil for the pasta. Add salt and the penne and cook for about 9 minutes until the pasta is barely tender. (The pasta should be slightly undercooked as it will cook more in the casserole.) Drain in a colander and set aside in a large bowl.

2. Meanwhile, steam the broccoli over 1 to 2 inches of water for about 5 minutes until tender. Add to the bowl with the penne.

3. Heat the oven to 350 degrees.

4. In a saucepan, heat the butter over medium heat. Add the onion and cook for about 3 minutes until softened. Stir in the garlic and flour and cook for 1 minute. Stir in the thyme and then slowly whisk in the broth and milk. Add the bay leaf, bring to the boil, reduce the heat and cook gently for 10 minutes. Add the chicken and cook for 2 to 3 minutes until the chicken is barely cooked through. Remove from the heat and season with salt, pepper and nutmeg. Add to the bowl with the pasta and broccoli along with the parsley and stir until the pasta is coated with the sauce. Taste and adjust the seasonings.

5. Oil a 2-quart $11\frac{1}{2}$-by-8-inch baking dish. Spoon the pasta mixture into the dish and smooth the top. Dot with spoonfuls of riccota and sprinkle with the Parmesan. Bake for about 20 minutes until the casserole is heated through and the top is lightly browned.

SHOPPING LIST

$\frac{3}{4}$ lb. boneless, skinless chicken breast
penne or other small tube-shaped pasta
broccoli
onion
garlic
bay leaves
ground nutmeg
parsley
dried thyme
chicken broth
flour
butter or margarine
low-fat ricotta cheese
Parmesan cheese
milk

QUICK MARINARA SAUCE

PASTA WITH WHITE CLAM SAUCE

This rich, red sauce can be prepared in less than an hour—which may not qualify as super quick but does not relegate it to the ranks of the red sauces requiring hours of slow, back-burner cooking. Keep the ingredients on hand and let the sauce cook while you make a salad, set the table, warm the bread and boil the pasta. You will never reach for a jar of prepared sauce again.

Makes about 3 cups
Preparation time: 10 minutes
Cooking time: 50 minutes

INGREDIENTS

2 tablespoons olive oil
1 small onion, chopped (about $\frac{1}{2}$ cup)
1 large clove garlic, finely chopped
35-ounce can plum tomatoes, with juice
$\frac{1}{2}$ teaspoon dried basil
$\frac{1}{2}$ teaspoon dried oregano
Salt and freshly ground pepper

1. Heat the oil in a medium saucepan over medium heat. Add the onion and garlic and cook, stirring, for about 5 minutes until softened. Chop the tomatoes coarsely and add them to the pan along with their juices. Add the basil and oregano. Bring the sauce to a simmer. Reduce the heat to low and simmer gently for about 45 minutes until the sauce is slightly thickened. Season with salt and pepper to taste and serve with pasta.

SHOPPING LIST

onion
garlic
35-oz. can plum tomatoes
basil
oregano
olive oil

Buy the clams at the fish store already shucked or, if you have no choice, use canned clams. The sauce will be nearly as good.

Serves 4 to 6
Preparation time: 10 minutes
Cooking time: about 20 minutes

INGREDIENTS

3 tablespoons olive oil
2 cloves garlic, finely chopped
3 tablespoons finely chopped shallot
$\frac{1}{3}$ cup finely chopped parsley
$\frac{1}{2}$ cup dry white wine or bottled clam juice
$1\frac{1}{2}$ cups chopped fresh clams, including their liquor
$\frac{1}{2}$ teaspoon salt
$\frac{1}{8}$ teaspoon pepper
$\frac{1}{8}$ teaspoon oregano
1 pound linguine or spaghetti

1. Heat the olive oil in a saucepan over medium heat. Add the garlic, shallot and parsley and cook, stirring, for 4 to 5 minutes. Add the wine, clams, salt, pepper and oregano and simmer for 15 minutes.

2. Meanwhile, cook the pasta in a large saucepan of boiling, salted water according to the package directions. Drain well and transfer to a warmed serving bowl. Add the sauce, toss quickly until well combined and serve immediately.

SHOPPING LIST

1 $\frac{1}{2}$ cups chopped fresh clams
1 lb. linguine or spaghetti
garlic
shallot
parsley
oregano
olive oil
dry white wine or bottled clam juice

LINGUINE WITH TUNA

T he smoky flavor of the roasted peppers and the fire of the hot pepper flakes give this dish a full, rounded flavor your family will surely like. For the best results we suggest albacore tuna packed in oil, but you can certainly use water-packed tuna.

Serves 4
Preparation time: 25 minutes, or less if
    using jarred peppers
Cooking time: 10 minutes

INGREDIENTS

2 large red bell peppers or 7-ounce jar
    roasted red bell peppers, drained and
    rinsed
3 tablespoons pine nuts
¼ cup olive oil
1 medium-size red onion, chopped
2 medium-size cloves garlic, chopped
¼ teaspoon hot red pepper flakes
1 tablespoon fresh chopped marjoram or
    1 teaspoon dried
Salt
6-ounce can tuna, preferably packed in oil,
    drained
2 tablespoons lemon juice
1 tablespoon capers
3 tablespoons chopped parsley
12 ounces linguine

1. If using fresh peppers, heat the broiler and broil them until charred. Put them in a bowl and cover tightly with plastic wrap. When cool enough to handle, stem, seed and peel them. Cut fresh or jarred roasted peppers into ¾- to 1-inch-wide strips, and then each strip into 1½-inch lengths.

2. Bring a large pot of water to the boil for the pasta.

3. Heat a medium frying pan (without oil) over medium-high heat. Add the pine nuts and cook, shaking the pan, for about 2 minutes until the nuts are lightly browned and fragrant. Watch them closely; once they begin to brown they will burn quickly. Remove the nuts from the pan.

4. Reduce the heat to medium and add the oil to the pan. Add the onion and cook for about 5 minutes until softened. Add the garlic and red pepper flakes and cook for 1 minute. Add the peppers and marjoram and cook for 3 to 4 minutes until the peppers are heated through and the flavors are blended. Season to taste with salt.

5. Break the tuna up into a serving bowl. Add the lemon juice, capers and parsley.

6. Add salt to the boiling pasta water and then the pasta and cook for 8 to 10 minutes until the pasta is tender. Drain and add to the serving bowl along with the pepper mixture. Toss the pasta until coated with the sauce. Sprinkle with the pine nuts and serve.

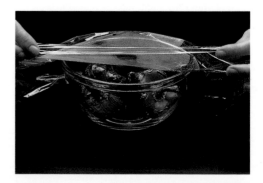

PASTA WITH MUSHROOMS AND RED WINE

If you like the earthy flavor of wild mushrooms, this recipe is for you. The red wine heightens that flavor all the more so that the sauce stands up very well to the bland pasta, making this a dish to remember. The stems of shiitake mushrooms are inedibly tough and must be completely removed; you will find that they detach easily in one piece from the cap.

Serves 4
Preparation time: 20 minutes
Cooking time: 40 minutes

INGREDIENTS

3 tablespoons olive oil
2 medium onions, chopped
2 medium cloves garlic, chopped
½ pound assorted wild mushrooms, such as shiitake, cremini, oyster or chanterelles, sliced
½ pound white mushrooms, sliced
Salt and freshly ground pepper
½ cup dry red wine
¼ cup chicken broth or water
2 teaspoons chopped fresh marjoram or ½ teaspoon dried
2 teaspoons chopped fresh sage or ½ teaspoon dried
1 bay leaf
12 ounces fettuccine
2 tablespoons chopped parsley

1. In a large saucepan, heat 2 tablespoons of the oil over medium-high heat. Add the onion and cook for about 5 minutes until lightly browned. Stir in the garlic and cook for just a few seconds until fragrant.

2. Reduce the heat to medium, add the mushrooms and sprinkle with ¼ teaspoon salt. Cook for about 5 minutes until the mushrooms begin to render their juices. Add the wine, broth, marjoram, sage and bay leaf. Bring to the boil, reduce the heat and simmer, partially covered, for 15 minutes. Increase the heat and boil, uncovered, until the liquid is reduced and slightly thickened. (The time will depend on the size of the pan.) Season to taste with salt and pepper.

3. Bring a large pot of water to the boil for the pasta. Add salt and the fettuccine and cook for about 10 minutes until tender. Drain in a colander, return to the pot and toss with the remaining tablespoon of oil.

4. Heat the mushroom sauce to a simmer and pour over the pasta. Add the parsley and toss until the fettuccine is coated with the sauce.

SHOPPING LIST

fettucine
½ lb. assorted wild mushrooms
½ lb. white mushrooms
parsley
marjoram (fresh or dried)
sage (fresh or dried)
bay leaves
garlic
onion
chicken broth
olive oil
dry red wine

ZITI WITH TURKEY MEATBALLS

Using ground turkey and fat ziti makes this an updated version of everybody's favorite: spaghetti and meatballs. Substitute beef for the turkey if your family prefers a more conventional approach.

Serves 4 to 6
Preparation time: 15 minutes
Cooking time: 30 minutes

INGREDIENTS

Meatballs:
¾ cup fresh Italian or French bread crumbs
¾ cup low-fat milk
1¼ pounds ground fresh turkey
1 large egg
2 tablespoons chopped fresh parsley
2 tablespoons finely chopped onion
1 clove garlic, finely chopped
Salt and freshly ground pepper
All-purpose flour for dredging
3 tablespoons olive oil plus additional, if necessary
Sauce:
1 small onion, chopped
1 clove garlic, finely chopped
1 28-ounce can crushed tomatoes
½ cup dry red wine
1½ teaspoons dried Italian seasoning
Salt and freshly ground pepper
1 pound ziti or other tube-shaped pasta, freshly cooked and hot
Grated Parmesan cheese (optional)

1. Soak the bread crumbs with the milk in a bowl, then drain and squeeze out the excess liquid. In a large bowl, combine the soaked bread, turkey, egg, parsley, onion and garlic and season to taste with salt and pepper. Mix well. Taking scant tablespoonfuls, form the mixture into balls. Dredge the balls in flour, shaking off the excess.

2. Heat the oil in a large frying pan over medium-high heat. Add the meatballs and cook for about 5 minutes, shaking the pan frequently, until browned all over. Remove the meatballs from the pan, drain on paper towels and reserve.

3. To make the sauce: Reduce the heat to low and return the pan to the heat. If necessary, add another tablespoon of the oil to the pan. Add the onion and garlic and cook, stirring often, for about 3 minutes until softened. Increase the heat to medium and add the tomatoes, red wine and Italian seasoning. Bring the sauce to a boil. Reduce the heat to low and add the reserved meatballs. Simmer for 20 minutes, stirring occasionally. Season with salt and pepper to taste.

Serve the meatballs over the freshly cooked hot pasta with Parmesan cheese, if desired.

SHOPPING LIST

1 ¼ lbs. ground fresh turkey
Italian or French bread crumbs
1 lb. ziti or other tube-shaped pasta
parsley
onion
garlic
1 28-oz. can crushed tomatoes
Italian seasoning
flour
milk
Parmesan cheese
dry red wine

BAKED MACARONI AND CHEESE WITH HAM

Good old-fashioned baked macaroni and cheese never lets you down. For a meatless meal, leave out the ham.

Serves 6
Preparation time: 20 minutes
Cooking time: 45 minutes

INGREDIENTS

3 tablespoons butter or margarine
2 tablespoons flour
4 cups low-fat milk
1 tablespoon Dijon mustard
$\frac{1}{4}$ teaspoon salt
$\frac{1}{8}$ teaspoon freshly grated nutmeg
$\frac{1}{8}$ teaspoon cayenne pepper
1 onion, chopped
$\frac{1}{4}$ pound mushrooms, sliced
$\frac{1}{2}$ pound smoked, cooked ham, cut into
   $\frac{1}{4}$-inch pieces
$2\frac{1}{2}$ cups grated cheddar cheese
$\frac{3}{4}$ pound elbow macaroni
$\frac{1}{2}$ cup grated Parmesan cheese

1. Heat water for the pasta in a large saucepan.

2. Heat the oven to 400 degrees.

3. Heat 2 tablespoons of the butter in a 2-quart saucepan over low heat until foaming. Add the flour and cook, stirring for 2 minutes. Gradually stir in the milk and continue to stir until the mixture is smooth. Stir in the mustard, salt, nutmeg and cayenne.

4. Heat the remaining butter in a large skillet over medium heat. Add the onions and cook, stirring, for 4 or 5 minutes until softened. Add the mushrooms and ham and cook for an additional 10 or 12 minutes until the mushrooms are tender and the excess liquid has evaporated.

5. Gradually add the cheddar cheese to the white sauce, stirring after each addition, until melted. Add the mushroom mixture and stir well to combine.

6. Meanwhile, cook the pasta for 12 to 15 minutes until tender. Drain well in a colander.

7. Spoon half the macaroni into a buttered, 3-quart baking dish. Add half the sauce and stir gently to combine. Top with the remaining macaroni and pour the remaining sauce over it. Sprinkle with the Parmesan cheese and bake for 20 minutes.

SHOPPING LIST

$\frac{1}{2}$ lb. smoked, cooked ham
$\frac{3}{4}$ lb. elbow macaroni
onion
$\frac{1}{4}$ lb. mushrooms
fresh nutmeg
cayenne pepper
Dijon mustard
flour
butter or margarine
low-fat milk
cheddar cheese
Parmesan cheese

PASTA WITH TUNA AND CAPERS

Kids love shell-shaped pasta and its configuration is just right for a chunky sauce such as this one—the tuna clings to the crevices in the shells, while it would slip right off thin strands. With a can of tuna, a can of tomatoes and a jar of capers you can whip up a delicious, wholesome meal in less than an hour. And this is such a nice change from tuna-noodle casserole.

Serves 4
Preparation time: 15 minutes
Cooking time: 35 minutes

INGREDIENTS

3 tablespoons olive oil
1 small red onion, thinly sliced
28-ounce can whole tomatoes, drained and
    chopped
6½-ounce can water-packed tuna, drained
Salt and freshly ground pepper
¾ pound small pasta shells
2 tablespoons capers
4 tablespoons finely chopped parsley

1. Heat water for the pasta in a large saucepan.

2. Heat the oil in a large skillet over moderate heat. Add the onion and cook, stirring, for 5 to 8 minutes until softened. Add the tomatoes and cook for about 20 minutes. Stir in the tuna, season with salt and pepper to taste, and cook for another 5 minutes.

3. Meanwhile, cook the pasta in boiling salted water for 12 to 15 minutes until tender. Drain in a colander and then put in a warmed serving bowl.

4. Stir the capers and parsley into the sauce. Pour over the pasta and toss to combine. Serve immediately.

How Much Pasta?
Even the most seasoned cooks are sometimes baffled by the problem of how much pasta will feed how many people. As a general rule, a pound of dry pasta serves up to six people. If you are feeding hungry teenagers, a pound might only satisfy four or five. If the teens are on the high school football team, figure on a pound of pasta for three or four linebackers.

SHOPPING LIST
¾ lb. pasta shells
1 small red onion
capers
parsley
28-oz. can whole tomatoes
6 ½ oz.-can water-packed tuna
olive oil

PASTA WITH MIXED VEGETABLES

The vegetables are arranged in a specific way to ensure that they cook evenly in the microwave. When covering anything with plastic for microwave cooking, it is a good idea to turn back a corner to give built-up steam a way to escape. The Parmesan cheese adds great flavor but you may opt to leave it out if you are watching calories and fat.

Serves 4 to 6
Preparation time: 15 minutes
Cooking time: 16 to 20 minutes

INGREDIENTS

1½ cups thinly sliced carrots
2 medium-size zucchini, cut into
   2-by-⅛-inch strips
2 cups cauliflower florets
1 cup quartered mushrooms
4 tablespoons butter or margarine
½ teaspoon salt
2 tablespoons finely chopped onion
1 tablespoon all-purpose flour
⅛ teaspoon freshly ground pepper
1 cup low-fat milk
2 tablespoons grated Parmesan cheese,
   optional
3 tablespoons chopped parsley
½ pound linguine or vermicelli, cooked and
   drained

1. Arrange the carrots around the outside of a 12-inch round microwave-safe platter. Make a circle of cauliflower and zucchini strips in alternating groups inside the carrot border. Put the mushrooms in the center of the platter.

2. Put 2 tablespoons of the butter or margarine in a glass measure and microwave on High (100 percent) for 30 to 40 seconds until melted. Combine the melted butter with ¼ teaspoon of the salt and spoon the mixture over the vegetables. Cover with plastic wrap, turning back one corner to vent. Microwave on High (100 percent) for 6 to 10 minutes, rotating the platter after 4 minutes. Let the vegetables stand, still covered, for 2 minutes before testing for doneness; they should be crisp-tender.

3. To make the sauce, put 2 tablespoons of butter in a 1-quart microwave-safe measure. Microwave on High (100 percent) for 30 to 45 seconds or until melted. Stir in the onion and microwave on High (100 percent) for 1 minute, until the onion is soft. Stir in the flour, the remaining salt and the pepper. Add the milk gradually, stirring until the mixture is smooth. Microwave on High (100 percent) for 3 to 5 minutes, stirring every minute, until the sauce is slightly thickened. Stir in 1 tablespoon of the cheese, if desired, and 2 tablespoons of parsley.

4. Toss the pasta with the remaining butter, cheese and parsley. Spoon the vegetables over the pasta and top with the sauce.

SHOPPING LIST

½ lb. linguine or vermicelli
2 medium zucchini
carrots
cauliflower
mushrooms
onion
parsley
flour
low-fat milk
Parmesan cheese

BOLOGNESE SAUCE

Robust, meaty Bolognese Sauce may be made days ahead and reheated as needed with no loss of flavor but, rather, an enhancement. On the other hand, it can be made shortly before serving. This full-bodied sauce is best served with sturdy strands of spaghetti.

Makes about 3 cups
Preparation time: 15 minutes
Cooking time: about 50 minutes

INGREDIENTS

1 tablespoon butter or margarine
1 tablespoon olive oil
1 medium-size onion, finely chopped
2 cloves garlic, finely chopped
1 carrot, finely chopped
2 stalks celery, sliced
$\frac{1}{4}$ pound ground lean pork
$\frac{1}{4}$ pound ground lean beef
$\frac{1}{4}$ pound bacon or prosciutto, diced
$\frac{1}{2}$ cup tomato puree
$\frac{1}{2}$ cup beef broth
$\frac{1}{2}$ cup red wine
$\frac{1}{4}$ pound mushrooms, sliced
$\frac{1}{2}$ teaspoon dried oregano
Salt and freshly ground pepper

1. Heat the butter with the oil in a large sauce-pan over medium heat. Add the onion, garlic, carrot and celery and cook for about 5 minutes, until the onion is softened.

2. Crumble the pork and beef into the pan and add the bacon, turning the mixture quickly with a fork. Cook gently for 10 minutes. Drain off and discard the accumulated fat.

3. Thin the tomato puree with a few spoonfuls of the broth. Add it to the pan with the remaining broth and the wine. Stir in the mushrooms and the oregano and season with salt and pepper to taste. Lower the heat, cover the pan and simmer for 30 minutes. Adjust the seasonings if necessary and serve over freshly cooked pasta.

SHOPPING LIST

$\frac{1}{4}$ lb. ground lean pork
$\frac{1}{4}$ lb. ground lean beef
$\frac{1}{4}$ lb. bacon or prosciutto
onion
garlic
carrots
celery
$\frac{1}{4}$ lb. mushrooms
dried oregano
beef broth
tomato puree
olive oil
butter or margarine
red wine

POULTRY

Most families eat chicken at least once a week and generally more often. And why not? It is low in fat and high in protein—and, compared to other meats, does not cost much. This is equally true for the chicken's close cousin, the turkey, which is finding its way to America's supper tables more and more often. Both birds' mild flavor goes well with nearly any combination of ingredients so that with very little effort the simple chicken or turkey becomes a fiery feast, an earthy repast or a light and delicate meal.

In this chapter we have concentrated on chicken and turkey, with a quick nod to Cornish game hens. These are the fowl most often consumed by the American family, and chicken certainly leads the way. If possible, purchase poultry fresh and unfrozen. Freezing, according to many people, may not significantly alter the taste or texture of chicken and turkey but nonetheless, it is *best* when it is fresh. Unwrap the bird when you get home, rinse it off and dry it with paper towels and then re-wrap it in clean wax paper and plastic for refrigerator storage. As with fish, it is a good idea to keep the poultry near the back of the refrigerator on the lowest shelf where it is coldest. Eat the chicken or turkey within a day or two. Be sure to cut chicken on a clean cutting board and, even more importantly, wash the board and knife thoroughly after you have finished with the poultry and before you use it again. This eliminates the possibility of spreading bacteria. Plastic, nonporous cutting boards are the best sort to use for chicken and turkey.

We are well aware that most families are too busy to get to the market every time they want chicken or turkey and so will choose to freeze either whole birds or parts to have on hand for everyday meals. This is sensible planning and does save time and energy when you need it most—at the end of a long working day! Try to freeze poultry that has not been frozen once already. Unwrap the bird, rinse and pat it dry and then wrap it well in plastic and foil. Mark the package with the date and try to eat the chicken or turkey within a month of freezing. Let frozen poultry defrost overnight and all the next day in the refrigerator, or, if your schedule permits, on the counter for a few hours. If the day is particularly hot, however, keep a close watch on the bird. Raw chicken and turkey can spoil relatively quickly. As soon as the bird seems thawed, refrigerate it until it is time to cook it. The microwave is a big help when it comes to thawing poultry and can make dinner possible even when you have neglected to take the frozen bird from the freezer earlier in the day.

We offer an array of poultry recipes designed to tempt the entire family. There are simple, practically unadorned preparations such as Herb-Marinated Chicken and Grilled Lemon Chicken. For more exotic fare, try the Moroccan Cornish Hens or the Chicken with Coconut Sauce. Oven Deviled Chicken with Yogurt and Arizona Chicken are sure to be hits with the entire family—down to the preschoolers in the crowd—and for sheer fun, we suggest Turkey Fajitas and Plymouth Chili. The selection is large and varied and we hope this chapter will get frequent use so that, before long, the following pages are comfortably dog-eared!

OVEN-DEVILED CHICKEN
WITH YOGURT

Your kids will thank you every time you make this chicken. It tastes equally good served piping hot in midwinter or served cold in midsummer, and is a great choice for picnics. No need to watch the chicken as it cooks—it crisps all by itself. If your family likes spicy food, add more cayenne pepper. It might be easier for you to marinate the chicken in the yogurt-mustard mixture for the entire day while you are at work. If so, the flavor will be even better.

Serves 4
Preparation time: 5 minutes
Cooking time: 55 minutes

INGREDIENTS

½ cup plain low-fat yogurt
3 tablespoons Dijon mustard
¾ teaspoon Tabasco sauce
½ teaspoon salt
3- to 3½-pound chicken, cut into pieces, rinsed and patted dry
2½ cups fresh bread crumbs
¼ teaspoon cayenne pepper
2 tablespoons olive or vegetable oil

1. Line a 9-by-13-inch baking dish with heavy-duty aluminum foil. Spray the dish lightly with non-stick vegetable oil spray. Heat the oven to 400 degrees.

2. In a large bowl, stir together the yogurt, mustard, Tabasco and salt. Add the chicken and stir until the chicken is well coated.

3. In a medium bowl, combine the bread crumbs and cayenne pepper. Roll each piece of chicken in the bread crumbs. Put the chicken in the prepared pan and drizzle with the olive oil. Bake for 50 minutes to 1 hour until golden brown and the juices run clear when the chicken in pierced. Serve hot, warm or at room temperature.

SHOPPING LIST

3 to 3 ½ lbs. chicken
Dijon mustard
Tabasco sauce
bread crumbs
cayenne pepper
olive or vegetable oil
low-fat yogurt

TURKEY FAJITAS

Think twice about introducing your family to these fajitas; you may soon tire of the ceaseless begging for them night after night! But perhaps you won't mind—they are painlessly easy to make and since the toppings (salsa, guacamole and sour cream) can be changed, substituted or eliminated, a fajita to suit every taste is not out of the question. When these rather messy but fun tortilla sandwiches were first imported across the border to Texas, they always contained strips of grilled steak. Ours are filled with healthier turkey—but with no loss of flavor.

Serves 4
Preparation time: 10 minutes
Cooking time: 5 minutes

INGREDIENTS

1½ pounds sliced turkey breast (uncooked)
½ teaspoon ground cumin
¼ teaspoon ground coriander (optional)
Juice of 1 lime
2 teaspoons vegetable oil
8 flour tortillas
Salt and freshly ground pepper
Shredded lettuce
Sour cream or plain yogurt
Santa Fe Guacamole (page 273)
Five-Alarm Salsa (page 273)
Coriander sprigs

1. Heat the oven to 350 degrees.

2. Rub the turkey with the cumin and coriander and put it in a shallow non-aluminum bowl. Add the lime juice and oil and turn the turkey pieces to make sure they are well coated. Marinate for 10 minutes.

3. Meanwhile, wrap the tortillas in foil and heat in the oven for about 10 minutes until warmed through.

4. Heat the broiler. Sprinkle the turkey lightly with salt and pepper and broil for 2 to 3 minutes until opaque on one side. Remove the thinner slices at this point as they will be cooked through. Turn the remaining slices and broil for about 1 minute more until cooked through.

5. Cut the turkey into 1-inch-wide strips and serve wrapped in the warmed tortillas and topped with the lettuce, sour cream, Santa Fe Guacamole, Five-Alarm Salsa and coriander sprigs.

SHOPPING LIST

1 ½ lbs. sliced turkey breast (uncooked)
8 flour tortillas
lettuce
1 lime
3 medium avocados
3 lbs. medium tomatoes
onions
garlic
2 chili peppers (fresh or canned)
ground cumin
sour cream or plain yogurt

ARIZONA CHICKEN

Redolent with the flavors so favored in the great American Southwest, this "couldn't be easier" chicken recipe is adapted from one for Red-Chili Marinade developed by Rick Bayless. If you have the time, let the chicken marinate in the spice paste for several hours in the refrigerator.

Serves 4
Preparation time: 10 minutes
Cooking time: 45 minutes

INGREDIENTS

2 medium-size cloves garlic, finely chopped
¼ cup orange juice or cider vinegar
1 tablespoon vegetable oil
2 tablespoons mild paprika or chili powder
1½ teaspoons ground cumin
1 teaspoon dried oregano
½ teaspoon cinnamon
½ teaspoon hot red pepper flakes
½ teaspoon ground coriander (optional)
½ teaspoon salt
2 tablespoons water
4 pounds chicken parts
Lime wedges

1. Heat the oven to 375 degrees.

2. Put all the ingredients except the chicken and lime in the bowl of a food processor and process to a smooth paste.

3. Put the chicken in a large baking dish or small roasting pan. Spread the spice paste over the chicken and bake for 40 to 45 minutes until the chicken is cooked through. Serve with lime wedges.

Paprika
To obtain the fullest flavor from paprika (and curry and chili powder), sauté it for a moment or two in hot butter or oil.

SHOPPING LIST

4 lbs. chicken parts
garlic
dried oregano
ground cumin
cinnamon
hot red pepper flakes
ground coriander
1 lime
orange juice or cider vinegar
mild paprika or chili powder
vegetable oil

WALNUT-CHEESE CHICKEN BREASTS

T he filling for these breasts is pushed right under the skin, a method which serves two delicious purposes. First, the filling becomes even more tasty as it bastes in the chicken juices during baking. Secondly, the chicken breasts stay nice and moist, since the filling provides a shield from the drying heat of the oven. Beware of over-stuffing the chicken— excess filling will seep out during cooking.

Serves 4
Preparation time: 15 minutes
Cooking time: 40 minutes

INGREDIENTS

¾ cup part-skim ricotta cheese
½ cup finely chopped walnuts
¼ cup grated Parmesan cheese
2 tablespoons fresh bread crumbs
2 tablespoons chopped fresh basil or parsley
Salt and freshly ground pepper
4 chicken breast halves, with bones and
　skin
Olive oil
¼ cup dry white wine or vermouth

1. Position a rack in the top of the oven. Heat the oven to 375 degrees. Lightly oil a medium-sized baking dish.

2. In a medium bowl, combine the ricotta, walnuts, Parmesan, bread crumbs and salt and pepper to taste. Slip your fingers between the skin

and meat of one chicken breast. Stuff about one-fourth of the cheese filling under the skin. Repeat with the remaining breasts. Arrange the breasts in the prepared baking dish. Brush the breasts with olive oil, sprinkle with the wine and season with salt and pepper to taste.

3. Bake the chicken breasts for 35 to 40 minutes, basting occasionally, until the juices run clear when the chicken is pierced. Serve hot, warm or at room temperature.

SHOPPING LIST

4 chicken breast halves, with bones and skin
basil or parsley
chopped walnuts
olive oil
bread crumbs
part-skim ricotta cheese
Parmesan cheese
dry white wine or vermouth

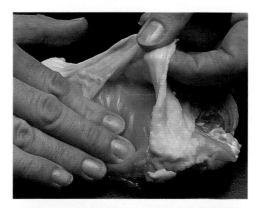

CHICKEN BASQUAISE

Try this sauce and cooking method with pork chops or fish fillets, too. Serve the chicken with boiled potatoes and a plain vegetable such as broccoli or peas.

Serves 4
Preparation time: 15 minutes
Cooking time: 40 minutes

INGREDIENTS

6 skinless, boneless chicken breasts,
   $1\frac{1}{2}$ to 2 pounds
Salt and freshly ground pepper
2 tablespoons olive oil
2 medium-size onions, thinly sliced
$\frac{1}{2}$ teaspoon dried thyme
$\frac{1}{4}$ teaspoon dried rosemary
$1\frac{1}{4}$ pounds red and green peppers, sliced
Pinch of cayenne
2 medium-size cloves garlic, finely chopped
1 pound tomatoes, cored, peeled, seeded and
   chopped, or 1-pound can whole peeled
   tomatoes, drained
$\frac{1}{4}$ cup dry white wine or $\frac{1}{4}$ cup liquid from
   canned tomatoes
2 teaspoons capers (optional)

1. Lightly sprinkle the chicken breasts with salt and pepper. Heat 1 tablespoon of oil over medium-high heat in a frying pan large enough to hold the chicken. Cook the chicken for about 2 minutes until lightly browned on each side. Remove from the pan.

2. Lower the heat to medium. Add the onions and the herbs to the pan and cook for 5 minutes, stirring often. Add the peppers and cook for about 10 minutes more, stirring often, until the vegetables are softened. Stir in the cayenne and salt and pepper to taste. Add the garlic and the tomatoes and stir in the white wine. Cover and cook for 10 minutes more.

3. Return the chicken to the pan. Cover and cook for 5 to 10 minutes, turning the chicken once or twice, until it is cooked through. Remove the chicken to a serving platter.

4. Stir the capers into the sauce, if desired. If the sauce is thin, boil over high heat until reduced. Taste and adjust the seasoning. Spoon the sauce over the chicken and serve.

SHOPPING LIST

6 skinless, boneless chicken breasts
(1 $\frac{1}{2}$ to 2 lbs.)
onions
1 $\frac{1}{4}$ lbs. red and green peppers
garlic
1 lb. tomatoes (fresh or canned)
capers
dried thyme
dried rosemary
cayenne
olive oil
dry white wine or $\frac{1}{4}$ cup liquid from
canned tomatoes

CHICKEN CHOUCROUTE

On a blustery night when the family needs a warming, filling meal, try this tasty chicken and cabbage dish. It is especially good with the Potato Skillet Cake found on page 220.

Serves 4
Preparation time: 15 minutes
Cooking time: 1 hour

INGREDIENTS

1 tablespoon olive or vegetable oil
4 pounds chicken parts
Salt and freshly ground pepper
2 large onions, thinly sliced
2 large carrots, sliced into thin rounds
1 large head green cabbage (1¾ to 2
   pounds), very thinly sliced
¼ cup chicken broth or water
¼ cup white wine vinegar
1 bay leaf

1. Heat the oil in a large frying pan over medium-high heat. Sprinkle the chicken with salt and pepper and cook for 15 to 20 minutes until well browned on all sides. Remove from the pan.

2. Lower the heat to medium. Add the onions and carrots and cook for 5 minutes, scraping up the browned bits from the bottom of the pan. Add the cabbage and cook for about 10 minutes, stirring, until wilted. Add the broth, vinegar and bay leaf and season to taste with salt and pepper. Bring to a simmer and simmer for 2 minutes, stirring occasionally.

3. Lower the heat to medium-low. Put the chicken on top of the cabbage, cover and cook for 20 to 25 minutes until the chicken is tender and the juices run clear when pierced. Serve the chicken on the bed of cabbage.

SHOPPING LIST
4 lbs. chicken parts
onions
carrots
green cabbage (1 ¾ to 2 lbs.)
bay leaves
chicken broth
white wine vinegar
olive or vegetable oil

HERB-MARINATED CHICKEN

1. Crush the garlic cloves and rub them over the chicken. Put the chicken with the garlic in a non-aluminum container and sprinkle with pepper. Add the remaining ingredients except salt and turn the chicken to coat it in the mixture. Let the chicken marinate for 1 to 2 hours, turning several times.

2. Light the charcoal grill. Remove the chicken from the marinade and sprinkle it lightly with salt. Grill the chicken, skin side down, for about 10 minutes until the skin is crisp and golden brown. Turn the chicken and continue grilling for about 20 minutes until the juices run clear when the chicken is pierced with a knife at its thickest point. Baste frequently with the marinade during cooking.

We readily admit that this recipe takes a while longer than an hour and therefore may not deserve the "quick" label, but since most of the time is taken up with marinating, we thought you would want to include it in your menu planning. It is a wonderful way to serve chicken on a weekend when you have a little time for advance preparation but not much for fiddling in the kitchen. Lemon juice and olive oil make a classic marinade for chicken. Balsamic vinegar mellows the acidity of the lemon.

Serves 4
Preparation time: 10 minutes, plus marinating time
Cooking time: 30 minutes

INGREDIENTS

2 large cloves garlic
4 chicken breast halves (about 3 pounds), with bones and skin
Salt and freshly ground pepper
½ cup olive oil
¼ cup lemon juice
2 tablespoons balsamic vinegar
2 teaspoons dried thyme
2 teaspoons dried rosemary
2 bay leaves, crushed
6 sprigs parsley

SHOPPING LIST

4 chicken breast halves (about 3 lbs.) with bones and skin
bay leaves
parsley
garlic
lemon
dried thyme
dried rosemary
balsamic vinegar
olive oil

GRILLED GINGER-SESAME CHICKEN WINGS

In the summer, grill a large batch of these sesame-flavored chicken wings and sit back as your family heartily enjoys a casual supper on the deck, porch or picnic table. These wings also make great cocktail party food. We use two kinds of sesame oil in the recipe—a light-colored oil for cooking, which is found in health food stores, and the familiar amber-colored Oriental sesame oil, which is found in supermarkets and Asian markets. The latter provides the good sesame flavor.

Serves 4 to 6
Preparation time: 15 minutes, plus marinating time
Cooking time: 20 minutes

INGREDIENTS

4 pounds chicken wings
1½ tablespoons chopped fresh ginger
1 jalapeno pepper, stemmed, seeded and chopped
2 medium-size cloves garlic, chopped
2 tablespoons brown sugar
6 tablespoons low-sodium soy sauce
¼ cup sherry
2 tablespoons sesame or vegetable oil
2 teaspoons Oriental sesame oil

1. Light the charcoal grill.

2. Remove the smallest section of each wing at the joint and discard.

3. In a non-aluminum container, combine the remaining ingredients and stir to blend. Add the chicken wings and turn to coat them in marinade. Let the wings marinate, turning several times, while the grill heats, or for at least 40 minutes.

4. Remove the wings from the marinade and grill them, brushing often with the marinade, for about 20 minutes until the skin is crisp and lacquered and the meat is tender.

SHOPPING LIST

4 lbs. chicken wings
fresh ginger
1 jalapeno pepper
garlic
brown sugar
low-sodium soy sauce
sherry
sesame oil
vegetable oil

CHICKEN AND SPRING VEGETABLE STIR FRY

Adapted from a recipe for a ragout of spring vegetables from the Greens restaurant cookbook by Deborah Madison, this recipe marries Oriental technique with Western ingredients. The classic stir fry, enhanced by the wonderful combination of chicken and asparagus, should be served with boiled or steamed rice.

Serves 4
Preparation time: 25 minutes
Cooking time: 20 minutes

INGREDIENTS

3 tablespoons olive oil
1 pound boneless, skinless chicken breast, cut crosswise into thin slices
2 cups firmly packed thinly sliced Chinese cabbage
3 ounces snow peas, stems removed
1 cup chopped scallion
1 teaspoon chopped fresh ginger
1 tablespoon butter
6 ounces white mushrooms, sliced
½ pound asparagus, trimmed and cut diagonally into 1½- to 2-inch lengths
2 small carrots, peeled and sliced diagonally into ⅛- to ¼-inch slices
½ cup dry white wine
½ cup water
¼ cup chopped parsley

1. In a large frying pan, heat 1 tablespoon of oil over high heat. Add the chicken and cook, stirring, for 2 to 3 minutes until the chicken is opaque. Remove the chicken to a bowl.

2. Add 1 more tablespoon of oil to the pan. Add the cabbage, snow peas, scallion and ginger and cook, stirring, 3 to 4 minutes until the cabbage wilts. Remove to the bowl with the chicken.

3. Reduce the heat to medium-high and add 1 tablespoon of oil and the butter to the pan. Add the mushrooms, asparagus and carrots and cook for about 3 minutes until the mushrooms wilt. Add the wine and water, cover and cook gently for about 5 minutes until the vegetables are tender. Remove the cover, increase the heat to high and boil for 1 to 2 minutes until the liquid is reduced and thickened. Return the reserved chicken and vegetables to the bowl along with the parsley and stir to coat with the sauce.

SHOPPING LIST

1 lb. boneless, skinless chicken breast
Chinese cabbage
snow peas
scallion
ginger
6 oz. white mushrooms
½ lb. asparagus
carrots
parsley
olive oil
butter
dry white wine

MOROCCAN CORNISH HENS

If you are feeding children, half a hen will do for a serving, which nicely stretches this recipe. You can also reduce the cooking time by 10 to 15 minutes if you sever the hens completely into halves. If so, use four lemons and nestle the squeezed lemon halves beneath each hen half.

Serves 4
Preparation time: 10 minutes
Cooking time: 50 to 55 minutes

INGREDIENTS

4 cornish game hens, about $1\frac{1}{2}$ pounds each
4 large cloves garlic
1 teaspoon salt
1 tablespoon paprika
1 teaspoon cumin seed
$\frac{1}{4}$ cup olive oil
2 large lemons, halved

1. Preheat the oven to 400 degrees.

2. Using a sharp, heavy knife, split each hen along its back, and open up flat. Place the hens skin side up on roasting pans large enough to hold them flat without crowding. Squeeze the juice of half a lemon over each hen. Place a squeezed half underneath each hen.

3. Using a sharp knife, chop the garlic with the salt until very finely chopped. Scrape the garlic into a small bowl and add the paprika and cumin. With the back of a spoon crush the mixture against the side of the bowl. Gradually add the oil, mixing continuously until a thin paste forms. (Alternatively, crush the garlic, salt, paprika and cumin in a mortar and pestle. Gradually mix in the olive oil until smooth.) With a spoon, coat each hen evenly with the paste.

4. Bake for 50 to 55 minutes, basting often with the pan juices, until the hens' juices run clear yellow when pierced with a fork.

SHOPPING LIST

4 cornish hens, about 1 ½ lbs. each
garlic
2 lemons
paprika
cumin seed
olive oil

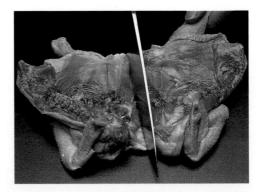

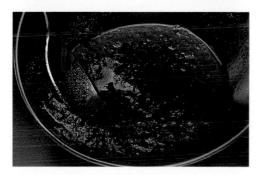

147

GRILLED CHICKEN WITH NEW ENGLAND BARBECUE SAUCE

The barbecue sauce is not a marinade—you brush it on the chicken only toward the end of cooking and then pass it at the table. This is typical of how red barbecue sauces are employed during cooking. They simply and purely flavor the chicken with a sweet, true taste unobtainable any other way. They do not tenderize, as do marinades. In the summer, try this chicken grilled.

Serves 4
Preparation time: 2 minutes
Cooking time: 25 minutes

INGREDIENTS

Barbecue Sauce (page 275)
$\frac{1}{2}$ teaspoon garlic salt
$\frac{1}{4}$ teaspoon freshly ground black pepper
$\frac{1}{8}$ teaspoon ground red hot pepper
4 chicken breast halves, with bones and
    skins, rinsed and patted dry

1. Make the Barbecue Sauce. Set aside $\frac{1}{2}$ cup and reserve the rest for another use.

2. In a small bowl, mix the garlic salt, black pepper and red pepper. Sprinkle the chicken breasts with the spice mixture and allow to stand at room temperature for about 20 minutes. Heat the broiler to high.

3. Lightly oil a broiler rack and put the chicken on it. Broil the breasts about 5 inches from the heat for 25 to 30 minutes, turning them often. During the last 10 minutes of cooking time, brush the chicken with the barbecue sauce. Serve immediately with additional barbecue sauce, if desired.

Defrosting Chicken
  To defrost chicken parts in the microwave, remove packaging and place in the dish required for the recipe. (Defrosting will be more rapid without the insulation of plastic wrap and foam meat trays.) Microwave on Medium-Low (30%) for 5 to 7 minutes per pound.
  After half the defrosting time, turn the chicken upside down. Separate the parts as soon as possible. If some areas of the chicken have thawed while others are still frozen, use small pieces of aluminum foil to cover the thawed areas.
  Remove thin or bony pieces (such as wings or drumsticks) from the oven as soon as they thaw. Leave breasts and thighs in the oven for the remaining time, because they take longer to defrost. Rinse in cool water and pat dry with paper towels before cooking.

SHOPPING LIST
4 chicken breast halves, with bones and skins
onion
garlic
garlic salt
ground red hot pepper
Dijon mustard
maple-flavored syrup
cider vinegar
12-oz. bottle chili sauce

PENNSYLVANIA DUTCH CHICKEN POT PIE

Do not expect anything much resembling a pie when you follow this recipe. It is more of a chicken stew fortified with pasta and earning its name because the ingredients are similar to those found in chicken pot pies. The pasta is a stand-in for a pastry crust. The pasta also makes it more nutritious. This pie—or should we say stew?—can be made ahead of time and reheated.

Serves 6
Preparation time: 30 minutes
Cooking time: 1 hour

INGREDIENTS

4 pounds chicken parts
2 onions sliced
1 carrot, cut into 1-inch pieces
1 stalk celery, cut into 1-inch pieces
1 bay leaf
½ teaspoon salt
¼ teaspoon peppercorns
2 cups sliced carrots
¼ pound bow-shaped pasta or broad egg noodles
1 cup fresh or frozen peas

1. Put the stewing hen in a large covered saucepan or Dutch oven with the onions, carrots, celery, bay leaf, salt and peppercorns. Add water to cover and bring to the boil over medium-high heat, skimming off any foam that rises to the surface. Reduce the heat to low, cover the pan and simmer for about 45 minutes until the chicken is tender.

2. Lift the chicken from the pan and strain the liquid. Discard the vegetables. When the chicken is cool enough to handle, remove and discard the skin. Pull the meat from the bones and cut it into 1-inch pieces.

3. Pour the strained cooking liquid into a large saucepan and season with salt and pepper to taste. Bring to the boil over medium-high heat. Add the sliced carrots, reduce the heat to medium and cook for 5 minutes. Stir in the noodles and cook for 8 to 9 minutes until just tender. Stir in the peas and the cooked chicken, heat through and serve.

SHOPPING LIST

4 lbs. chicken parts
¼ lb. bow-shaped pasta or broad egg noodles
onions
carrots
celery
bay leaves
peppercorns
fresh or frozen peas

PLYMOUTH CHILI

Our version of the now-famous Cincinnati Chili may call for ground turkey rather than beef but does not stint on the sheer fun of the dish. The only thing it stints on is fat. In Cincinnati, ingenious Greek short-order cooks serve beef chili over bowls of steaming hot spaghetti, top it with beans, grated cheese and onions and sometimes call it "five-way" chili. You figure it out. We named our chili after the site where the pilgrims first landed as a tribute to Thanksgiving and Tom Turkey. But wherever you find yourself—Ohio, Greece, Massachusetts or your own kitchen—just set the fixings for this dish on the table and let the family at it. They'll love it!

Serves 6 to 8
Preparation time: 10 minutes
Cooking time: 35 minutes

INGREDIENTS

2 tablespoons olive oil
1 large onion, coarsely chopped (about 1 cup)
1 large clove garlic, chopped
1¼ pounds ground turkey
About 1 tablespoon chili powder
½ teaspoon dried oregano
½ teaspoon cinnamon
8-ounce can tomato sauce
½ cup water
Salt and freshly ground pepper
1 pound tubular pasta, such as penne, freshly cooked and hot

16-ounce can kidney beans, drained and heated
4 ounces cheddar cheese or low-fat mozzarella, grated
1 cup finely chopped onion

1. Heat the oil in a large saucepan over medium heat. Add the onion and garlic and cook for 5 minutes, stirring occasionally, until softened. Add the turkey and cook, stirring, until the meat is no longer pink. Add the chili powder, oregano, cinnamon, tomato sauce, water and salt and pepper to taste. Bring the mixture to a simmer, then reduce the heat to low and cook, partially covered, for 30 minutes, adding additional water if necessary.

2. Serve on top of cooked pasta, topped with desired amounts of beans, cheese and chopped onions.

Beans
Many packaged beans do not require presoak-
ing. Read the directions to find out whether or not
they should be soaked.

CHICKEN BREASTS
WITH APPLES

With this recipe, you cook the apples, the chicken and the sauce all in the same frying pan, but in stages. This would be delicious, too, with medallions of pork that have been pounded thin.

Serves 4
Preparation time: 5 minutes
Cooking time: 15 minutes

INGREDIENTS

3 tablespoons butter or margarine
1 tablespoon finely chopped shallot or onion
$\frac{1}{4}$ teaspoon dried thyme
$1\frac{1}{2}$ cups sliced, tart apples, such as Granny Smiths
$\frac{1}{2}$ cup flour
Salt and freshly ground pepper
2 tablespoons vegetable oil
2 whole, boneless, skinless chicken breasts, cut in half and pounded thin
$\frac{1}{4}$ cup half-and-half
$\frac{1}{2}$ cup chicken broth
4 tablespoons apple juice or cider
1 tablespoon cornstarch

1. Heat 2 tablespoons of butter in a frying pan over medium heat. Add the shallot, thyme and apple slices in a single layer. Cook for 3 minutes, turning once, until slightly softened. Transfer the mixture to a bowl and keep warm.

2. Season the flour with salt and pepper. Dredge the chicken breasts in the seasoned flour and shake off the excess.

3. Add the remaining butter and the oil to the pan and heat over medium heat. Cook the chicken breasts for 3 to 4 minutes on each side until lightly colored. Discard any fat remaining in the pan. Transfer the chicken to a warmed serving dish and cover with the apple mixture.

4. Pour the half and half, chicken broth and 3 tablespoons of the apple juice into the pan and cook until the sauce is hot. Dissolve the cornstarch in the remaining apple juice and stir into the sauce. Cook briefly, stirring, until the sauce begins to thicken.

5. Pour the sauce over the chicken and apples and serve immediately.

SHOPPING LIST
2 whole boneless, skinless chicken breasts
shallot or onion
2 large tart apples
dried thyme
cornstarch
chicken broth
butter or margarine
half-and-half

CHICKEN WITH COCONUT SAUCE

This tender chicken with its mild, exotic flavor is a specialty of Indonesia where much use is made of the readily available fresh coconuts and coconut milk. Lemongrass, hot chili and lime paste and coconut milk may be hard to find if you do not live in a large city with access to ethnic markets, but if you know of a shop selling Thai or Indonesian ingredients, please try this. You will be glad you did.

Serves 4
Preparation time: 10 minutes
Cooking time: 40 minutes

INGREDIENTS

2 onions, peeled and quartered
2 cloves garlic, peeled
1-inch piece fresh ginger, peeled
1-inch piece fresh lemongrass or 1
    teaspoon powdered lemongrass
1 teaspoon hot chili
1 teaspoon lime paste
2 cups coconut milk
1 teaspoon ground coriander
1 teaspoon turmeric
1 teaspoon salt
8 chicken thighs

1. Put the onions, garlic, ginger, lemongrass and hot chili and lime paste in a food processor or blender. Add ¼ cup of the coconut milk and process to make a paste. Add the remaining coconut milk, the coriander and the turmeric and process until smooth.

2. Pour the mixture into a heavy saucepan and bring to a simmer. Rub the salt into the chicken and add the chicken to the pan. Reduce the heat to low, cover the pan and cook the chicken for 25 minutes or until the juices run clear when a thigh is pierced.

3. Remove the chicken from the pan to a serving platter and keep warm. Turn the heat to high and cook the sauce for 10 to 15 minutes until it is reduced and thickened. Taste and add salt if necessary. Pour the sauce over the chicken and serve.

> *Fresh Ginger*
> *Keep fresh ginger root in the freezer and remove slices as needed.*

SHOPPING LIST

8 chicken thighs
onions
garlic
fresh ginger
lemongrass (fresh or powdered)
hot chili
lime paste
coconut milk
ground coriander
turmeric

ZUCCHINI STUFFED WITH SMOKED TURKEY

Hollowed-out zucchini make tasty containers for all sorts of fillings. This one, composed of a flavorful combination of smoked turkey, walnuts, vegetables and cheese, is a meal in itself. And they are fun to serve, too. Buy the smoked turkey at the local deli or specialty food market. It adds a depth of flavor you cannot get from other turkey meat, but if you cannot find it smoked, substitute roast turkey.

Serves 4
Preparation time: 30 minutes
Cooking time: 20 minutes

INGREDIENTS

2 pounds zucchini
3 tablespoons butter or margarine
1 cup finely chopped onion
¼ cup thinly sliced celery
¼ cup finely chopped red or green pepper
¼ cup finely chopped walnuts
1½ cups cooked smoked turkey
8-ounce can whole tomatoes, chopped
1 cup fresh whole wheat bread crumbs
¼ teaspoon freshly ground pepper
½ cup shredded mozzarella cheese
¼ cup grated Parmesan cheese

1. Heat the oven to 350 degrees. Cut the zucchini in half lengthwise. Scoop out the seeds and pulp with a spoon, leaving ¼-inch-thick shell. Chop the zucchini pulp and reserve.

2. Cover the bottom of a large frying pan with about ½ inch of water. Add salt and bring to the boil over high heat. Add the zucchini shells and lower the heat to a simmer. Cook, covered, for 5 minutes, until the shells are bright green and partially cooked. It may be necessary to cook the shells in 2 batches.

3. Remove the zucchini to a colander and rinse with cold water. Pat dry and put the shells in a baking dish.

4. Heat the butter in a large frying pan over medium heat. Add the onions, celery, peppers, walnuts and reserved zucchini pulp and cook for 5 or 6 minutes until the onions are just tender. Remove the pan from the heat and stir in the smoked turkey, tomatoes, breadcrumbs and black pepper. Mound the mixture into the zucchini shells.

5. Combine the mozzarella and Parmesan in a bowl. Sprinkle over the stuffed zucchini shells. Bake for about 25 minutes, until the zucchini is heated through and the cheese is golden.

SHOPPING LIST

1 ½ cups cooked smoked turkey
2 lbs. zucchini
onion
celery
1 red or green pepper
8-oz. can whole tomatoes
whole wheat bread crumbs
chopped walnuts
mozzarella cheese
Parmesan cheese

CHICKEN WITH SUMMER TOMATOES

This lovely chicken dish is best in the summer when you can get vine-ripened tomatoes bursting with good flavor, but do not hesitate to make it other times of the year. Use plum tomatoes, hydroponic fruit or drained canned tomatoes. You will not be disappointed.

Serves 6 to 8
Preparation time: 30 minutes
Cooking time: 1½ hours

INGREDIENTS

2 chickens, about 2½ pounds each
Salt and freshly ground pepper
2 teaspoons fresh thyme or 1 teaspoon dried
1 lemon, halved
2 tablespoons olive oil
2 tablespoons butter or margarine
2 small onions, finely chopped
2 cloves garlic, finely chopped
2 pounds tomatoes, peeled and chopped
1 teaspoon dried oregano or 1 tablespoon
   chopped fresh oregano
½ cup white wine
1½ cups chicken broth
2 tablespoons chopped chives

1. Heat the oven to 350 degrees. Season each chicken cavity with salt, pepper, thyme and a lemon half. Close each cavity and truss the birds.

2. Heat the olive oil and butter in a large casserole and, starting with the breast side down, cook the chickens for about 20 minutes until golden, turning occasionally. Transfer the birds to a platter.

3. Add the onion and garlic to the pan and cook for 5 minutes over medium heat. Add the tomatoes, oregano, wine and broth and cook over high heat for 10 to 15 minutes, until the tomatoes give off most of their liquid and the sauce is slightly thickened.

4. Return the chicken to the casserole and baste with the sauce. Cover and place in the oven for 1 hour or until the juices run clear when a leg is pierced.

5. Put the chickens on a carving board to rest briefly. Skim any fat from the juices in the pan and cook over high heat to reduce the liquid and intensify the flavor. Taste for seasoning and keep warm. Carve the chicken and serve. Pass the sauce separately.

Tomatoes
To remove the skins from tomatoes and peaches, plunge them in boiling water for ten seconds and then into a bowl of cold water for ten seconds. If the peel does not slip off easily repeat the procedure.
Do not slice tomatoes until you are ready to eat them or the seeds will fall out and make the plate watery.

SHOPPING LIST

2 chickens, about 2 ½ lbs. each
1 lemon
onions
garlic
2 lbs. tomatoes
chives
thyme (fresh or dried)
chicken broth
olive oil
white wine

CHICKEN WITH ROASTED SHALLOTS AND GARLIC SAUCE

Twenty-five cloves of garlic!? Yes—no misprint here. By the time the garlic has cooked with the chicken for nearly an hour, much of its pungency is diffused and all that is left is subtle, mild flavor. This chicken recipe is a little fancier and fussier than some of the others, so you might want to make it on a weekend or on an evening when you feel like spending time in the kitchen. The final result is splendid. Perhaps a budding chef in the family will help peel the cooked garlic, which actually is not as tedious as peeling fresh garlic; the skin slips right off.

Serves 4
Preparation time: 15 minutes
Cooking time: 1 hour

INGREDIENTS

12 shallots, peeled
$3\frac{1}{2}$-pound chicken
2 tablespoons lemon juice
2 tablespoons butter or margarine, softened
25 cloves garlic, unpeeled
$\frac{1}{4}$ cup white wine
$\frac{1}{2}$ cup chicken broth
2 tablespoons butter or margarine
Salt and freshly ground pepper

1. Heat the oven to 425 degrees.

2. Bring a saucepan of water to the boil over high heat. Plunge the shallots into the boiling water for 2 minutes. Drain in a colander and let cool.

3. Spread the shallots and garlic cloves in the bottom of a roasting pan. Rub the chicken all over with the lemon juice and softened butter, truss it and put it on a rack in the roasting pan. Pour in the wine and $\frac{1}{4}$ cup of the chicken broth. Roast the chicken for 20 minutes. Baste the chicken occasionally with the pan juices.

4. Reduce the oven temperature to 325 degrees and continue roasting and basting for 20 to 30 minutes, until the chicken legs move freely. Remove the chicken to a warmed platter, cover and let rest for 15 minutes.

5. Meanwhile, remove the garlic and shallots and spoon off as much fat as possible from the pan. Add the remaining $\frac{1}{4}$ cup of chicken broth. Peel the garlic and force it through a strainer back into the roasting pan. Put the pan over medium high heat and bring the liquid to the boil. Cook, stirring, for about 2 minutes. Whisk in the butter and season with salt and pepper to taste.

6. Carve the chicken and add any released juices to the sauce. Put the chicken on a serving platter and arrange the shallots around the outside. Pass the sauce separately.

SHOPPING LIST

3 ½ lbs. chicken
garlic
12 shallots
1 lemon
chicken broth
butter or margarine
white wine

GRILLED
LEMON CHICKEN

Lots of lemon juice makes this chicken moist and delicious. You will have to plan ahead for this, since the chicken must marinate for 3 or 4 hours. Leave it in the refrigerator all day while you are at the office, if that is easier on your schedule.

Serves 4 to 6
Preparation time: 15 minutes plus marinating
Cooking time: 35 to 40 minutes

INGREDIENTS

2 3-pound chickens, quartered
2 tablespoons grated lemon rind
$\frac{1}{2}$ cup fresh lemon juice
4 cloves garlic, crushed
1 teaspoon crushed black peppercorns
1 teaspoon crushed canned green
  peppercorns
$\frac{1}{2}$ cup olive oil
2 red onions, cut into $\frac{1}{4}$-inch slices

1. Combine the chicken pieces, lemon rind, lemon juice, garlic, wine, peppercorns and olive oil in a large bowl. Toss until the chicken is thoroughly coated. Cover the bowl and let the chicken marinate in the refrigerator, turning occasionally, for 3 to 4 hours.

2. Heat the broiler or light the charcoal grill.

3. Put the onion slices on a plate and brush them with some of the marinade. Lift the chicken from the marinade and put the dark pieces on a broiler pan or grill. Cook the dark meat under the heated broiler or on the very hot grill for about 15 minutes, turning and basting frequently with the marinade. Add the pieces of white meat and the onion slices to the pan and cook for another 20 minutes. Serve as soon as all the chicken is crisp and golden.

Chicken
When frying chicken, cook the legs first and then add the breasts later. Dark meat takes longer to cook than white meat.
Truss all chicken and other poultry before roasting or the wings and thighs will be overcooked.
When preparing a chicken for a salad or sandwiches, poach it in chicken broth to keep it moist and flavorful.
When chicken is cooked in a casserole, the leg meat shrinks, exposing the bone. For a more attractive appearance, trim off the bone ends and wing tips using poultry shears.
When boning a chicken breast, be sure to remove the white tendon or it will contract during cooking, causing the chicken meat to shrink.

SHOPPING LIST

2 3-lb. chickens
1 lemon
garlic
2 red onions
black peppercorns
canned green peppercorns
olive oil

BELGIAN CHICKEN CASSEROLE

In Belgium, this light, vegetable-filled dish is called *waterzooi*. A cross between a robust soup and a light stew, it is usually served in bowls. Because the chicken is cooked with the skin, the vegetables are especially well flavored; but after cooking the skin is removed, making this a relatively low-fat meal. If you choose to, you can omit the egg and milk sauce. The texture and flavor may not be as good but the calories and cholesterol will be substantially reduced.

Serves 4
Preparation time: 10 minutes
Cooking time: about 35 minutes

INGREDIENTS

3 pounds chicken parts
Freshly ground pepper
2 tablespoons butter or margarine
4 leeks, sliced or 2 onions, finely chopped
2 stalks celery, sliced
2 carrots, sliced
2 cups chicken broth
2 large egg yolks
2 tablespoons milk
3 tablespoons finely chopped parsley
1 teaspoon salt

1. Season the chicken pieces to taste with pepper.

2. Put the butter in a $2\frac{1}{2}$-quart microwave-safe casserole and microwave on High (100 percent) for 40 to 60 seconds until melted. Put the vegetables in the casserole and arrange the chicken pieces on top. Add the broth, cover and cook on Medium-High (70 percent) for 30 to 35 minutes until the chicken is cooked.

3. Lift the chicken from the casserole and let it cool. When it is cool enough to handle, remove and discard the skin.

4. Combine the egg yolks and milk and stir thoroughly. Stir the egg-milk mixture into the casserole. Return the chicken to the casserole and microwave on High (100 percent) for 2 to 3 minutes until the sauce is lightly thickened and the chicken is hot. Stir in the parsley and salt and serve immediately.

SHOPPING LIST

3 lbs. chicken parts
leeks
celery
carrots
parsley
chicken broth
eggs
milk
butter or margarine

STIR-FRIED
TURKEY BREAST

East meets west in this recipe when all-American turkey is stir fried after marinating in Asian spices. The result is worthy of international attention—or at least the attention of your family, who will love this quick, easy dish. Plan on several hours for marinating.

Serves 4
Preparation time: 15 minutes plus marinating
Cooking time: 10 minutes

INGREIDENTS

1½ pounds boneless, skinless turkey breast,
   cut into strips
2 tablespoons sesame oil
1 tablespoon soy sauce
1 teaspoon honey
¼ teaspoon dried cumin
½ teaspoon freshly ground black pepper
Pinch of cayenne pepper
2 tablespoons peanut oil
6 scallions, chopped
½ cup peanuts
Salt

1. Put the turkey strips in a bowl. Add the sesame oil, soy sauce, honey, cumin, black pepper and cayenne. Mix to coat the turkey. Cover the bowl and refrigerate for 2 hours.

2. Heat the peanut oil in a wok or large skillet over high heat. Add the turkey and stir-fry for 5 minutes. Add the scallions and peanuts and cook, tossing, for 8 or 9 minutes more. Season to taste with salt.

Chopsticks
When eating with chopsticks, imagine you are picking up a butterfly. This will prevent you from gripping the sticks so anxiously that they cross.

Peanut Oil
Peanut oil reaches the highest temperature of all cooking oils and is the first choice for Chinese cooking and deep-fat frying.

SHOPPING LIST
1 ½ lbs. boneless, skinless turkey breast
scallions
dried cumin
cayenne pepper
honey
sesame oil
soy sauce
peanut oil
½ cup peanuts

TURKEY SCALLOPINI WITH TOMATO AND VINEGAR SAUCE

Here is a no frills treatment for turkey cutlets that you can make with the supplies stored away in your cupboard. The light tomato sauce is underlined with the tang of vinegar and is so easy to make, dinner is ready in minutes. To cut back a little on calories, use a non-stick skillet and eliminate some of the oil. Most companies market turkey cutlets in one-pound packages which hold four or five cutlets, each weighing about three or four ounces.

Serves 4
Preparation time: 10 minutes
Cooking time: 15 minutes

INGREDIENTS

½ cup all-purpose flour
Salt and freshly ground pepper
1 pound turkey cutlets (4 or 5 cutlets, about 4 ounces each)
3 tablespoons olive oil, plus additional oil if necessary
2 tablespoons chopped shallots or onion
¼ cup red wine vinegar
1 cup peeled, seeded chopped fresh plum tomatoes or well-drained canned plum tomatoes
2 tablespoons drained capers (optional)
½ teaspoon dried tarragon or 1½ teaspoons fresh

1. Heat the oven to 250 degrees.

2. Combine the flour, salt and pepper in a shallow dish. Dredge the cutlets with the flour mixture, shaking off the excess.

3. Heat 1 tablespoon of the oil in a large skillet over medium-high heat. Cook the cutlets in batches, without crowding the pan, for about 4 minutes, turning once, until golden brown on both sides. Add additional oil to the pan if necessary. Transfer the cutlets to a platter, cover lightly with aluminum foil and keep warm in the oven.

4. Add 2 tablespoons of oil to the skillet and heat over medium-high heat. Add the shallots and cook, stirring, for about 30 seconds until softened. Add the vinegar and allow to bubble for 2 minutes until the liquid is almost evaporated. Add the tomatoes, capers, tarragon and salt and pepper to taste. Bring to a boil and serve the sauce immediately with the cutlets.

SHOPPING LIST

1 lb. turkey cutlets (4 or 5 cutlets, about 4 oz. each)
shallots or onion
capers
tarragon (dried or fresh)
flour
plum tomatoes (fresh or canned)
olive oil
red wine vinegar

TURKEY DIVAN

This is a great way to use up leftover turkey—and if you have none left over, it is worth a trip to the deli for sliced turkey. When you buy a whole turkey or a turkey breast, buy a little more than you will need right away, since there are so many delicious ways to use the leftovers. If you do not have chicken broth on hand to use in this recipe, substitute a teaspoon of crumbled bouillon or bouillon granules. Simply add it to the melted butter—no need to dissolve it in hot water.

Serves 4
Preparation time: 5 minutes
Cooking time: 10 minutes

INGREDIENTS

2 tablespoons butter or margarine
3 tablespoons all-purpose flour
1 tablespoon chicken broth
¼ teaspoon dry mustard
1½ cups low-fat milk
¼ cup mayonnaise
1 teaspoon lemon juice
2 cups fresh or frozen broccoli florets
¾ pound cooked, sliced turkey
2 tablespoons grated Parmesan cheese, optional

1. Put the butter in a 1-quart glass measure and microwave on High (100 percent) for 30 seconds until melted. Whisk in the flour, broth and mustard. Gradually stir in the milk. Microwave on High (100 percent) for 2 to 3 minutes until slightly thickened. Stir in the mayonnaise and lemon juice.

2. Put the broccoli in an 8-inch square microwave-safe pan and cover with plastic wrap. Turn back a corner to vent. Microwave on High (100 percent) for 2 to 4 minutes until the broccoli is crisp-tender.

3. Arrange the turkey slices on top of the broccoli. Pour the sauce over the turkey and sprinkle with the Parmesan, if desired. Microwave on High (100 percent) for 6 or 7 minutes until thoroughly heated.

SHOPPING LIST

¾ lb. cooked turkey
1 lemon
broccoli (fresh or frozen)
flour
dry mustard
mayonnaise
low-fat milk
Parmesan cheese
butter or margarine

BROILED CHICKEN WITH MUSTARD AND LEMON

Few chicken recipes are as easy or as tasty as this one. Spread the mustard-based, herb-filled baste on the chicken pieces and broil them. Try this on the grill, too.

Serves 4
Preparation time: 10 minutes
Cooking time: 40 minutes

INGREDIENTS

2½ pounds chicken parts
1 tablespoon vegetable oil
2 tablespoons Dijon mustard
2 tablespoons chopped parsley
2 tablespoons chopped chives
2 teaspoons dried marjoram
2 tablespoons fresh lemon juice

1. Brush the broiling rack with oil to prevent the chicken from sticking. Heat the broiler.

2. Dry the chicken thoroughly with paper towels. Combine the mustard, parsley, chives, marjoram and lemon juice. Brush the mixture over the chicken.

3. Broil the chicken 6 inches from the heat for 20 minutes on each side, basting every 5 minutes. Serve the chicken immediately or let cool to room temperature.

Lemons
Room temperature lemons yield more juice than chilled ones. To get the most juice, roll the lemon under the palm of your hand on the kitchen counter, pressing hard, before squeezing it. When you grate lemon rind, use a dry pastry brush to brush away any little pieces that stick to the grater.

SHOPPING LIST

2 ½ lbs. chicken parts
parsley
chives
1 lemon
vegetable oil
Dijon mustard
dried marjoram

POACHED CHICKEN BREASTS WITH ORANGE SAUCE

Poaching the chicken breasts preserves their tenderness and moistness—be sure, though, to keep the poaching liquid at a simmer and do not let it boil. We generally associate orange sauce with roast duck but it works equally well with chicken. The combination of watercress and orange sections makes a colorful and tasty garnish, although you could easily disregard them.

Serves 4
Preparation time: 10 minutes
Cooking time: 30 minutes

INGREDIENTS

1 cup orange juice
¾ cup chicken broth
2 scallions, chopped
2 6-ounce boneless chicken breasts
1½ tablespoons cornstarch
3 tablespoons cold water
1 bunch watercress, optional
1 large orange, peeled and sectioned,
   optional

1. Combine the orange juice, broth and scallions in a small saucepan. Place over moderate heat and simmer for 2 minutes. Put the chicken breasts in the poaching liquid and cover the pan. Poach for 15 to 20 minutes over low heat, until the chicken is tender and cooked through. Using a slotted spoon, remove the chicken from the pan, cover and keep warm.

2. Combine the cornstarch with the water in a small bowl and stir until smooth. Slowly pour the mixture into the poaching liquid, stirring constantly. Cook over moderate heat, stirring, for 3 to 4 minutes.

3. Bring a saucepan of water to the boil over high heat. Add the watercress to the pan and cook for 15 seconds, until wilted. Drain immediately through a colander.

4. Arrange the watercress on serving plates. Put the chicken on top of the watercress and spoon the sauce over the chicken. Serve the chicken garnished with orange sections.

SHOPPING LIST

2 6-oz. boneless chicken breasts
scallions
1 orange
watercress
1 can chicken broth
cornstarch

MEAT

Times are changing, there is no denying. We eat less red meat today than we did 10 years ago and far less than we did 20 years ago. But that does not mean we do not like it. Sometimes nothing will do except a slice of juicy steak, a bite of tender lamb or a forkful of sweet pork. And why not? Few main courses satisfy in precisely the same way.

Red meat is a good source of protein and iron as well as necessary vitamins. Some of it is high in fat and cholesterol, but eaten in moderation, a healthy adult or child can enjoy its full, robust flavor several times a month. We suggest you avoid those cuts that are heavily marbled with fat—which makes them tender and juicy but not too good for you. Select instead less expensive, leaner cuts with good color and little visible fat. Before cooking, trim any fat from the meat.

The following recipes are bursting with the wonderful flavor provided only by meat. The portions are smaller than some—about four ounces of meat per person—but are often embellished with a judicious amount of tasty vegetables or grains so that no one feels deprived. We offer several stir frys for fast cooking, offset by the comparatively slow cooking meals that you can forget about once they are in the oven. A number of the recipes are terrific grilled over charcoal, but we always provide broiling instructions as well for those readers who do not enjoy grilling or have no access to it. Grilling and broiling are particularly good cooking methods for meat as the fat drips away during cooking. Read through the following recipes for some good, sound ideas about how to incorporate everybody's favorite beef, lamb and pork into a healthy diet. Your family will appreciate it.

Dry meats on paper towels before frying or they will not brown. Do not salt meat before frying it. The salt causes the blood to rise to the surface and be lost in the hot fat and the meat will become dry and stringy and stick to the pan. Wait until the meat is turned before salting it.

Cook tough meats in a liquid; cook tender meats by dry heat, either by roasting or broiling.

To test the doneness of meat, press it with your finger. The more "done" it is, the greater will be the resistance.

The larger a roast, the longer will be its keeping potential. To extend its refrigerator life, marinate it and turn it in the marinade every day for up to 5 days.

If a piece of meat is smaller than 3 pounds in weight, do not attempt to roast it—it will become dry before it is fully cooked.

Roast meats and poultry on a rack so that the underside does not fry in its own fat.

Allow all roasts to stand for 15 minutes to allow the juices to reassemble. This will make carving easier and the meat will be moist and flavorful.

SOUTHWESTERN PORK STIR FRY

This quick fry-up is a surefire way to please a family with a penchant for Mexican and Tex-Mex fare. For the family who likes it hot (and some do), use fresh jalapeno or serrano peppers—for extra fire, toss the ribs and seeds of the peppers into the pan. For those who prefer their food a little milder, opt for canned green chilies, located in the Mexican food department of the supermarket. If you want to cut back on calories, use a non-stick frying pan and rely on one tablespoon of oil to fry the pork; this cuts out about 200 calories. Serve the pork with Cumin Rice (page 237).

Serves 4
Preparation time: 20 minutes
Cooking time: 10 minutes

INGREDIENTS
1 pound boneless pork tenderloin, cut into
   2-by-¼-inch strips
¼ cup plus 2 tablespoons olive oil, divided
1 tablespoon lime juice
1 large zucchini, scrubbed and trimmed
1 medium-size red or green pepper
1 small red onion
1 medium-size clove garlic
1 tablespoon finely chopped fresh jalapeno
   peppers or 2 tablespoons canned green
   chilies
1 cup fresh or defrosted corn kernels
1 tablespoon chili powder
Salt and freshly ground pepper
1 teaspoon cornstarch
½ cup beef broth

1. Combine the pork, ¼ cup of olive oil and the lime juice in a medium-sized, non-corrosive bowl. Let stand at room temperature for 20 minutes.

2. Meanwhile, prepare the vegetables. Slice the zucchini into ¼-inch rounds. Cut the red or green pepper into ¼-inch-wide strips, discarding the seeds, ribs and stem. Thinly slice the red onion. Finely chop the garlic.

3. Heat the remaining 2 tablespoons of olive oil in a large skillet until hot. Remove the pork from the marinade and pat dry. Cook the pork for 2 minutes, stirring often. Add the zucchini, red or green pepper, onion, garlic, jalapeno pepper or green chilies, corn, chili powder and salt and pepper to taste. Cook for 2 minutes more, stirring often.

4. Dissolve the cornstarch in the beef broth. Add to the skillet and cook just until the liquid comes to the boil and thickens. Serve immediately.

SHOPPING LIST
1 lb. boneless pork tenderloin
1 lime
1 large zucchini
1 medium red or green pepper
1 small red onion
garlic
1 jalapeno pepper (or canned green chili)
1 ear corn (or frozen kernels)
beef broth
olive oil
cornstarch

BEEF WITH PEPPERS AND CARROTS

Lean sirloin steak goes quite far when it is cooked with vegetables. Here, wrapped in simple paper towels, the meat cooks quickly with peppers and carrots for a fast, tasty meal. The steak is so tender to begin with, it needs only brief marinating for good, gingery flavor. We recommend using only white paper towels for microwave cooking.

Serves 2 to 3
Preparation time: 15 minutes plus marinating
Cooking time: 5 to 7 minutes

INGREDIENTS

2 tablespoons low-sodium soy sauce
2 teaspoons vegetable oil
$\frac{1}{2}$ teaspoon ground ginger
Freshly ground pepper
$\frac{1}{2}$ pound boneless sirloin steak, cut into $\frac{1}{4}$-inch strips
2 medium-size carrots, cut into $\frac{1}{4}$-inch strips
1 green pepper, cut into $\frac{1}{4}$-inch strips
4 tablespoons water

1. Combine the soy sauce, vegetable oil, ginger and pepper to taste in a small bowl. Add the steak and stir to coat it. Let the meat marinate for 15 minutes.

2. Lay 4 attached sheets of paper towel on the counter. Divide them into 2 pieces so that each one has 2 connecting sheets. Divide the carrots and peppers between the 2 sheets, laying the vegetables directly on the perforations. Lift the sirloin strips from the marinade and divide them equally between the 2 sheets of toweling on top of the vegetables.

3. Fold the paper towels over the food and then fold over the ends to make enclosed packets. Put both packets, perforated sides up, on a microwave-safe tray or plate. Sprinkle each packet with 2 tablespoons of water and microwave on High (100 percent) for 5 to 7 minutes until the vegetables are crisp-tender. Serve immediately.

SHOPPING LIST

$\frac{1}{2}$ lb. boneless sirloin steak
carrots
1 green pepper
ground ginger
low-sodium soy sauce
vegetable oil

GRILLED FLANK STEAK

Flank steak is an inexpensive cut of meat that benefits from marinating. While it will do fine marinated all day in the refrigerator, a quick soak on the kitchen counter once you get home in the evening flavors and tenderizes it just enough. Lemongrass, available at Oriental markets, adds an exotic, lemony flavor to this marinade but if you cannot find it, do not let that stop you from trying the recipe.

Serves 4
Preparation time: 10 minutes
Cooking time: 15 minutes

INGREDIENTS

$\frac{1}{4}$ cup lime juice
2 tablespoons vegetable oil
2 tablespoons Oriental sesame oil
3 tablespoons low-sodium soy sauce
2-inch piece fresh ginger, thinly sliced
2 scallions, chopped
2 stalks lemongrass, thinly sliced, optional
6 sprigs coriander
$\frac{1}{2}$ teaspoon hot red pepper flakes
2 pounds flank steak

1. Combine all of the ingredients except the steak in a large non-aluminum container. Add the steak and turn to coat in the marinade. Let the meat marinate while the grill heats.

2. Heat the broiler or light the charcoal grill. Broil or grill the steak 4 to 5 minutes on each side for medium-rare, brushing occasionally with the marinade. Let the cooked steak rest for 10 minutes before cutting it into thin slices. Spoon a little marinade over the steak, avoiding the ginger and lemongrass, and serve.

SHOPPING LIST

2 lbs. flank steak
scallions
1 lime
ginger
lemongrass
coriander
hot red pepper flakes
vegetable oil
Oriental sesame oil
low-sodium soy sauce

GREEK MEATLOAF WITH TOMATO SAUCE

Honey and vinegar, a common combination in Greek cooking, flavor the lowly meatloaf and raise it to new gustatory heights. Since half the tomato sauce is heated and served with the cooked meatloaf (the other half is spread on top), you can leave the ketchup bottle in the kitchen. If you prefer, try a combination of equal proportions of ground beef, pork and veal. Leftovers make great sandwiches, such as the Meatloaf Sandwich with Mustard and Horseradish (page 15).

Serves 4
Preparation time: 25 minutes
Cooking time: 1 hour to 1 hour and
    10 minutes

INGREDIENTS

2 tablespoons plus 1 teaspoon olive oil
3 medium cloves garlic, chopped
2 11-ounce cans Italian plum tomatoes, drained, seeded and coarsely chopped
$\frac{1}{4}$ cup red wine vinegar
1 tablespoon honey
Salt and freshly ground pepper
2 pounds very lean (90 percent lean, if possible) ground beef
1 medium-size onion, finely chopped
1 egg
$\frac{1}{2}$ cup fresh whole wheat bread crumbs (about 1 slice bread)
$\frac{1}{2}$ cup chopped parsley
1 tablespoon chopped fresh oregano or 1 teaspoon dried

1. Heat 1 teaspoon oil in a medium saucepan over medium heat. Add 1 clove of garlic and cook for 1 minute. Add the tomato and cook for about 5 minutes. Add the vinegar and honey and simmer for 20 to 25 minutes until thickened. Season to taste with salt and pepper.

2. Meanwhile, heat the oven to 350 degrees. Lightly combine the remaining ingredients, 1 teaspoon of salt and $\frac{1}{2}$ teaspoon of pepper, being careful not to mash the meat, and pack the mixture into a loaf pan. Bake for 30 minutes. Spread the meatloaf with a little more than half of the tomato mixture and bake for another 30 minutes.

3. Bring the remaining tomato mixture back to a simmer. Slice the meatloaf and serve the tomato sauce on the side.

LONDON BROIL WITH GARLIC-MUSTARD CRUST

London broil is another smart buy at the meat counter as it is far less expensive than other steaks. Cooked this way, a thin, tasty crust encases the meat, trapping all the good juices inside. Everyone loves red meat once in a while and this method makes it easy and economical to serve.

Serves 4
Preparation time: 10 minutes
Cooking time: 10 to 12 minutes

INGREDIENTS

2 tablespoons Dijon mustard
2 medium-size cloves garlic, chopped
2 teaspoons chopped fresh rosemary
Freshly ground pepper
1 tablespoon olive oil
2 pounds London broil, about $1\frac{1}{2}$ inches
    thick

1. Combine the mustard, garlic and rosemary in a small bowl. Whisk in the oil and season with pepper.

2. Heat the broiler. Put the steak on a broiler pan and broil for 2 minutes on each side to sear the meat. Spread the meat with half the mustard mixture and broil for 3 to 4 minutes. Turn the meat, spread with the remaining mustard mixture and broil for 3 to 4 minutes until rare. Let the meat rest for 10 minutes before cutting into thin slices and serving.

SHOPPING LIST

2 lbs. London broil, about 1 ½-in. thick
garlic
rosemary
Dijon mustard
olive oil

PROVENCALE LEMON-LAMB CASSEROLE

This is a simplified version of a *gardiane*, a lamb and vegetable casserole popular in the South of France. In that heady corner of the world, no two cooks prepare the dish in precisely the same way, but the concept is similar. Ours gets added sparkle from the addition of lemon and mint, which marry beautifully with the other ingredients.

Serves 4
Preparation time: 15 to 20 minutes
Cooking time: 45 minutes

INGREDIENTS

3 tablespoons olive oil
4 shoulder lamb chops, about 6 ounces
   each, about $\frac{1}{2}$-inch thick
1 medium-size onion, coarsely chopped
2 medium-size carrots, chopped into
   $\frac{1}{4}$-inch-thick pieces
2 large Idaho potatoes, peeled and cut into
   $\frac{1}{8}$-inch-thick slices
9-ounce package frozen artichoke hearts,
   thawed
1 medium-size clove garlic, finely chopped
$\frac{1}{3}$ cup beef broth or dry white wine
Grated rind and juice of 1 small lemon
1 tablespoon chopped fresh mint or 1
   teaspoon dried
Salt and freshly ground pepper
Chopped fresh mint, for garnish, optional

1. Heat the oven to 400 degrees.

2. Heat the oil in a large ovenproof frying pan over high heat. Add the chops and cook for about 4 minutes, turning once, until the chops are browned on both sides. Transfer the chops to a plate, reserving the fat from the pan.

3. Add the onion and carrots to the pan and cook, stirring often, until the onion is softened. Add the artichokes, potatoes and garlic and cook, stirring often, for about 5 minutes until the potatoes are limp. Add the beef broth, lemon rind, lemon juice, mint and any juices from the chops and bring the mixture to a simmer, scraping any browned bits from the bottom of the pan with a wooden spoon. Season the vegetables with salt and pepper and place the lamb chops on top. Cover the skillet and put it in the oven. Bake for 15 minutes. Uncover the skillet and bake for another 15 minutes until the lamb chops are well-done. Serve immediately sprinkled with the chopped mint, if desired.

SHOPPING LIST

4 shoulder lamb chops, about 6 oz. each,
$\frac{1}{2}$-in. thick
onion
carrots
2 large Idaho potatoes
garlic
1 lemon
mint (fresh or dried)
9-oz. pkg. frozen artichoke hearts
beef broth or dry white wine
olive oil

STIR-FRIED BEEF WITH CELERY AND PEPPERS

If you are concerned with your family's sodium intake, use light soy sauce for this recipe as it is lower in salt than regular soy sauce, yet still adds good flavor. For a hotter dish, use mostly hot peppers in the pepper mix.

Serves 4 to 6
Preparation time: 20 minutes
Cooking time: 15 minutes

INGREDIENTS

1 pound flank or sirloin steak, trimmed and
   thinly sliced
1 tablespoon dry sherry
3 tablespoons soy sauce
1 tablespoon cornstarch, optional
4 tablespoons peanut oil
4 slices fresh ginger
2 cloves garlic, crushed
2 cups stemmed, seeded and thinly sliced
   mixed hot and sweet peppers
½ cup thinly sliced celery
½ cup thinly sliced carrots

1. Put the steak in a large bowl. Add the sherry, soy sauce and cornstarch and toss until the meat is well coated.

2. Heat 2 tablespoons of the oil in a wok or large frying pan over high heat. As soon as the oil starts to smoke, lower the heat to medium. Add the ginger and garlic and stir fry for 30 seconds. Add the peppers and stir fry for 3 minutes, until tender but still crisp. Remove the peppers from the pan with a slotted spoon and set aside.

3. Add the celery and carrots to the wok and stir fry for 3 minutes, until tender but still crisp. Remove from the pan with a slotted spoon and set aside. Add the remaining oil to the pan and increase the heat to high. When the oil begins to smoke, add the beef with its marinade to the pan and stir fry for 2 to 3 minutes, until the meat has lost its pink color. Return all the vegetables to the pan and toss until just heated through. Discard the sliced ginger and serve immediately with boiled rice.

```
•••••••••••••••••••••••••••••••
          SHOPPING LIST

    1 lb. flank or sirloin steak
              garlic
           fresh ginger
      hot and sweet peppers
              celery
              carrots
            dry sherry
            soy sauce
            peanut oil
            cornstarch
•••••••••••••••••••••••••••••••
```

GRILLED LEG OF LAMB WITH CUMIN AND LEMON

A marinated leg of lamb is one of the great meats to cook on an outdoor grill, but apartment dwellers should not despair. It tastes mighty good broiled, too. This recipe is adapted from one developed by Michael McLaughlin, who uses lime juice and jalapenos for a Southwestern flair. We have selected ingredients to give the exotic flavor of the foods of Morocco. Leftovers may be used in Lamb Sandwiches with Raita (page 22).

Serves 8 to 10
Preparation time: 10 minutes, plus marinating
Cooking time: 20 to 25 minutes

INGREDIENTS
1 medium-size onion
6 medium-size cloves garlic
½ cup olive oil
¼ cup lemon juice
1½ teaspoons ground cumin
1 tablespoon paprika
1 teaspoon cayenne
1 teaspoon ground coriander
1 teaspoon salt
¼ cup chopped fresh coriander
8- to 8½-pound leg of lamb, boned and butterflied

1. Combine all of the ingredients except the lamb in a food processor and process to a paste. Spread the paste over the lamb in a large non-aluminum container and let the meat marinate while the broiler heats, or overnight.

2. Heat the broiler or light the charcoal grill. Broil or grill the lamb, covered, for 10 to 12 minutes on each side until the thickest parts of the leg are medium-rare. (Cooking time will depend on how completely the leg has been butterflied. If the large muscles are intact, the leg may take somewhat longer to cook. And if you do not cover the grill, the cooking time will certainly be longer.)

3. Let the lamb rest 10 minutes before cutting into thin slices.

BEEF AND VEGETABLE KEBABS

U sing a more expensive cut of meat such as sirloin saves you time because it does not need to be marinated, as would chuck or round. The mixture of butter (or margarine) and oil with garlic and hot pepper sauce keeps the kebabs moist and adds flavor. It is most important to brush it over the vegetables. You could cut back a bit on the amount of butter and oil if you want fewer calories.

Serves 4
Preparation time: 30 minutes
Cooking time: 10 to 15 minutes

INGREDIENTS

4 small, thin-skinned potatoes
1½ to 2 pounds beef sirloin, trimmed and
   cut into 1½-inch cubes
1 large green pepper, cut into 1½-inch
   pieces
1 large red pepper, cut into 1½-inch pieces
2 tablespoons butter or margarine, melted
4 tablespoons olive oil
1 clove garlic, finely chopped
2 drops hot pepper sauce

1. Heat the broiler or light the charcoal grill. Let the coals get medium hot.

2. Gently scrub the potatoes under running water but do not peel them. Cook them in 2 inches of boiling water in a covered saucepan for 15 to 20 minutes. Cool and cut into quarters.

3. Thread the meat and vegetables onto four metal skewers, alternating pieces of meat, pepper and potato. Combine the melted butter or margarine with the garlic and hot pepper sauce.

4. Broil or grill the kebabs for 10 to 15 minutes suspended over a broiler pan or set over the medium-hot coals, turning and brushing with the butter mixture as they cook.

> **SHOPPING LIST**
> 1 ½ to 2 lbs. beef sirloin, cubed
> 1 large green pepper
> 1 large red pepper
> garlic
> 4 small, thin-skinned potatoes
> hot pepper sauce
> olive oil
> butter or margarine

BROILED LAMB CHOPS
WITH HERBS

What could be simpler—and quicker—to prepare than broiled lamb chops? And what could be more delicious? The oil and herb marinade, easily prepared a day ahead or when you get home in the evening, adds flavor and succulence.

Serves 4 to 6
Preparation time: 15 minutes plus marinating
Cooking time: 12 to 16 minutes

INGREDIENTS

⅓ cup olive oil
3 garlic cloves, crushed
1 teaspoon freshly ground black pepper
1 teaspoon dried thyme
1 teaspoon dried basil
1 teaspoon dried rosemary, crumbled
2 tablespoons red wine vinegar
Salt
12 lamb rib chops

1. Combine the oil, garlic, black pepper, thyme, basil, rosemary and vinegar in a shallow dish. Add salt to taste. Add the lamb chops to the mixture and turn to make sure they are well coated. Cover the dish and marinate the lamb for 20 to 30 minutes or in the refrigerator overnight.

2. Heat the broiler. Remove the chops from the marinade and put them on a broiler pan. Broil the lamb about 2 inches from the heat source for 6 to 8 minutes on each side.

Leftovers
If you are planning to have leftovers from a roast, slice the meat from both ends, leaving the rarer center for other uses.

Cooked foods should be wrapped and chilled as soon as possible after it becomes apparent that they are indeed leftovers. A roast that sits naked and exposed to the air for several hours and cheeses that have sweated out their butter fat while you entertained your guests so charmingly in another room can never be restored to their former greatness.

Leftover cooked meats and vegetables are best reheated in a microwave oven or stir-fried in a wok. They need only be reheated—not recooked.

Add mustard, horseradish, herbs, spices, lemon juice or a freshly cooked vegetable to leftovers to brighten the taste of the preparation.

It is better to add various leftovers to several new dishes rather than emptying the refrigerator in one impulsive sweep and dumping everything into a casserole. The idea may seem virtuous and economical, but the results will not taste good.

SHOPPING LIST

12 lamb rib chops
garlic
dried thyme, basil and rosemary
olive oil
red wine vinegar

LAMB BROCHETTES
WITH FENNEL

These brochettes are oven cooked for ease and simplicity. The result is juicy, tender chunks of lamb subtly flavored with fennel. Fresh fennel—that is, in bulb form rather than the dried seeds—is fairly easy to find in the produce section of many supermarkets. Its unmistakable aniseed flavor has traditionally been paired with fish but it combines equally well with meats such as lamb.

Serves 4
Preparation time: 10 minutes plus 30 minutes
   marinating
Cooking time: 10 to 12 minutes

INGREDIENTS

⅓ cup olive or vegetable oil
½ cup red wine vinegar
1 tablespoon finely grated orange rind
1 teaspoon dried thyme
1 teaspoon crushed fennel seeds
Salt and freshly ground pepper
1 pound boneless leg or loin of lamb, cut
   into 1-inch cubes
1 large fennel bulb, white part only, cut
   into 1¼-inch pieces

1. Heat the oven to 425 degrees.

2. Combine ½ cup of the oil with the vinegar, orange rind, thyme and fennel seeds in a glass or china dish. Add salt and pepper to taste. Add the lamb, turning until it is well coated. Let the meat marinate at room temperature for 30 minutes, turning once.

3. Remove the lamb from the marinade and pat it dry. Brush the fennel pieces with the remaining oil and season with salt and pepper.

4. Thread 4 metal skewers with alternating pieces of lamb and fennel. Suspend the skewers over a baking pan so that the juices will drip into the dish and the heat from the oven can circulate around them. Cook 10 to 12 minutes for medium-rare meat, turning once.

SHOPPING LIST

1 lb. boneless leg or loin of lamb, cubed
1 orange
dried thyme
fennel seeds
olive or vegetable oil
red wine vinegar

PORK AND RICE WITH MUSHROOMS

Here is a simple and filling one-dish meal that requires no more than a mixed green salad to round it out. The pork and mushroom combination cooks gently with the rice while providing good, full flavor. And it tastes great reheated the next day.

Serves 4
Preparation time: 25 minutes
Cooking time: 25 to 30 minutes

INGREDIENTS

1 teaspoon ground ginger
Salt and freshly ground pepper
1 pound pork tenderloin or other lean pork, cut into thin strips
6 to 7 scallions
2 tablespoons butter or margarine
2 tablespoons vegetable oil
2 cloves garlic, finely chopped
½ pound mushrooms, sliced
½ cup long-grain rice
1¼ cups chicken broth or water

1. Combine the ginger with salt and pepper to taste. Sprinkle the mixture over the meat, turning so that the seasonings are well distributed. Chop the scallions fine, reserving 2 tablespoons of the green part for garnish.

2. Heat the butter and oil in a wok or large frying pan over medium heat. Add the scallions and garlic and cook for 5 minutes.

3. Remove the scallions and garlic from the pan. Add the meat, a batch at a time to avoid overcrowding, and cook until lightly browned, about 10 minutes in all. When the last batch is cooked, stir in the mushrooms and rice.

4. Return all the meat, the scallions and the garlic to the pan. Pour in the broth and bring to the boil. Stir the meat and turn the heat to very low. Cover the pan and cook for 25 minutes, until the liquid is absorbed and the pork and rice are tender. If necessary, add 2 to 3 tablespoons more liquid and cook for 5 more minutes. Sprinkle with the reserved scallion greens before serving.

SHOPPING LIST

1 lb. pork tenderloin or other lean pork
scallions
garlic
½ lb. mushrooms
ground ginger
long-grain rice
chicken broth
vegetable oil
butter or margarine

SHERRY MARINATED PORK CHOPS

You will have to plan ahead for these pork chops since they need to marinate for eight hours or so in the refrigerator. You could put them in the marinade in the morning before leaving for work, or even start them the night before. Either way, the marinade tenderizes and flavors the meat before becoming a tasty sauce with the thinly sliced onions.

Serves 4
Preparation time: 10 minutes plus marinating
Cooking time: about 25 minutes

INGREDIENTS

½ cup vegetable oil
3 tablespoons steak sauce
3 tablespoons dry sherry
3 tablespoons red wine vinegar
1 tablespoon Worcestershire sauce
1 tablespoon packed brown sugar
1 teaspoon dried marjoram
4 pork loin chops, about 1 inch thick
1 medium-size onion, thinly sliced

1. Combine all but 1 tablespoon of the oil with the steak sauce, sherry, vinegar, Worcestershire sauce, brown sugar and marjoram in a glass or ceramic bowl. Stir until well mixed and then add the pork chops. Turn to coat, cover and marinate for at least 8 hours or overnight. Turn the chops occasionally if you can.

2. Remove the chops from the marinade and pat dry with paper towels. Reserve the marinade.

3. Heat a microwave browning dish on High (100 percent) for 5 minutes. Carefully sprinkle the dish with the reserved tablespoon of oil and lay the pork chops on top. Microwave on High (100 percent) for 1 minute on each side. Pour the marinade over the chops and top with the sliced onion. Cover and microwave on Medium (50 percent) for 18 to 22 minutes, turning the chops over after 10 minutes, until the meat is tender and juices run clear.

SHOPPING LIST

4 pork loin chops, about 1-in. thick
onion
dried marjoram
packed brown sugar
steak sauce
dry sherry
red wine vinegar
Worcestershire sauce
vegetable oil

CURRY BEEF SATE

After just a brief soaking in a piquant curry mixture, strips of lean beef are ready for the microwave. In minutes, you have a tasty main course to serve with rice and a green salad. Make the marinade and add the beef to it after you have put the rice on to cook. Supper is ready in minutes. The microwave will not brown the beef, although the Worcestershire sauce will help color it. For more of a browned look, add a teaspoon of microwave browning sauce to the marinade, which you can buy at the supermarket.

Serves 4
Preparation time: 10 minutes
Cooking time: 3 to 4 minutes

INGREDIENTS

1¼ pounds beef top round, very thinly sliced
2 tablespoons peanut or vegetable oil
2 tablespoons grated onion
1 tablespoon brown sugar
1 teaspoon curry powder
1 teaspoon Worcestershire sauce
½ teaspoon hot pepper sauce
Salt, optional

1. Combine all the ingredients except the salt in a large glass or ceramic bowl and mix well. Let the mixture stand for 10 minutes.

2. Thread the beef slices on four 8-inch wooden skewers, distributing them evenly. Put the skewers on a microwave-safe rack set in a shallow microwave-safe baking dish. Be sure not to over-crowd the dish—the meat may be cooked in 2 batches if necessary, but reduce the cooking time for each batch if you do so. Brush the meat with any remaining curry mixture.

3. Microwave on High (100 percent) for 3 to 4 minutes, rotating the dish once. Sprinkle lightly with salt, if desired, just before serving.

SHOPPING LIST

1 ¼ lbs. beef top round
onion
curry powder
brown sugar
Worcestershire sauce
hot pepper sauce
peanut or vegetable oil

FISH AND SEAFOOD

Good news! Supermarkets everywhere are spreading shaved ice on refrigerated counters and setting out fresh fish and seafood for everyday consumption. Now, even landlocked Americans can enjoy fresh fish as often as they want, which helps a lot in menu planning, since fish is quick to prepare as well as nutritious and low in fat and calories—nearly the perfect food. Many types of fish meld nicely with ingredients such as tomatoes, mushrooms, potatoes and cucumbers. Others stand up to grilling and quick cooking with no more fuss than a squeeze of lemon or a splash of white wine. All taste good and are good for you, too.

Recent studies show that a diet which regularly includes fish aids in the prevention of heart disease. This is not only true of the much publicized fishes with omega-3 fatty acids, such as tuna, but of leaner, lighter fish as well. Evidently, eating nearly any sort of fish twice a week significantly reduces the risk of heart attack. Fish is high in protein, B vitamins, thiamin, riboflavin and niacin, too, and many supply needed amounts of iodine, copper and iron.

Crustaceans such as lobster and shrimp tend to be quite high in cholesterol and calories. But these seafoods are so delicious it would be a shame to abandon them completely. Instead categorize them as you do red meat: moderate amounts do no harm. In fact, they may do more good than harm if you consider the psychological lift you get from indulging in shrimp every now and then.

Fresh fish has no odor. The eye should have a gleam and the skin be very shiny.

There are two classifications for fish: fresh and saltwater. They may be lean or fatty. Lean fish are generally fried, sautéed in butter, poached or steamed—in other words, cooked in a liquid in one form or another. Fatty fish are best cooked by *dry heat, by being baked, broiled or grilled over charcoal.*

To test the doneness of fish, use a sharp knife to flake it near the bone. If there is any visible blood, continue cooking. If it is white and opaque and flakes easily, it is cooked sufficiently. (Test it early on: fish cooks very quickly.)

GRILLED TUNA WITH ORANGE MINT CHUTNEY

If you decide to grill the steaks over a charcoal fire, be sure the fire is not too hot. Once the coals have turned ash gray, see if you can hold your hand about five inches from them for five or six seconds. If you have to pull away from the heat after one or two seconds, the coals are sending out too much heat and you should wait a few minutes before cooking. These steaks are good served as they are or placed on top of a leafy bed of seasonal greens and sprinkled with some of the remaining marinade, or a squeeze or two of lemon and orange juice and a little olive oil.

Serves 4
Preparation time: 10 minutes plus marinating
    time
Cooking time: 6 minutes

INGREDIENTS

1 medium-size orange
2 tablespoons lemon juice
1 tablespoon soy sauce
½ teaspoon dried thyme
¼ teaspoon fennel seed, crushed (optional)
1 medium-size clove garlic, crushed
Freshly ground pepper
¼ cup olive oil
4 6- to 8-ounce tuna steaks, about 1-inch
    thick
Orange Mint Chutney (page 272)

1. Finely grate the rind from the orange into a shallow non-corrosive baking dish. Cut the orange in half and squeeze the juice into the baking dish. Add the lemon juice, thyme, fennel, garlic and pepper to taste and mix well. Gradually whisk in the olive oil until smooth. Add the tuna to the marinade and turn to coat all sides. Let the tuna marinate at room temperature for 30 to 45 minutes.

2. Light the charcoal grill or heat the broiler to medium-hot. Remove the tuna from the marinade, reserving the marinade. Cook the steaks, 5 to 6 inches from the heat, for 6 minutes, turning once and basting often with the remaining marinade. Serve immediately with Orange Chutney.

BAKED COD WITH POTATOES, PEPPERS AND GARLIC

This is a dish that owes its origins to the simple fish preparations eaten in fishing villages along the coast of France. Like most good peasant food, it could not be easier or tastier and surely will please anyone who enjoys simple food, simply cooked.

Serve 4
Preparation time: 25 minutes
Cooking time: 25 minutes

INGREDIENTS

1½ pounds baking potatoes, cut into
    ⅛- to ¼-inch slices
Salt and freshly ground pepper
½ large or 1 small red pepper, quartered
    and thinly sliced
1 medium-size red onion, thinly sliced
2 large cloves garlic, finely chopped
¼ cup plus 1 tablespoon olive oil
2 tablespoons chopped parsley
1 teaspoon chopped fresh thyme or
    ¼ teaspoon dried
1½ to 2 pounds cod steaks, about 1 inch
    thick
Juice of ½ lemon

1. Bring a large saucepan of water to the boil. Add the potatoes and salt to taste, and simmer for 3 to 4 minutes until just tender. Drain and pat dry.

2. Combine the potatoes with the red pepper, onion, garlic, ¼ cup oil, herbs, salt and pepper to taste, and toss gently.

3. Heat the oven to 400 degrees. Coat a baking dish large enough to hold the cod with the remaining tablespoon of oil. Sprinkle the cod lightly on both sides with salt and pepper and put it in the baking dish. Squeeze the lemon juice over the cod. Cover with the potato mixture and smooth the top. Bake for 20 to 25 minutes until the cod is just opaque. Serve the cod on a bed of the potato mixture.

Selecting Fish
Whenever possible, buy fresh fish. If a recipe calls for lemon or grey sole and you can only find it frozen, but there is some fresh fluke or flounder, buy the fresh fish. The characteristics of the two fish are so similar they can be cooked the same way. This is not to say that all frozen fish is bad—flash freezing techniques have come a long way and much of the frozen fish available today is very good. You will have to experiment on your own.

When you buy fresh fish, try to do so from a reliable fish store. Get to know the merchant. He can be a big help when it comes to selecting what is freshest and best on the ice-covered counter. The fish should look firm and wet and have no odor at all. Whole fish should have clear eyes and glistening scales. Unwrap the fish when you get home, rinse it off and wrap it in fresh plastic, wax paper or foil. Store it on the back of the lowest shelf of the refrigerator where it is coldest and eat it the same day or the next, if you can. If not, wrap it well in plastic and set it in a container holding ice. Change the ice as it melts in the refrigerator. The fish should keep for three or four days if it was nice and fresh to begin with.

SHOPPING LIST

1 ½ to 2 lbs. cod steaks, about 1-in. thick
1 small red pepper
1 red onion
garlic
parsley
1 lemon
1 ½ lbs. baking potatoes
thyme (fresh or dried)
olive oil

FLOUNDER WITH WHITE WINE AND MUSHROOMS

Here is a classic way to prepare flounder fillets. The white wine and mushrooms dress up the light fish just enough to make it special but not fussy. Flounder is generally easy to find, but, of course, you can substitute sole in the recipe.

Serves 4
Preparation time: 20 minutes
Cooking time: 25 minutes

INGREDIENTS

2 tablespoons olive or vegetable oil
Butter or margarine
$\frac{3}{4}$ pound white mushrooms, thickly sliced
$\frac{1}{2}$ teaspoon dried thyme
Salt and freshly ground pepper
1 medium-size clove garlic, chopped
1 large scallion, chopped
$1\frac{1}{2}$ to 2 pounds skinned flounder fillet,
    each fillet halved lengthwise
$\frac{1}{2}$ cup dry white wine
$\frac{1}{4}$ cup water
1 bay leaf
2 tablespoons chopped parsley

1. Heat the oil and 1 tablespoon of butter in a large pan over medium heat. Add the mushrooms and thyme and cook, stirring, until the mushrooms release their juices. Sprinkle them lightly with salt and simmer until the liquid has been reabsorbed and the mushrooms are dry, 5 to 10 minutes (cooking time will depend on the size of your pan). Add the garlic and cook 2 to 3 minutes longer, taking care not to burn it. Season to taste with pepper.

2. Butter a second frying pan large enough to hold the fish in one layer. Scatter the scallions over the pan. Score the skin side of the fillets (there is a white membrane on that side) in a few places to prevent the fillets from curling. Hold the fillets with the scored side down. Fold the thin tail pieces under the fillets to protect them from overcooking; if the fillets are very thin, fold them completely in half. Arrange the fillets in the pan and sprinkle lightly with salt and pepper. Pour the wine and water into the pan, add the bay leaf and gently bring the liquid to a simmer over medium heat. Cover and poach very gently (the fish will fall apart if cooked too vigorously) for 5 to 10 minutes, depending on the size of your fillets, until the fish is opaque at the center.

3. Carefully remove the fillets from the liquid with a spatula and shake them over the pan to drain as much as possible. Arrange them on a serving plate, cover and keep warm. Pour the fish cooking liquid into the pan with the mushrooms and add the parsley. Bring to the boil and boil for 2 to 3 minutes until the liquid is reduced and thickened. Adjust the seasonings and pour the mushroom mixture over the fish.

SHOPPING LIST

1 $\frac{1}{2}$ to 2 lbs. skinned flounder fillet
$\frac{3}{4}$ lb. mushrooms
garlic
scallions
parsley
bay leaves
dried thyme
olive or vegetable oil
butter or margarine
dry white wine

SZECHUAN SCALLOPS ON A BED OF NOODLES

The hardest part of Chinese cooking is chopping the vegetables. Maybe you can commandeer the kids to help cut the pepper and scallion and chop the ginger and garlic. Once the food is prepared, stir-frying is a quick, easy, low-fat way to cook. Using a non-stick skillet helps reduce the fat even more, as you can cut back on the amount of oil needed for the crisp noodle bed. If you think the noodle bed seems like too much effort to make, serve the scallops with plain white rice—although we're sure if you try it, you will love the noodles.

Serves 4
Preparation time: 20 minutes plus marinating
Cooking time: 20 minutes

INGREDIENTS

1 tablespoon soy sauce
1 tablespoon dry sherry
1 tablespoon rice vinegar
1 teaspoon brown sugar
¼ teaspoon dried red pepper flakes
1 pound bay scallops, or sea scallops cut into 1-inch pieces
8 ounces fresh or dried Chinese noodles or dried spaghetti
3 tablespoons vegetable oil
1 tablespoon finely chopped fresh ginger
¼ cup chopped scallion
1 medium-size clove garlic, chopped
1 medium-size red pepper, stemmed, seeded and ribbed, cut into 1-inch-wide strips
3 scallions, cut into 1-inch lengths

1 can sliced water chestnuts, drained and rinsed
2 teaspoons cornstarch
½ cup chicken broth

1. Combine the soy sauce, sherry, vinegar, brown sugar and red pepper flakes in a medium-sized non-corrosive bowl. Add the scallops and stir to coat them with the marinade. Let marinade for 30 minutes at room temperature.

2. Meanwhile, cook the noodles in boiling salted water, 2 minutes for fresh, 7 to 8 minutes for dried. Drain the noodles in a colander, rinse under cold running water and drain again. Add 1 tablespoon of the oil to noodles in the colander and mix with your hands until the noodles are coated with the oil.

3. Heat the oven to 225 degrees. Line a baking sheet with paper towels. Pour another tablespoon of oil into a large non-stick skillet, swirling the oil to coat the sides. Heat the oil over medium heat until very hot. Add the noodles to the skillet in a thick layer. Cook for about 5 minutes until the underside is golden brown. Cover the noodles with a plate and invert them onto the plate. Slide the noodles, uncooked side down, into the skillet and cook for 5 minutes more until golden brown. Transfer the noodles to the prepared baking sheet and keep warm in the oven.

4. Heat the remaining tablespoon of oil in the non-stick skillet over medium heat until very hot. Add the ginger, chopped scallion and garlic and stir-fry for 30 seconds. Add the red pepper, sliced scallions and water chestnuts and stir-fry for 1 minute. Add the scallops and their marinade and stir-fry for 1 minute, just until the scallops turn opaque.

5. Dissolve the cornstarch in the broth. Add the broth to the skillet and heat just until boiling. Serve the scallops over the noodle bed, cutting the noodles into wedges to serve.

SHOPPING LIST

1 lb. bay scallops or sea scallops
fresh or dried Chinese noodles or dried spaghetti
scallions
garlic
ginger
1 medium red pepper
1 can water chestnuts
chicken broth
cornstarch
brown sugar
soy sauce
dry sherry
rice vinegar

SALMON SCALLOPS
WITH CUCUMBER SAUCE

This is a good dish to serve in the spring when the salmon is especially fresh in the markets and you want to celebrate the warmer days and bluer skies. If you have time—or will need time later on—mix the cucumbers and yogurt in the morning before work. Remember, however, to allow time for the cucumbers to drain so that the sauce will not be watery.

Serves 4
Preparation time: 30 minutes
Cooking time: 4 minutes

INGREDIENTS

1 medium-size cucumber, peeled and halved
   lengthwise
1 teaspoon salt
½ cup plain yogurt
1 tablespoon chopped fresh dill
4 4- to 5-ounce pieces skinless, boneless
   salmon fillets
Salt and freshly ground pepper
Non-stick vegetable spray
¼ cup dry vermouth

1. With a teaspoon, scoop the seeds from the cucumber halves. Cut the cucumber shells into a ¼-inch dice and place in a strainer. Sprinkle with salt, toss and set aside to drain for about 15 minutes. Rinse well under cold running water, drain and squeeze the cucumbers by the handful to remove excess moisture. Combine the cucumbers in a small bowl with the yogurt and dill and mix lightly. Refrigerate until ready to serve.

2. Season the salmon with salt and pepper to taste. Spray a large non-stick skillet with vegetable spray and place over medium-high heat. Add the salmon and cook one minute. Add the vermouth, reduce the heat to medium-low, cover and cook for 3 minutes until the salmon is just cooked through. Using a slotted spatula, transfer the salmon to serving plates. Serve immediately with cucumber sauce.

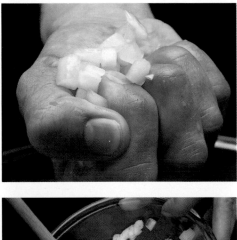

SHRIMP WITH GARLIC SAUCE

Shrimp
Double the quantity when buying shrimp in the
shell to allow for the weight of the shell.

Shrimp and garlic is a combination made in food lovers' heaven, and this pairing is no exception. Round out the meal with crusty bread and a crisp green salad. By the way, an inexpensive device called a shrimp deveiner makes speedy work of peeling shrimp. Or, if you are familiar with the fish store, buy the shrimp already peeled—they will be more expensive but you will save a lot of time.

SHOPPING LIST

1 ¼ lbs. medium shrimp
garlic
1 medium sweet red pepper
1 lemon
parsley
crushed red pepper flakes
olive oil
dry sherry

Serves 4
Preparation time: 10 minutes
Cooking time: 5 minutes

INGREDIENTS

½ cup olive oil
4 medium-size cloves garlic, thinly sliced
1 medium-size sweet red pepper, stemmed, seeded and cut in a ⅛-inch dice
1¼ pounds medium shrimp, peeled
3 tablespoons lemon juice
3 tablespoons dry sherry
¼ teaspoon crushed red pepper flakes or to taste
Salt
3 tablespoons finely chopped parsley, for garnish

1. Heat the oil in a large skillet over medium-high heat. Add the garlic, pepper and shrimp. Cook for about 2 minutes, stirring constantly, just until the shrimp turn pink. Increase the heat to high. Add the lemon juice, sherry, hot red pepper and salt to taste and bring to a boil. Serve immediately, sprinkled with parsley.

SWORDFISH WITH TOMATO SAUCE

Swordfish is a firm, meaty fish with a delicate flavor that takes well to simple preparations such as this one. Tuna, snapper and sea bass would taste good, too, prepared this way.

Serves 4
Preparation time: 10 minutes
Cooking time: 15 minutes

INGREDIENTS

3 tablespoons olive oil
$1\frac{1}{2}$ to 2 pound swordfish steaks,
 $\frac{3}{4}$- to $\frac{1}{2}$-inch thick
Salt and freshly ground pepper
$\frac{3}{4}$ pound Italian plum tomatoes, seeded and
 cut into $\frac{1}{2}$-inch pieces
1 large scallion, chopped
1 tablespoon balsamic vinegar
1 tablespoon chopped basil

1. Heat 1 tablespoon of oil in a large frying pan over medium-high heat. Sprinkle the fish lightly with salt and pepper and cook for 4 to 5 minutes on each side until the fish is opaque at the center. Remove from the pan and keep warm on a serving plate.

2. Add the remaining 2 tablespoons of oil to the pan along with the tomatoes and scallions. Cook over medium-high heat for 3 to 4 minutes until the tomatoes are softened. Add the vinegar and cook for 1 minute. Stir in the basil and season to taste with salt and pepper.

3. Spoon the tomato sauce over the fish and serve.

Marinating Fish
Fish is well suited to marinating, particularly thick, dense tuna and swordfish steaks, which seem to benefit from the gentle flavoring. However, be sure not to marinate the fish for too long. As a rule, an hour or two is all the fish can take before the acid in the marinade begins to break down certain enzymes in the fish so that it actually begins "cooking." If this happens, the texture of the fish, after you have cooked it over heat, may be cottony. When you marinate fish, be sure to use a non-corrosive dish (glass or porcelain is a good choice) and, unless otherwise directed, keep the covered dish in the refrigerator the whole time.

SHOPPING LIST
1 ½ to 2 lbs. swordfish steaks, ¾ to ½-in. thick
scallions
¾ lb. Italian plum tomatoes
basil
balsamic vinegar
olive oil

RED SNAPPER WITH TOMATOES

We have included mussels in this recipe for added flavor and fun. If it seems like too much trouble to prepare them, disregard the instructions for cooking them and just make the quick tomato sauce, still using the red wine. Perhaps you will want to make the dish with the mussels on a weekend night when company is expected. The cooking times are based on four smallish snapper fillets with a combined weight of 1½ pounds. If you buy fewer *larger* fillets, increase the cooking time by four to six minutes. Be sure to cook the fish until it is opaque and feels firm when you press it with your fingers. Red snapper is a firm white-fleshed fish with wonderful flavor. It is sold across the country and when kept whole, is a lovely red color.

Serves 4
Preparation time: 20 minutes
Cooking time: 40 minutes

INGREDIENTS

16 mussels or more, if desired
¾ cup dry red wine
2 tablespoons olive oil
1 medium onion, chopped
½ teaspoon dried oregano
1 medium green bell pepper, cut into strips
2 ounces white mushrooms, sliced
2 medium cloves garlic, chopped
¾ pound tomatoes, cored, seeded and coarsely chopped

¼ cup water
1 bay leaf
Salt and freshly ground pepper
1½ pounds snapper fillet

1. Debeard the mussels and scrub them well with a vegetable brush under running water. In a large pot, combine the wine and mussels, cover and cook over high heat until the mussels have opened. Remove the mussels and strain the wine through a coffee filter or paper towels and reserve. Discard any mussels that have not opened.

2. In a large oven-proof (if possible) frying pan, heat the oil over medium heat. Add the onion and oregano and cook for about 5 minutes until the onion is soft. Add the bell pepper and mushrooms and cook for about 5 minutes. Stir in the garlic and cook for about 30 seconds until the garlic is fragrant. Add the tomatoes along with the strained wine, the water and the bay leaf, cover and simmer for about 15 minutes until thickened. Season to taste with salt and pepper.

3. Heat the oven to 400 degrees. If the frying pan is oven-proof, arrange the fillets in a single layer over the sauce. If the pan is not oven-proof, pour the sauce into a baking dish large enough to hold the fillets and arrange the fish on top. Sprinkle lightly with salt and pepper and bake for 3 minutes. Add the mussels and bake for an additional 3 to 5 minutes until the fish is opaque in the center.

SHOPPING LIST

1 ½ lbs. snapper fillet
16 mussels
onion
1 medium green bell pepper
white mushrooms
garlic
bay leaves
dried oregano
olive oil
dry red wine

FISH CAKES WITH CORN

2 tablespoon lemon juice
$\frac{1}{2}$ teaspoon paprika
$\frac{1}{4}$ teaspoon salt
Freshly ground pepper
$\frac{1}{2}$ cup yellow cornmeal
Five-Alarm Salsa (page 273.)

Glancing at the long list of ingredients, you may decide to turn the page and try another recipe. Please don't. These fish cakes are sure to be a crowd pleaser in your family, as appropriate for a weekend breakfast (without the salsa) as they are for a light supper. Since they are bound with potato rather than bread crumbs, they are very moist and on the delicate side. Take care that they do not fall apart when you dredge them with cornmeal. Another advantage to these cakes is that they freeze very well before the final cooking. Wrap them in wax paper and foil for freezing and let them thaw in their wrapping in the refrigerator during the day. Cooking them just before serving is quick work.

Serves 4
Preparation time: 35 minutes
Cooking time: 10 to 15 minutes

INGREDIENTS

10-ounce baking potato, peeled, quartered lengthwise and cut into 1- to 1½-inch chunks
1 pound cod fillets
$\frac{3}{4}$ cup corn kernels or kernels from 1 ear of fresh corn
2 scallions, chopped
$\frac{1}{4}$ cup chopped parsley
1 medium jalapeno pepper, stemmed, seeded and finely chopped
Olive or vegetable oil
3 tablespoons whole milk
1 egg, lightly beaten

1. Put the potato in a saucepan with water to cover. Bring to the boil, reduce the heat and cook gently for about 15 minutes until the potato is tender. Drain in a colander and then return the potato to the pot and dry it out over low heat for about 10 seconds. Mash the potato with a large fork. Don't mash completely smooth—some lumps provide good texture in the fish cakes.

2. Meanwhile, put about $\frac{1}{4}$ inch of water in a frying pan large enough to hold the fish in a single layer. Add the fish and bring the water to a simmer. Cover and cook gently until the fish is opaque in the center. (The cooking time will depend on the thickness of the fish, but you can figure on about 10 minutes per inch of thickness.) Gently remove the fish from the pan and drain on paper towels.

3. Rinse the pan and add about $\frac{1}{2}$ inch of fresh water. Bring the water to the boil, add the corn and cook for 3 to 5 minutes until the corn is tender. Drain in a colander and put into a mixing bowl along with the scallions, parsley, jalapeno and potato. Add 3 tablespoons of oil, the milk, egg, lemon juice, paprika and salt and season to taste with pepper. Mix well. Flake the cod into the mixture and mix just to combine. Taste and adjust the seasonings.

4. Combine the cornmeal and a pinch of salt and pepper on a plate. Using about $\frac{1}{4}$ cup for each cake, shape the fish mixture into 12 3-inch patties, each about 1 inch thick. Carefully dredge the patties in the cornmeal.

5. Lightly film a large frying pan with oil. Working in batches and adding a little oil for each new batch, cook the fish cakes over medium-high heat for 2 to 3 minutes on each side until the coating is lightly browned. Serve the fish cakes with the salsa.

PAELLA

We are extremely partial to this dish and have included squid as one of the ingredients as well as expensive and sometimes hard to find saffron threads. You may omit both and still have a smashing dish, robust enough to satisfy the healthiest appetites. In Spain, where paella originated, every kitchen boasts at least one broad-bottomed paella pan, but you can make it in a large frying pan. Arborio rice, an Italian short-grain rice that is easy to find in the U.S., mimics the short-grain rice grown in Valencia, Spain, that is traditionally used in Paella. The result is a creamier consistency than you will get with long-grain rice, which of course you may use instead. A well-flavored stock is nice in this dish, but the ingredients themselves have so much flavor that water is just fine. Use small or medium-size shrimp; these do not need to be deveined.

Serves 4
Preparation time: 20 minutes
Cooking time: 35 minutes

INGREDIENTS

2 tablespoons olive oil
$1\frac{1}{2}$ to $1\frac{3}{4}$ pounds chicken thighs
Salt and freshly ground pepper
2 medium-size onions, chopped
1 small green bell pepper, cored, seeded and
    cut into 1-inch pieces
1 small red bell pepper, cored, seeded and
    cut into 1-inch pieces
$\frac{1}{2}$ teaspoon paprika
2 medium-size cloves garlic, chopped

$\frac{3}{4}$ pound tomatoes, cored and quartered
$2\frac{2}{3}$ cups chicken broth or water
6 threads saffron, optional
1 bay leaf
$1\frac{1}{2}$ cups arborio or long-grain rice
1 pound small or medium-size shrimp,
    rinsed
$\frac{1}{2}$ pound squid, cleaned and cut into wide
    rings, optional
2 tablespoons chopped parsley

1. Heat 1 tablespoon of oil in a large deep frying pan or a soup pot over medium-high heat. Sprinkle the chicken with salt and pepper and cook for about 3 minutes on each side until the meat is nicely browned. Remove from the pan.

2. Add 1 more tablespoon of oil to the pan along with the onion, peppers and paprika. Cook for about 5 minutes until the vegetables are tender and the onions are golden. Add the garlic and cook for a few seconds until fragrant. Then add the tomatoes and $\frac{1}{4}$ teaspoon of salt (if you are using salted broth, omit the salt) and cook, stirring occasionally, for about 3 minutes.

3. Add the broth, saffron and bay leaf and bring the mixture to the boil. Return the chicken to the pot along with the rice, shrimp, squid and parsley. Reduce the heat and simmer, covered, for about 20 minutes until the rice is cooked and the liquid has evaporated. If the liquid evaporates too fast, lower the heat rather than adding more liquid. Serve the Paella immediately.

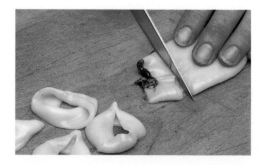

PORTUGUESE PORK AND CLAM SUPPER

Inspired by the gutsy seafood stews of Portugal's sea coast, this full bodied dish calls for a relatively small amount of pork tenderloin combined with juicy clams and fragrant vegetables. Let everyone at the table scoop the clam meat from the shells. Serve this with a generous loaf of French or Italian bread to sop up the liquid.

Serves 4
Preparation time: 15 minutes
Cooking time: 20 minutes

INGREDIENTS

2 tablespoons olive oil
1 pound pork tenderloin, cut into 12 1-inch cubes
1 teaspoon paprika
Salt and freshly ground pepper
1 large onion, coarsely chopped
1 large red bell pepper, seeded and coarsely chopped
2 medium-size cloves garlic, coarsely chopped
1 cup dry white wine or chicken broth
½ teaspoon dried oregano
1 bay leaf
32 medium-size littleneck clams, well scrubbed
2 tablespoons chopped parsley
Lemons wedges, for garnish

1. In a large kettle, heat the olive oil over medium-high heat. Add the pork cubes and season with the paprika, salt and pepper. Cook, stirring often, for 6 to 8 minutes until the pork is browned on all sides. With a slotted spoon, transfer the pork to a side dish and set aside.

2. Reduce the heat to medium, add the onion, bell pepper and garlic and cook, stirring often, for about 3 minutes until the onions are softened. Return the pork cubes with any juices to the kettle, add the wine, oregano and bay leaf and bring to a simmer. Cook, covered, for 5 minutes. Add the clams and cook, covered, for another 5 minutes, shaking the kettle often, until all of the clams have opened. Discard any that do not open.

3. Season lightly with salt and pepper and sprinkle with the parsley. Garnish with the lemon wedges and serve immediately.

SHOPPING LIST

1 lb. pork tenderloin, cubed
32 medium little neck clams
garlic
onion
1 large red bell pepper
1 lemon
bay leaves
parsley
paprika
dried oregano
olive oil
dry white wine or chicken broth

GRILLED SHRIMP AND CORIANDER PESTO

This is a wonderful way to serve shrimp and pasta. The Corinader Pesto tastes delicious with the lime-soaked seafood, but if you prefer to make it with traditional basil pesto, the dish is equally good. You might even consider buying commercial pesto found in the refrigerator sections of many supermarkets and specialty stores. You could also substitute lemon juice for the lime juice or use drained canned tuna in place of shrimp. If you fail to soak the wooden skewers, they may burn over the charcoal. Metal skewers work well, too and we recommend them in the broiler. Rest them on the edges of a broiling pan for cooking.

Serves 4
Preparation time: 45 minutes
Cooking time: 5 to 6 minutes

INGREDIENTS

1 pound medium-sized shrimp, unshelled
1½ tablespoons lime juice
Light olive or vegetable oil
Salt and freshly ground pepper
12 ounces spaghetti
Coriander Pesto (page 274)
¾ cup chopped, seeded tomato

1. Heat the broiler or light the charcoal grill.

2. Shell the shrimp, leaving the tails attached, and devein them. Rinse the shrimp well and pat them dry. Whisk together the lime juice and 3 tablespoons of oil. Add the shrimp and let them marinate while the grill is heating or for at least ½ hour.

3. Bring a large pot of water to the boil for the pasta. Add salt and the pasta and cook for 11 to 13 minutes until the pasta is tender. Drain in a colander.

4. Meanwhile, skewer the shrimp, sprinkle them lightly with salt and pepper and broil or grill them for 2 to 3 minutes on each side until they are opaque at their centers. Pull the shrimp off the skewers and put them in a serving bowl with the pesto and tomato. Add the pasta and toss to coat with the sauce.

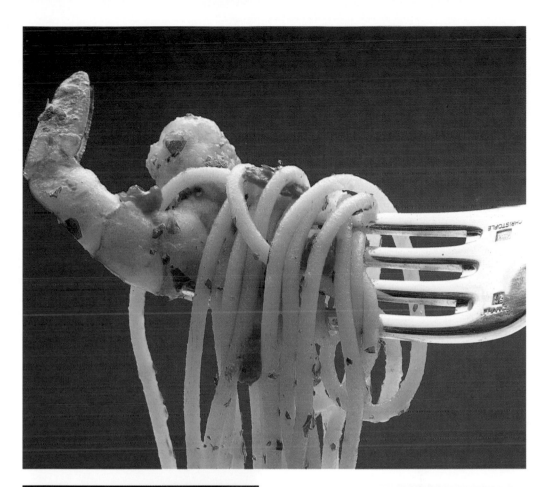

COD WITH WHITE WINE, ZUCCHINI AND TOMATOES

2. Wrap the plastic around each fillet to form a sealed package. Put the packages in the microwave in a single layer. Cook on High (100 percent) for 9 to 11 minutes. Let stand for 2 to 3 minutes before serving.

T his is an updated version of cooking fish in parchment. In this recipe, we use plastic wrap and cook the fish in the microwave. Microwave cooking is ideal for fish, which requires gentle, fast heating. When you open the plastic wrapped around the fish and vegetables, the aroma will be so enticing even your most reluctant child will come running.

Frozen fish fillets for poaching and breaded fish for frying should not be defrosted before cooking. Whole fish and fish for broiling, pan-frying or deep-fat frying should be completely thawed; if it is not fully defrosted, the outside will be cooked before the center. Dry fish thoroughly on paper towels before cooking or fat will splatter over the stove.

The most effective way of finding hidden bones in uncooked fish is to run your fingertips from the head end down to the tail. Remove small bones with your fingers or eyebrow tweezers.

If you must freeze raw fish, put it in a well-rinsed milk carton or similar container, fill the container with cold water and freeze immediately.

Serves 4
Preparation time: 5 minutes
Cooking time: 11 minutes

INGREDIENTS

4 6-ounce cod fillets
4 tablespoons dry white wine
4 teaspoons lemon juice
4 tablespoons butter or margarine
1 small zucchini, thinly sliced
2 plum tomatoes, chopped
$\frac{1}{2}$ teaspoon dried thyme
Salt and freshly ground pepper

SHOPPING LIST

4 6-oz. cod fillets
1 small zucchini
2 plum tomatoes
1 lemon
dried thyme
butter or margarine
dry white wine

1. Tear off four pieces of plastic wrap, each large enough to wrap around one fish fillet. Put one fillet in the center of each piece of plastic. Add 1 tablespoon of wine, 1 teaspoon of lemon juice, 1 tablespoon of butter and a fourth of the zucchini and tomatoes to each fillet. Sprinkle each with a little thyme and season with salt and pepper to taste.

VEGETABLES

We wish we could guarantee that these recipes will convince the youngsters you know to eat their vegetables. What we can promise, however, is that the following formulas will brighten your table, invite you to try a wider variety of vegetables and, hopefully, provide new ideas for perking up old, familiar standbys. Serve the Zucchini Gratin with broiled pork chops, the Carrot and Scallion Stir Fry with a roasted turkey breast or the Sweet Potato Fries with burgers. For a delicious twist on a classic summer meal, try the Roasted Corn and Cherry Tomatoes with Herbs with grilled chicken; on a cold winter's night, offer the Guilt-Free Mashed Potatoes and Honeyed Curried Carrots with meatloaf. A simple repast suddenly becomes a meal to reckon with when the vegetable dishes are as full of good flavor as these are.

Most of the recipes in this chapter are for side dishes although a few could be meatless main courses. Either way, begin with fresh or frozen vegetables, depending on the recipe. If the vegetables are fresh, try to buy them unbruised, since bruised produce rapidly loses vitamins A and C. Wash them well—three minutes under running water with soap is recommended to rid fruits and vegetables of pesticide residue—and peel those that require it with sharp knives or vegetable peelers to reduce the likelihood of bruising. Not all vegetables should be stored in the refrigerator, although it is a good place for most. Potatoes and onions do best kept in a cool, dark bin but should not be stored with each other as one hastens spoilage in the other. Garlic, too, does poorly in the refrigerator and tomatoes, unless cut or very ripe, are candidates for the kitchen counter or windowsill. Carrots, celery, squash, broccoli, asparagus, lettuce and other green vegetables should be kept in the fridge.

Certainly there are times when the easiest recourse is to pull a packet of frozen green beans or peas from the freezer. We recognize this and applaud the food companies for providing such good variety and quality in frozen produce, but we also hope you will take advantage of the ever increasing selection of fresh vegetables available in supermarkets and greengrocers. Try some of these recipes or create a few of your own using our basic techniques for stir frying, steaming, oven cooking and so on. Who knows—your kids may ask for second helpings!

Vegetables
If you succumb to the temptation of buying a basket of soft, slightly overripe vegetables such as tomatoes, arrange them in the refrigerator in a single layer to make them last as long as possible.

If vegetables are prepared in advance, parboil them and drain them in a colander. Rinse immediately under cold running water to crispen the texture and brighten the color. Reheat in boiling water or saute in hot butter just before serving.

SAUTEED CHERRY TOMATOES WITH HERBS

Vary the herbs for these tomatoes—try a good handful of chopped basil or some thyme in the summer. A splash of balsamic vinegar adds tang, too.

Serves 4
Preparation time: 10 minutes
Cooking time: 3 minutes

INGREDIENTS

2 tablespoons olive oil
1 pound cherry tomatoes, stemmed and cut in half
2 scallions, chopped
2 teaspoons chopped parsley
2 teaspoons chopped fresh mint
Salt and freshly ground pepper

1. Heat the oil in a large frying pan over medium-high heat. Add the tomatoes and scallions and cook for 2 to 3 minutes until the tomatoes are just heated through. Sprinkle with the herbs and salt and pepper to taste, and serve immediately.

SHOPPING LIST

1 lb. cherry tomatoes
scallions
parsley
mint
olive oil

LONE STAR STIR-FRY OF SPICY VEGETABLES

When you are in the market for something colorful and spicy to perk up a meal centered around plain grilled chicken or fish steaks, toss these ingredients into a frying pan. You are all set in two to three minutes.

Serves 4
Preparation time: 15 minutes
Cooking time: 5 minutes

INGREDIENTS

2 tablespoons olive oil
1 red onion, thinly sliced
1 sweet red, yellow or green bell pepper, ribbed and cut into 2-inch-by-½-inch strips
½ cup fresh or frozen corn kernels
1 medium-size clove garlic, finely chopped
1 tablespoon lime juice
2 teaspoons chili powder
Salt and freshly ground pepper

1. In a medium frying pan over medium-high heat, cook the onion in the olive oil for 1 minute.

2. Add the remaining ingredients and cook, stirring often, for about 2 minutes until the vegetables are crisp-tender. Serve immediately.

SHOPPING LIST

1 red onion
1 sweet red, yellow or green bell pepper
garlic
1 ear corn (or frozen kernels)
1 lime
chili powder
olive oil

ZUCCHINI GRATIN

Although it is at its very best in the summer when you can find it in backyard gardens and farm stands, zucchini is available most of the year. This is a simple and delicious way to serve it—no stirring, no tending. Try it with the Herb-Marinated Chicken on page 141, the Flounder with White Wine and Mushrooms on page 189 or with plain broiled hamburgers or chicken.

Serves 4
Preparation time: 10 minutes
Cooking time: 20 minutes

INGREDIENTS

2 tablespoons olive oil
1 pound zucchini, thinly sliced
Salt and freshly ground pepper
3 tablespoons grated Parmesan cheese

1. Heat the oven to 450 degrees.

2. Brush an 8- by 11-inch baking dish with 1 tablespoon oil. Arrange overlapping slices of zucchini in the dish and sprinkle with salt and pepper. Drizzle with the remaining tablespoon of oil and sprinkle with the cheese. Bake for 15 to 20 minutes until the zucchini is tender and the cheese is golden brown.

SHOPPING LIST

1 lb. zucchini
olive oil
Parmesan cheese

ROASTED CORN

I f you have never tried roasted corn, give it a chance. One of the nicest things about roasting corn is that once the foil-wrapped ears are in the oven, you can go about the business of getting the rest of the meal on the table without a second thought. Here, we have spread the ears with sage butter and then roasted them so that there is no need for extra butter on the dinner table. This saves on calories and fuss. Sage tastes just wonderful with corn, but use any sort of herb to flavor the butter—thyme or dill would be delicious, too.

Serves 4 to 6
Preparation time: 10 minutes
Cooking time: 20 to 25 minutes

INGREDIENTS

6 tablespoons butter or margarine, softened
2 tablespoons chopped fresh sage or 2
   teaspoons dried
8 ears fresh corn, husks and silks removed
Salt and freshly ground pepper

1. Heat the oven to 500 degrees.

2. In a small bowl, mix together the butter and herbs until combined.

3. Put each ear of corn on a 12-inch-square piece of aluminum foil. Rub some butter on each ear. Roll the foil around the corn to enclose it completely, twisting the ends shut.

4. Place the wrapped corn in one layer on a baking sheet. Roast for 20 to 25 minutes until tender. To serve, unwrap the corn and pass the salt and pepper at the table.

Corn

Sweet corn, like the summer tomato, has a short season and at no other time during the year is it as good. Buy it from a farm stand if you can, where you can be pretty sure it was picked the same day. As soon as the ears are taken from the stalk the sugar in the corn begins a rapid conversion into starch and the corn soon loses its glorious sweetness. The best tasting corn is that cooked straight from the garden, with no stops on the way to the kitchen. When you get sweet corn home, leave it in its husks until it is time to cook it. Store the ears in the refrigerator or a cool place. If you plan to boil the corn, drop the shucked ears in boiling water and let it cook for four or five minutes after the water has returned to the boil.

Corn that is a day or so old or that has been permitted to get too large in the field is good in soups, casseroles, breads and stews. Either cut or scrape the kernels from the cob. Cut them by inserting the blade of a sharp knife behind the kernels and cutting straight down. To scrape corn, run the tip of a knife through the center of the kernels in every row. Turn the knife over and push down at an angle to scrape the kernels off into a waiting bowl. You will get a good mixture of flesh and corn milk, the perfect consistency to make creamed corn, corn pudding and to moisten some cornbreads.

SHOPPING LIST

8 ears fresh corn
sage (fresh or dried)
butter or margarine

CARROT AND SCALLION STIR FRY

Because they cook so quickly, grated vegetables retain a lot of the vitamins that are otherwise discarded with the cooking water. In this recipe, we combine two vegetables that are available all year long in a fast and easy side dish to serve with roasts, grilled meats and fish. The use of the non-stick frying pan and the broth rather than oil makes this a low-fat and low-calorie dish your family will appreciate. Use the food processor to grate the carrots or the large-holed side of a hand-grater.

Serves 4 to 6
Preparation time: 10 minutes
Cooking time: 5 minutes

INGREDIENTS

¼ cup chicken broth
1 pound carrots, trimmed, peeled and
    grated
2 medium-size scallions, chopped
1 teaspoon dried tarragon
Salt and freshly ground pepper

1. Heat the chicken broth in a medium-sized non-stick frying pan over medium heat until very hot. Add the carrots, scallion and tarragon and stir fry for 2 minutes until the carrots are hot but still crisp.

2. Season with salt and pepper to taste and serve immediately.

CRISP POTATO CAKES

Just when you thought there was not another way to cook potatoes here come these easy little cakes. Their crispness will delight your children, and if you want a little extra flavor, try brushing them with garlic- or herb-flavored oil or sprinkling chopped fresh herbs over them before baking. Nicely rounded potatoes yield even, round slices. Be sure to use a judicious amount of oil on the baking sheets, otherwise the cakes will stick and fall apart when you try to lift them off. You can make these a day or two ahead of time, refrigerate them once cooked and then reheat them in a 450 degree oven for about five minutes until hot.

Makes 8 potato cakes
Preparation time: 10 minutes
Cooking time: 15 minutes

INGREDIENTS

3 to 4 tablespoons olive oil
2 large, well-rounded baking potatoes, about 1 pound
Salt and freshly ground pepper

1. Heat the oven to 450 degrees. Brush 2 baking sheets generously with olive oil.

2. Peel and slice the potatoes about $\frac{1}{8}$-inch thick. Using about 6 slices per cake, arrange the slices on the baking sheets to make 8 rings of overlapping slices. Brush with the remaining oil and sprinkle slightly with salt and pepper. Bake for about 15 minutes until the potatoes are tender and the edges of the cakes are lighlty browned. Two or three times during cooking press the cakes down with a spatula so that the slices adhere to one another. Serve 2 potato cakes per person.

Olive Oil

According to connoisseurs, Italian olive oil from Lucca, Tuscany, is the best in the world. The oil is pressed from tree-ripened olives; oil from the first pressing is termed "extra virgin" and is the finest. The best olive oil is clear and golden. Green-colored oils are fruitier and cloudy ones are inferior.

Most good olive oils will maintain their freshness indefinitely if kept in a tightly sealed bottle or can, in a relatively cool, dry place away from direct light. In very hot, humid climates, olive oil may need to be kept in the refrigerator, which will make it cloudy but has little effect on flavor.

Olive oil contains no cholesterol and is very digestible. Tests conducted by the American Heart Association's Nutrition Committee proved that using olive oil in place of saturated fats in the diet reduces blood cholesterol levels.

Low heat should be used when cooking with olive oil because it smokes at a lower temperature than other edible oils. It should not be used for deep-fat frying.

SHOPPING LIST

2 large baking potatoes
olive oil

STEAMED BROCCOLI
WITH WARM BALSAMIC
VINEGAR

Steamed broccoli never tasted so good! The warm dressing gives the old standby jazzy flavor. The dash of balsamic vinegar provides a lovely sweetness and complements the tomato, but if you do not have balsamic on hand, omit the lemon juice and use ordinary red wine vinegar instead. The broccoli may be served hot, at room temperature or cold, and tastes wonderful with grilled meats, poultry or fish.

Serves 4
Preparation time: 15 minutes
Cooking time: 20 minutes

INGREDIENTS

1 bunch broccoli, about 1½ pounds
3 tablespoons olive oil
1 plum tomato, seeded and chopped
1 clove garlic, finely chopped
¼ teaspoon hot red pepper flakes
1 tablespoon balsamic vinegar
¼ teaspoon grated lemon rind
About 1 teaspoon lemon juice
Salt and freshly ground pepper

1. Trim the woody ends and cut the broccoli into florets. Peel the stems with a vegetable peeler, halve them lengthwise, and cut them into 1- to 1½-inch lengths. Steam the broccoli on a vegetable steamer over 1 inch of boiling water for 15 to 20 minutes until tender.

2. Meanwhile, heat the oil with the tomato, garlic and red pepper flakes in a small saucepan over low heat until just warm. Whisk in the vinegar and lemon rind and add lemon juice to taste. Season with salt and pepper to taste. Pour the dressing over the broccoli in a serving bowl. Taste and adjust the lemon juice and seasonings.

Orange And Lemon Rind
To remove orange and lemon rinds from a grater, bang the grater briskly on the counter or brush the rind from the grater with a pastry brush.

SHOPPING LIST
1 bunch broccoli
1 plum tomato
garlic
1 lemon
hot red pepper flakes
olive oil
balsamic vinegar

GUILT-FREE
MASHED POTATOES

These potatoes are moistened and flavored with a low-fat mixture of yogurt and ricotta cheese—no butter and cream to add calories and fat. Mash potatoes with a potato masher, fork or hand-held electric mixer—not in a food processor, which will make them gluey.

Serves 4 to 6
Preparation time: 15 minutes
Cooking time: 20 minutes

INGREDIENTS

2 pounds boiling potatoes, peeled and cut into 1-inch chunks
½ cup plain low-fat yogurt
½ cup part-skim ricotta cheese
Salt and freshly ground pepper
Chopped fresh herbs such as chives, basil or parsley

1. Put the potato chunks in a large saucepan and add cold water to cover. Cover the pan and bring to the boil over high heat. Reduce the heat to medium and boil, uncovered, for about 15 minutes until the potatoes are tender. Drain the potatoes well and return them to the saucepan. Shake the potatoes over medium heat to evaporate the excess moisture. Remove the pan from the heat.

2. In a blender or food processor, blend the yogurt and ricotta until smooth. Using a potato masher or a hand-held mixer at medium speed, beat the yogurt mixture into the potatoes. Continue beating until the potatoes have the consistency you desire. Season with salt and pepper to taste and serve.

Potatoes
We buy and consume potatoes so readily we barely notice them. After all, they are always in the markets, always inexpensive and every kitchen has a few lying about. But the lowly potato is the stuff of greatness. As a staple of so many cuisines, it has nourished families for generations. It, like the tomato, is a native of the new world but, also like the tomato, quickly became an integral part of the European diet and points beyond.

There may be more than 400 varieties of potato but most growers only produce a few disease-resistant types which are vaguely named. These generally fall into the category of baking potatoes (russets, long whites) and boiling potatoes (round whites and reds). New potatoes are just that: young potatoes of any sort and thus "new." We may associate red potatoes with new potatoes but it is the size and age that earns the moniker. Baking potatoes have a higher starch content than boiling potatoes and as a rule the two ought not to be interchanged for culinary uses. The age of the potato also contributes to the starch content; older spuds are starchier. High-starch varieties are, as mentioned, best for baking; those with lower starch do well boiled and used in salads. The starch content does not mean the potatoes are fattening. A medium-size potato has fewer than 100 calories and when it is boiled, it loses about 20 of those. And potatoes are good sources of vitamin B and potassium.

SHOPPING LIST

2 lbs. boiling potatoes
chives, basil or parsley
plain low-fat yogurt
part-skim ricotta cheese

POTATO GRATIN

This recipe will work equally well with other root vegetables such as rutabagas, turnips or celery root. If you decide to use another vegetable, mix in some potatoes, too—about a third of the total. The starch in the potato thickens the broth and helps the consistency of the final dish.

Serves 4
Preparation time: 15 minutes
Cooking time: 40 minutes

INGREDIENTS

2 tablespoons olive oil
1 small leek or onion
1 medium clove garlic, chopped
1½ teaspoons chopped fresh sage or
    ½ teaspoon dried
2 pounds baking potatoes
Salt and freshly ground pepper
1¼ cups chicken broth or water
3 tablespoons grated Parmesan cheese,
    optional

1. Heat the oven to 400 degrees.

2. Heat the oil in a 9- or 10-inch cast iron or ovenproof frying pan over medium heat. Add the leek, garlic and sage and cook for about 5 minutes until the leek is softened. Add the potatoes, salt and pepper and stir gently to coat the potatoes with the leek mixture. Add the broth and bring to the boil. Gently flatten the mixture into the pan and transfer to the oven. Bake for 20 to 25 minutes until the potatoes are tender and the liquid has evaporated.

3. If using cheese, heat the broiler. Sprinkle the gratin with the cheese and broil until golden brown.

Frying
If you chill food thoroughly before frying it, the fibers will be tightly contracted and the fat will not be able to penetrate into the food itself.

Use 2 forks to dip foods in egg and breadcrumb coating and into batters—it is less messy than using your fingers.

Wait until you are ready to cook before dredging foods in flour or breadcrumbs or dipping in batter and the coating will not become soggy.

Do not fill deep-fat frying pans more than half full or the fat will spill over the edge when the food is added to the pan.

SHOPPING LIST

2 lbs. baking potatoes
leeks or onions
garlic
sage (fresh or dried)
chicken broth
olive oil
Parmesan cheese

217

CAPONATA

If you can, make caponata a few days ahead and let it mellow in the refrigerator. Serve it warm or at room temperature alongside hot or cold meat as a flavorful accent, or in dishes such as Lamb and Caponata with Pasta on page 118.

Serves 4 to 6
Preparation time: 35 minutes
Cooking time: 40 minutes

INGREDIENTS

¼ cup red wine vinegar
2 teaspoons tomato paste
1 tablespoon sugar
¼ cup chopped pitted green olives
3 tablespoons raisins
1 tablespoon capers
1 large eggplant (1½ to 1¾ pounds),
    unpeeled, cut into ½- to ¾-inch pieces
2 teaspoons coarse salt
7 tablespoons olive oil
Salt and freshly ground pepper
3 medium-size stalks celery, finely chopped
1 medium-size red onion, coarsely chopped

1. Combine the vinegar, tomato paste, sugar, olives, raisins and capers and set aside.

2. Put the eggplant in a colander set over a bowl and toss with the coarse salt. Weight the eggplant and let drain for 30 minutes. Rinse and drain in the colander; pat dry.

3. Heat 3 tablespoons of the oil in a large, heavy frying pan over medium-high heat. Add half of the eggplant and cook for 8 to 10 minutes until tender and lightly browned. Remove to a bowl. Heat 3 more tablespoons of oil in the frying pan. Add the remaining eggplant and cook for 8 to 10 minutes until tender and lighly browned. Remove to the bowl. Season the eggplant with salt and pepper to taste.

4. Heat the remaining tablespoon of oil in the frying pan over low heat. Add the celery and onion and stir to coat with the oil. Add ½ cup water, cover and cook gently for about 15 minutes until the vegetables are tender. Remove the cover, raise the heat and boil for 3 to 4 minutes until the liquid evaporates and the vegetables brown slightly. Season with salt and pepper to taste and remove to the bowl with the eggplant.

5. Reduce the heat to low. Add the vinegar mixture and cook gently for 1 minute, scraping up the browned bits on the bottom of the pan. Add to the vegetables and stir gently to combine. Taste and adjust seasonings.

POTATO SKILLET CAKE

Instead of a number of small potato cakes, make a single large one in a frying pan. The fast and simple side dish can be cut into wedges and served with roasts, grilled steaks or scrambled eggs. Everyone will love it—and why not? It's made from grated potatoes flavored with scallions and salt and pepper, all rapidly cooked until crispy. To reduce the amount of fat needed for easy turning, be sure to use a non-stick frying pan.

Serves 4 to 6
Preparation time: 10 minutes
Cooking time: 15 minutes

INGREDIENTS

2 tablespoons vegetable oil
1 tablespoon unsalted butter or margarine
2 large baking potatoes, peeled and
    shredded
2 scallions, finely chopped
Salt and pepper

1. Heat the oil and butter in a medium-size non-stick frying pan over medium-high heat. Add half the potatoes, spreading them out in an even layer. Sprinkle the scallions on top of the potatoes. Arrange the remaining potatoes in an even layer on top of the potatoes and season with salt and pepper.

2. Reduce the heat to medium-low, cover and cook for 6 to 8 minutes until the bottom of the potato pancake is golden brown. To turn the pancake, hold a dinner plate on top of the frying pan with one hand. With your other hand, flip the frying pan and the plate upside down at the same time so that the pancake falls out of the frying pan and onto the plate. Slip the potato pancake, browned side up, back into the frying pan. Cook, uncovered, for another 6 to 8 minutes until the underside of the potato pancake is cooked. Serve immediately cut into wedges.

SHOPPING LIST

2 large baking potatoes
scallions
vegetable oil
unsalted butter or margarine

ROASTED NEW POTATOES WITH RED PEPPERS

Olive oil and rosemary combine with tender new potatoes to make a side dish full of flavor and about as easy to assemble and cook as you could hope for. As the potatoes roast in the oven, they become brown and crispy on the outside and stay moist inside—both a function of the olive oil coating.

Serves 6
Preparation time: 10 minutes
Cooking time: 25 minutes

INGREDIENTS

2 pounds new potatoes, quartered
1 red pepper, stem and seeds removed, cut into 1-inch pieces
1 onion, cut into 1-inch pieces and separated
3 tablespoons olive oil
1 teaspoon dried rosemary
1 teaspoon grated lemon rind
Freshly ground black pepper

1. Heat the oven to 350 degrees.

2. Put the potatoes, red pepper and onion in a baking dish and pour in the olive oil. Add the rosemary and lemon rind and season to taste with black pepper. Toss until the ingredients are well coated.

3. Roast the potatoes in the preheated oven for 25 minutes or until they are tender and browned. If necessary, add more oil during cooking as it is absorbed by the potatoes. Serve the potatoes hot or at room temperature.

SHOPPING LIST

2 lbs. new potatoes
1 red pepper
onion
1 lemon
dried rosemary
olive oil

BROCCOLI AND CABBAGE STIR-FRY

Vegetables are satisfying to stir fry—they cook quickly yet retain their crispness and good flavor. Stir fried vegetables are a good, straightforward way to adorn a simple roasted chicken or baked pork chop without a lot of bother.

Serves 4
Preparation time: 10 minutes
Cooking time: 10 minutes

INGREDIENTS

2 tablespoons vegetable oil
1 large onion, finely chopped
1 clove garlic, finely chopped
2 stalks celery, thinly sliced
1 cup sliced broccoli
1 cup cut and trimmed string beans
1 cup shredded white cabbage
1 scallion, chopped
1 bunch watercress, chopped
1 tablespoon soy sauce

1. Heat the oil in a wok or heavy frying pan. Add the onion and garlic and stir fry for 1 minute. Add the celery and stir fry for 2 minutes. Add the broccoli and string beans and stir fry for 2 minutes. Add the cabbage, scallions and watercress and stir fry for 2 minutes. If any water has accumulated, let it evaporate over high heat.

2. Sprinkle the vegetables with the soy sauce. Toss well and transfer to a serving platter.

Stir Frying
The secret to success with stir frying is to take your time. That may sound contradictory, since by nature this is a speedy method of cooking, but it is important not to rush when adding the ingredients. Put them in the hot frying pan or wok in a logical order, beginning with the ones which will require the longest cooking. It is also important to use the right kind of oil (olive oil, for example, cannot get hot enough for stir frying before it begins to smoke). Supermarket vegetable oil is a fine choice for most stir frying. It is often made from soy oil, peanut oil or corn oil, all of which can withstand high heat. Be sure, too, that the food is as dry as possible. If there are drops of water on the vegetables, for instance, the food will steam rather than cook rapidly in the hot oil. This will also lower the temperature of the oil and spoil it for the rest of the ingredients.

SHOPPING LIST

broccoli
garlic
celery
½ lb. string beans
white cabbage
scallions
onions
watercress
olive oil
soy sauce

STEAMED SQUASH WITH CHIVES

SWEET POTATO FRIES

If you like the mild flavor of squash, try this easy method of cooking it. Use a vegetable steamer or a steamer tray that fits in the bottom of an everyday saucepan.

Serves 4
Preparation time: 10 minutes
Cooking time: 8 minutes

INGREDIENTS

2 medium-size zucchini
2 medium-size summer squash
3 tablespoons butter
2 tablespoons chopped fresh chives
Salt and freshly ground pepper

1. Cut the zucchini and the squash into ¼-inch slices.

2. Fill the bottom of a steamer with enough water to come to within an inch of the steamer tray. Cover the steamer and bring the water to a simmer over medium heat. Put the zucchini and squash on the steamer tray, cover the pan and cook for 8 minutes.

3. Heat the butter in a heavy saucepan over low heat. Add the chives and cook for 2 minutes. Add the steamed zucchini and squash and toss. Season with salt and pepper to taste and serve immediately.

SHOPPING LIST

2 medium zucchini
2 medium summer squash
chives
butter

We call them fries, but they are actually baked in a very hot oven so that the potato fingers turn nice and crunchy but you do not have the bother of frying food in hot, spattering oil. Sweet potatoes are delicious this way but regular baking potatoes would be good, too.

Serves 4
Preparation time: 10 minutes
Cooking time: 25 to 30 minutes

INGREDIENTS

2 pounds sweet potatoes, peeled and cut into ½-inch-thick fingers, 3 to 4 inches long
3 tablespoons vegetable oil
Salt and freshly ground pepper

1. Heat the oven to 450 degrees. Toss the potato fingers with the oil, salt and pepper in a large baking dish.

2. Bake the potatoes, shaking the pan every 5 to 10 minutes so that they cook evenly, for 25 to 30 minutes until the potatoes are tender and well carmelized.

SHOPPING LIST

2 lbs. sweet potatoes
vegetable oil

HONEYED CURRIED CARROTS

Sweet carrots, cooked with a pleasing blend of honey and orange juice and a touch of curry, are sure to become a regular part of your weekday meals. You can leave out the curry if your children are not sure they like it.

Serves 4 to 6
Preparation time: 10 minutes
Cooking time: 5 minutes

INGREDIENTS

1 tablespoon butter or margarine
1 pound carrots, peeled, trimmed and cut into ¼-inch rounds
2 teaspoons curry powder
½ cup orange juice
1 tablespoon honey
Salt and freshly ground pepper
Finely chopped parsley or coriander, for garnish

1. Heat the butter in a medium frying pan over medium-high heat. Add the carrots and curry powder and cook, stirring, for 30 seconds. Add the orange juice and honey. Bring the mixture to the boil and cook for 3 minutes.

2. Reduce the heat to low and cook for an additional 2 minutes until the liquid in the pan is almost evaporated and the carrots are crisp-tender. Season with salt and pepper to taste and sprinkle with chopped parsley. Serve immediately.

Coriander

Sometimes called cilantro or Chinese parsley, coriander is a flat-leafed green herb used extensively in Mexican, Middle Eastern, Chinese, Indian and Mediterranean food. It has a very distinctive flavor which has been described as "soapy" by those without a palate for it. Once your palate becomes accustomed to coriander, you will find numerous uses for it. It is good for pickling and in relishes (nearly always showing up in salsas) but also has a place in sauces for fish, lamb and pork. Coriander should be purchased fresh and used fairly soon after buying—it does not dry well. Do not confuse fresh coriander with coriander seeds. The two are completely different in flavor and uses. The seed is sharp flavored indeed and can spoil a dish calling for a sprinkling of chopped fresh coriander.

SHOPPING LIST

1 lb. carrots
parsley or coriander
curry powder
honey
orange juice
butter or margarine

SPAGHETTI SQUASH WITH GARLIC

Spaghetti squash is so called because its sweet-tasting flesh separates into thin strands resembling pasta. Serving it with melted garlic butter, as we suggest here, is easy and tasty for a side dish, but you can also try it with red sauce, such as the Quick Marinara Sauce on page 121, which turns it into a main course.

Serves 6
Preparation time: 10 minutes
Cooking time: 40 minutes

INGREDIENTS

1 large spaghetti squash
4 tablespoons butter or margarine
1 clove garlic, finely chopped
2 tablespoons chopped parsley
Salt and freshly ground pepper

1. Fill the bottom of a vegetable steamer with enough water to come to within 1 inch of the steamer tray. Cover the steamer and bring the water to a simmer over medium heat.

2. Cut the squash in half lengthwise and scoop out the seeds. Put the squash on the steamer tray, cut side down. Cover the pan and steam the squash for 40 minutes.

3. Heat the butter in a large frying pan over low heat. Add the garlic and cook, stirring, for 2 minutes.

4. Scoop the squash out of its skin, pulling it into strands. Add it to the garlic butter and toss. Add the parsley and season with salt and pepper to taste. Toss again and serve.

> #### Garlic
> To remove the skin from garlic cloves, smash them lightly with the flat side of a cleaver or the bottom of a small heavy saucepan.
> When chopping garlic, sprinkle a little salt on the chopping board. The salt will pick up the garlic juice. Add the salt to the cooking pan.

> #### Steaming
> Water is converted to steam at 212 degrees at or near sea level. This means there is no advantage in increasing the heat under a steamer pan as the food will not cook any more rapidly but the water will boil away very quickly. Maintain a slow steady boil and be sure the lid fits tightly.

> #### SHOPPING LIST
> *1 large spaghetti squash*
> *garlic*
> *parsley*
> *butter or margarine*

BRAISED ONIONS
WITH HERBS

Braised onions make an excellent side dish during the cold winter months when you want to serve food that is warm, nourishing and filling. As they cook, the onions become sweet and mild and make the perfect accompaniment to roasts. Use small fresh onions or already peeled, frozen onions.

Serves 4
Preparation time: 10 minutes
Cooking time: 35 minutes

INGREDIENTS

3 tablespoons butter or margarine
12 small onions (about 1½ pounds), blanched and peeled
¼ cup beef broth
2 teaspoons finely chopped garlic
2 teaspoons dried rosemary
1 bay leaf
Salt and freshly ground pepper

1. Heat the oven to 350 degrees.

2. Put the butter in a shallow flameproof dish, about 8 inches in diameter, over medium heat. When the butter starts to brown, add the onions and cook for 3 to 4 minutes, stirring frequently, until the butter is nut brown and onions start to darken.

3. Stir in the remaining ingredients and cover the dish. Bake in the oven for 30 minutes, until the onions resist only slightly when pierced with a skewer or knife. Remove the bay leaf before serving.

SHOPPING LIST

*12 small onions
garlic
bay leaves
dried rosemary
beef broth
butter or margarine*

VEGETABLE STEW
WITH DILL

This vegetable stew takes a little more than an hour to cook and requires a tiny bit of watching during the last half hour of cooking. The result is a chunky, satisfying dish without a trace of meat—just lots of good vegetables and their wholesome good flavor. Serve it as a main course or as a side dish.

Serves 4
Preparation time: 15 minutes
Cooking time: 1¼ hours

INGREDIENTS

4 tablespoons olive oil
2 tablespoons chopped onions
1 cup finely chopped carrots
½ cup cooked split peas
½ cup cooked lima beans
¾ cup cubed potatoes
¾ cup fresh green peas
¾ cup corn kernels
½ cup chicken broth
Salt and freshly ground pepper
1 cup chopped fresh spinach
3 tablespoons chopped fresh dill

1. Heat the oven to 350 deegrees.

2. Heat the oil in a large, heavy casserole or Dutch oven over low heat. Add the onions and cook for 5 to 8 minutes, until softened and translucent.

3. Stir in all the remaining ingredients except the spinach and dill. Bring to the boil over high heat.

4. Cover the pot and put in the oven for 30 minutes. Remove the cover and cook, stirring occasionally, for 30 to 40 minutes more or until the vegetables are tender and the pan juices are thickened. Add the spinach and dill and cook for 5 minutes more.

SHOPPING LIST
onions
carrots
split peas
lima beans
potatoes
green peas
1 ear corn
spinach
dill
chicken broth
olive oil

ARTICHOKES WITH BASIL BUTTER

Globe artichokes—those intriguing large vegetables with the spiky leaves—do superbly in the microwave. Be sure to eat the whole thing; the soft, tender heart, buried in the center of the globe, is the best part.

Serves 2
Preparation time: 5 minutes
Cooking time: 10 to 12 minutes

INGREDIENTS

2 artichokes, about 6 ounces each
1 small lemon, cut in half
6 tablespoons butter or margarine
1 teaspoon dried basil, crumbled
$\frac{1}{4}$ teaspoon finely chopped garlic
Freshly ground pepper

1. Trim the stems from the artichokes and pull off any tough leaves from the bottom. Cut about an inch off the top of each artichoke and trim the tips of the remaining leaves with scissors.

2. Rub the cut surfaces of the artichokes with the lemon. Wrap each artichoke in wax paper. Put the artichokes in a shallow microwave-safe dish. Miicrowave on High (100 percent) for 7 to 9 minutes, rotating the dish once. Remove the artichokes from the oven and let stand for 5 minutes.

3. Meanwhile, combine the butter, basil, garlic and 2 tablespoons of juice from the cut lemon in a small glass bowl. Microwave on High (100 percent) for 1½ to 2 minutes or until the butter has melted. Stir well and season with pepper to taste.

4. Serve the artichokes with the basil butter on the side.

> *A Note About Power Levels*
> *Since high power may vary in each oven, it is not enough simply to recommend high, medium, and low; we have used wattage numbers throughout to assist you in using your own microwave. To see if your wattage is the same as that used in the book, fill an 8-ounce glass measure with tap water. Cook on high for 3 minutes; if the water comes to a boil within this time, your timing matches the timing in the book. If it doesn't, adjust your timing accordingly.*

> **SHOPPING LIST**
>
> *2 artichokes, about 6 oz. each*
> *1 lemon*
> *garlic*
> *dried basil*
> *butter or margarine*

STEWED EGGPLANT AND ZUCCHINI

This pretty melange of summer garden vegetables can, with the microwave, be "stewed" in less than half an hour.

Serves 8
Preparation time: 15 minutes
Cooking time: 20 to 25 minutes

INGREDIENTS

1 onion, thinly sliced
1 green pepper, thinly sliced
2 cloves garlic, finely chopped
3 tablespoons vegetable oil
1 pound eggplant, cut into 1-inch pieces
2 medium-size zucchini, sliced
¼ pound mushrooms, sliced
¾ cup chopped tomatoes
1 teaspoon dried basil
1 teaspoon sugar
¼ teaspoon freshly ground pepper

1. Combine the onion, green pepper, garlic and oil in a large microwave-safe casserole dish. Cover and microwave on High (100 percent) for 4 to 5 minutes, until the onion is soft.

2. Stir in the remaining ingredients. Cover and microwave on High (100 percent) for 15 to 17 minutes, until the vegetables are just tender. Let stand, covered, for 5 minutes before serving. Or, let cool and serve at room temperature.

Green Vegetables
When people ask us, what does the microwave oven cook best, we answer, vegetables! It's reason enough to buy a microwave if you don't have one. Green vegetables remain bright green, they retain more vitamins, and they are tender-crisp when microwaved.

If you prefer the mushy olive-drab green beans Grandma used to cook all day, you may not like the microwave version immediately. Keep trying, and remember that al dente vegetables are not only fashionable but also much more healthful.

The most important factor in microwaving fresh green vegetables is the cooking time. This is determined by the weight and type of vegetable. You should have a scale in your kitchen to weigh the food. The weight of the vegetables at the store will not be the weight after trimming or preparation.

SHOPPING LIST

onion
1 green pepper
garlic
1 lb. eggplant
2 medium zucchini
¼ lb. mushrooms
2 medium tomatoes
dried basil
sugar
vegetable oil

WARM TOMATO AND ZUCCHINI WITH VINEGAR

This is a quick variation on a fresh summer salad. The vegetables are cooked only briefly to heighten their natural sweetness and good flavor. If you want, sprinkle the vegetables with ¼ cup of grated Parmesan just before serving.

Serves 4 to 6
Preparation time: 5 minutes
Cooking time: 6 minutes

INGREDIENTS

4 tablespoons olive oil
1 pound small zucchini, thinly sliced
2 tomatoes, chopped, juice reserved
1 onion, thinly sliced
¼ pound mushrooms, thinly sliced
2 to 3 tablespoons white wine vinegar
1 tablespoon chopped fresh thyme or 1
  teaspoon dried
1 tablespoon chopped fresh chives

SHOPPING LIST

1 lb. small zucchini
2 tomatoes
onions
¼ lb. mushrooms
chives
thyme (fresh or dried)
olive oil

1. Heat the oil in a large frying pan over medium heat. Add the zucchini, tomatoes, onion and mushrooms and cook for about 5 minutes, until the vegetables are tender.

2. Add the vinegar, thyme, chives and the reserved tomato juice and cook for 1 minute. Transfer the mixture to a bowl, toss and serve immediately.

EGGPLANT AND GARLICKY MUSHROOMS

This earthy vegetable mixture tastes just fine in the fall when you want bold taste and comforting texture. It is important to sprinkle the eggplant with salt, as the salt draws excess moisture from it. Otherwise, the dish may be too watery.

Serves 4
Preparation time: 15 minutes plus standing
Cooking time: 8 to 10 minutes

INGREDIENTS

1 pound eggplant
2 teaspoons salt
1 large clove garlic, finely chopped
1 tablespoon chopped fresh basil or parsley
1¼ cups sliced mushrooms
1 small green pepper, cut into thin strips
½ cup water
1 tablespoon olive oil

1. Trim the eggplant and cut it lengthwise into ¼-inch slices. Arrange the slices in a single layer on a large plate. Sprinkle them with the salt and let them stand for 10 minutes. Rinse thoroughly and drain in a large colander.

2. Lay a sheet of paper towel on a microwave-safe plate or tray. Put the eggplant slices in the center of the paper towel and top with the garlic, basil, mushrooms and pepper.

3. Fold the corners of the towel over the vegetables and top with another sheet. Tuck the corners under the packet. Pour the water evenly over the packet and microwave on High (100 percent) for 8 to 10 minutes, until the vegetables are tender. Rotate the dish once during cooking.

4. Remove the packet from the microwave and let it stand for 2 minutes. Arrange the vegetables in a bowl and sprinkle them with olive oil just before serving.

SHOPPING LIST

1 lb. eggplant
garlic
basil or parsley
½ lb. mushrooms
1 small green pepper
olive oil

RICE, GRAINS AND BEANS

You may not be aware of it, but you consume close to 150 pounds of grains every year. At least that is the estimated per capita consumption in the U.S., a number that has swelled in recent years and continues to grow as Americans recognize the nutritional benefits of grains as well as their good flavor. Most of those pounds are comprised of rice, but other grains, such as millet, couscous and bulgur are gaining in popularity. Combine a healthy amount of beans (legumes) with grain consumption and we can increase our recipe inventory, aid in our crusade for good health and save money all at the same time.

In this chapter we have assembled a collection of recipes for rice and other grains and for beans. We rely on lentils as the primary bean since they do not require the long soaking that other dried beans do, beans such as navy beans and black beans. (See the section in Chapter 2 on lentils, found on page 62, for more information on dried beans.) Both grains and beans are excellent sources of pro-

tein and while westerners have long gotten most of their protein from meat, the peoples of China and India have relied on grains for centuries as a dietary staple and the primary source of protein. Grains also contain most of the vitamins, amino acids and minerals needed for survival.

But aside from being wonderfully healthy, grains and beans taste good, too, and act as perfect backdrops for any number of other ingredients. These might include vegetables, seafood or cheese. They may be used to flavor the grain or bean only slightly or may become the primary focus of the dish. The recipes here are for side dishes that, for the most part, easily translate into main courses. You will find the grains in most supermarkets, but if you have trouble locating them, they are always available in health food stores. Try a few of the recipes that call for grains you may not be too familiar with, as well as the ones for rice. You will discover a whole new area of delicious and adaptable recipes to set on the table.

VEGETABLE COUSCOUS

In this recipe, large chunks of vegetables, greens and chick-peas are stewed until tender and then spooned over a generous helping of cooked couscous. Serve this as main course on a cold night when a robust vegetable stew—made in less than an hour—is just the thing. Make the stew ahead of time if you can and reheat if before serving. This might be a good choice for a busy weekend when you want something fast, easy and healthy which will keep in the refrigerator until everyone finally assembles for the evening meal. Couscous often is served with harissa, a hot chili pepper paste sold in specialty food stores. Put a little on the table if your family likes spicy condiments, straight or dissolved in a little of the cooking broth.

Serves 4
Preparation time: 25 minutes
Cooking time: 30 minutes

INGREDIENTS

1 tablespoon olive oil
1 medium-size onion
½ teaspoon ground coriander
½ teaspoon ground cumin
¼ teaspoon ground ginger
Pinch cinnamon
1 large new potato, unpeeled, cut into large chunks
2 medium-size carrots, halved lengthwise and cut into large chunks
2 medium-size turnips, cut into sixths or eighths
3 medium-size Italian plum tomatoes, cut into eighths
3 cups chicken broth
2 medium-size zucchini, halved lengthwise and cut into large chunks
½ cup cooked chick-peas
2 cups firmly packed leafy greens, such as spinach, chard, turnip greens or broccoli rabe
2 tablespoons chopped coriander
Pre-cooked couscous
Harissa (optional)

1. Heat the oil in a large pot over medium heat. Add the onion and spices and cook for about 5 minutes until the onion is softened.

2. Add the potato, carrots, turnips, tomato and broth. Bring the mixture to the boil, reduce the heat and cook gently for 5 minutes. Add the zucchini and continue cooking for about 20 minutes until the vegetables are very tender.

3. Stir in the chick-peas and greens, cover and cook for about 5 minutes longer until the chick-peas are cooked through and the greens are wilted. Stir in the coriander.

4. Meanwhile, make the instant couscous according to the package directions.

5. Divide the couscous between 4 bowls or deep plates. Spoon the vegetables over the grain along with some of the broth. Serve with harissa, if desired.

SHOPPING LIST

pre-cooked couscous
onion
1 large new potato
carrots
2 medium turnips
3 medium Italian plum tomatoes
2 medium zucchini
3 oz. chick-peas
spinach, chard, turnip greens or broccoli rabe
coriander (fresh and ground)
ground cumin
ground ginger
cinnamon
chicken broth
harissa
olive oil

STOVE TOP PILAF

The technique remains the same: onions are first softened in a bit of fat before the rice is added and allowed to cook for a few minutes. Next, liquid is added and cooks slowly with the rice until evaporated. What changes is the liquid. Water will do, but you really ought to use chicken, beef or fish stock, depending on the main course, to do justice to this wonderfully aromatic and flavorful side dish. A little white wine or vermouth boosts the overall flavor—substitute a quarter cup of broth with an equal amount of wine. Bottled clam juice is a good stand in for homemade fish broth, although you should dilute every cup of clam juice with one of water.

Serves 4 to 6
Preparation time: 10 minutes
Cooking time: 20 minutes

INGREDIENTS

1 tablespoon unsalted butter or margarine
1 tablespoon vegetable oil
¼ cup onions
1 cup long grain rice
¼ teaspoons dried thyme
2 cups chicken or beef broth or fish stock
Salt and freshly ground pepper

1. Heat the butter and oil in a small saucepan over medium heat. Add the onions and cook for 2 minutes, stirring often, until softened. Add the rice and thyme and cook for 1 minute, stirring often, until the rice turns opaque.

2. Add the broth and season with salt and pepper to taste. Bring to the boil. Cover the saucepan, reduce the heat to low and simmer for 20 minutes until the liquid is evaporated and rice is tender. Fluff the rice with a fork and serve immediately.

SHOPPING LIST

long-grain rice
onions
dried thyme
chicken or beef broth or fish stock
vegetable oil
butter or margarine

CUMIN RICE

Serve this mild yet distinctively flavored rice with dishes boasting of the flavors of sunny Mexico. Turkey Fajitas (page 134), South western Pork Stir Fry (page 166) and Oven Deviled Chicken (page 132) are good choices. For added flair, stir chopped coriander into the rice just before serving. Here is a good opportunity to try basmati rice, a fragrant rice from India that is increasingly available in supermarkets, specialty shops and health food stores. Plain long-grain rice is very nice in this recipe, too.

Serves 4 to 6
Preparation time: 10 minutes
Cooking time: 20 minutes

INGREDIENTS

1 tablespoon olive oil
¼ cup chopped scallions
1 cup basmati or long-grain rice
½ teaspoon ground cumin
2 cups chicken broth
Salt and freshly ground pepper
2 tablespoons chopped fresh coriander or
    parsley, optional

1. Heat the olive oil in a small saucepan over medium heat. Add the scallion and cook, stirring, for 1 minute until softened. Add the rice and cumin and cook, stirring, for another minute until the rice has turned opaque.

2. Add the chicken broth, salt and pepper to taste, and bring to the boil. Cover the saucepan, reduce the heat to very low and simmer for 20 minutes until the liquid is evaporated and the rice is tender. Fluff the rice with a fork, mix in the chopped coriander and serve immediately.

Rice
Do not raise the lid or stir rice as it cooks, or the grains will stick together.
To reheat rice, spread it in a buttered shallow dish and dot the surface with more butter. Season with salt and pepper and cover with foil. Place in the preheated 350-oven for 15 minutes and stir with a fork to make it fluffy.

SHOPPING LIST

basmati or long-grain rice
scallion
coriander or parsley
ground cumin
chicken broth
olive oil

WILD RICE WITH MUSHROOMS AND HAZELNUTS

Wild rice, which actually is not rice at all but the seed of grasses native to the region around the northern Great Lakes, is purely American and considered a rare treat. Afficionados consider the rice which grows in shallow lakes in Minnesota and is hand harvested by Native Americans to be the very best available. However, much of the wild rice sold today is cultivated and harvested by machinery and comes from California. This is good news for many of us as it means the nutty, crunchy grain-like food is far more accessible than it once was. The following preparation is very good, too, made with a combination of wild rice and white or brown rice.

Serves 4
Preparation time: 10 minutes
Cooking time: 30 minutes

INGREDIENTS

1 cup wild rice
5 cups water
¼ teaspoon salt
⅓ cup hazelnuts
2 tablespoons olive oil
¼ pound white mushrooms
1 teaspoon chopped fresh sage
⅓ cup chopped scallions
2 teaspoons low-sodium soy sauce
2 tablespoons chopped parsley
Freshly ground pepper

1. Rinse the rice and combine it in a medium saucepan with the water and salt. Bring the water to the boil, reduce the heat and simmer for about 30 minutes until the rice is tender. Drain in a colander.

2. Meanwhile, heat the oven to 425 degrees. Toast the hazelnuts in a baking dish for 5 to 7 minutes until they are fragrant and their skins begin to crack. Put the nuts in a towel and rub them vigorously against one another to remove the skin (some of the skin will not come off, but don't worry about it). Roughly chop the nuts.

3. Heat the oil in a medium frying pan over medium-high heat. Add the mushrooms and cook for 4 to 5 minutes until the mushrooms wilt. Add the scallions and cook for 1 to 2 minutes until the scallions are softened. Stir in the soy sauce and parsley.

4. When the rice is cooked, re-warm the mushroom mixture, add the cooked rice and hazelnuts and stir to blend. Season to taste with salt and pepper.

SHOPPING LIST
wild rice
¼ lb. white mushrooms
scallions
parsley
sage
hazelnuts
low-sodium soy sauce
olive oil

MILLET A L'INDIENNE

Millet has not yet acquired the cachet of some other grains but, if you're not already acquainted with it, this recipe is a good place to start. It is a highly nutritious grain with a flavor reminiscent of corn; this flavor is accentuated when the grain is lightly toasted. The three fragrant spices—cumin, coriander and cinnamon—as well as the raisins are what gives the dish an unmistakable flavor of India, where, by the way, millet is a valued staple.

Serves 4
Preparation time: 20 minutes
Cooking time: 25 minutes

INGREDIENTS

2 tablespoons sliced almonds
1 cup millet
1 tablespoon vegetable oil
1 small onion, chopped
$\frac{1}{4}$ teaspoon ground cumin
$\frac{1}{4}$ teaspoon ground coriander
$1\frac{1}{2}$-inch piece cinnamon stick
2 tablespoons raisins
$\frac{1}{2}$ teaspoon salt
2 cups boiling water
$\frac{1}{4}$ cup chopped parsley
Freshly ground pepper

1. Toast the almonds in a medium saucepan over medium heat for about 5 minutes until they are fragrant and lightly browned. Remove from the pan and set aside.

2. Toast the millet in the same pan over medium heat for 5 to 10 minutes until it is fragrant and some of the beads are lightly browned. Remove the millet from the pan and set aside.

3. Heat the oil in the same pan over medium-high heat. Add the onion, cumin, coriander and cinnamon and cook for about 5 minutes until the onion is lightly browned. Add the toasted millet, raisins, salt and water and bring to the boil. Reduce the heat and simmer, covered, for 16 or 17 minutes until the millet is tender but still has texture, and the water has been absorbed. Stir in the toasted almonds and parsley and season to taste with salt and pepper. Serve at once.

Millet
Millet is actually a catch-all term used to describe several different kinds of grass plants that produce tiny seeds. It thrives in poor soil and is much appreciated in northern India and northern China for its high protein, mineral and fiber content. Millet pancakes, breads and porridge are staples in China, while the Indians turn it into breads, pilaf and breakfast cereals. In a food-rich country like the United States, millet is primarily used in commercial birdseed mixtures—which is a pity, because although it tends to be bland on its own, a little imaginative seasoning can transform it into an interesting side dish.

SHOPPING LIST
millet
onion
parsley
ground cumin
ground coriander
1 ½-in. piece cinnamon stick
sliced almonds
vegetable oil

SEAFOOD RISOTTO

This risotto is a pleasant change from pasta and seafood and should be served as a main course with nothing more exotic accompanying it than a green salad or some steamed vegetables. If you do not have any Fish Stock on hand and do not have the time or inclination to make some, combine three cups of bottled clam juice with four cups of water.

INGREDIENTS

7 cups Fish Stock (page 48) or chicken broth
1 cup dry white wine
½ teaspoon crushed saffron threads, optional
3 tablespoons olive oil
1 small onion, finely chopped
1 stalk celery, finely chopped
1 small clove garlic, finely chopped
2 cups Italian Arborio rice
1 cup peeled, seeded and chopped ripe tomatoes, or canned Italian tomatoes
½ pound peeled and deveined shrimp
½ pound small scallops, cut into ½ inch cubes if large
Salt and freshly ground pepper
Chopped fresh basil or rosemary, for garnish

1. In a large saucepan, bring the Fish Stock or chicken broth, wine and optional saffron to a simmer over medium heat. Reduce the heat to low and keep the liquid at a simmer while cooking the risotto.

2. In a large heavy-bottomed saucepan, warm the olive oil over medium heat. Add the onion, celery and garlic and cook, stirring often, for about 3 minutes until the vegetables are softened. Add the rice and cook, stirring constantly, for about 1 minute until the rice turns opaque. Stir in the chopped tomatoes. Reduce the heat to medium-low and add 2 cups of the simmering broth, stirring constantly for 4 to 5 minutes. Add another 2 cups of the broth and cook, stirring constantly, for another 4 to 5 minutes until the liquid is almost evaporated.

3. Add the shrimp and scallops along with the remaining 2 cups of broth and cook, stirring constantly, for about 5 minutes until the rice is al dente and the seafood is cooked through. The risotto should be slightly wet and saucy not dry, so add very hot water toward the end of the cooking time if you need more liquid to keep the rice at the desired moistness and you have run out of broth. Season slightly with salt and pepper (the broth and seafood are salty). Transfer the mixture to a warm serving dish, sprinkle with the basil and serve immediately.

SHOPPING LIST

½ lb. small scallops
½ lb. shrimp
2 lbs. bones, heads and trimmings from sole, haddock or flounder
onion
celery
leeks
garlic
parsley
basil or rosemary
dried thyme
white peppercorns
2 tomatoes (or canned Italian tomatoes)
saffron threads
Italian arborio rice
dry white wine

LENTIL STEW

Combining grains and legumes is a satisfying way to get the protein you need with a minimum of fat. Here, we use lentils as the basis for a tasty stew enriched with cornmeal and corn kernel dumplings. Lentils are an especially good choice for a busy family because, unlike many beans which require lengthy soaking and cooking times, they are relatively quick to prepare.

Serves 6 to 8
Preparation time: 15 minutes
Cooking time: 45 minutes

INGREDIENTS

3 tablespoons olive oil
1 medium-size onion, finely chopped
3 medium-size carrots, peeled and cut into 1-inch chunks
2 stalks celery, cut into 1-inch chunks
1 medium-size clove garlic, finely chopped
1 pound lentils, rinsed and drained
16-ounce can Italian tomatoes, with juice
3 cups water
2 cups chicken broth
½ cup dry red wine
½ teaspoon ground cumin
½ teaspoon dried oregano
¾ cup all-purpose flour
¼ cup yellow cornmeal
2 teaspoons baking powder
½ teaspoon salt
1 tablespoon unsalted butter, chilled
⅓ cup low-fat milk
1 large egg

½ cup fresh or frozen and defrosted corn kernels
2 tablespoons chopped parsley
Salt and freshly ground pepper

1. In a large saucepan, cook the onions, carrots, celery and garlic, covered, over medium heat for about 6 minutes until the vegetables are softened. Stir in the lentils, tomatoes with juice, water, broth, wine, cumin and oregano and simmer over low heat, covered, for about 30 minutes, stirring often, until the lentils are tender.

2. Sift the flour, cornmeal, baking powder and salt into a medium-sized bowl. Using a pastry blender or fork, cut the butter into the dry ingredients until the butter is the size of small peas. In a measuring cup, lighly beat the milk with the egg and pour into the flour mixture. Add the corn kernels and parsley and stir until just combined. Drop the dough, a tablespoon at a time, into a simmering lentil stew. Cover and cook for 10 minutes until the dumplings are done and the lentils are tender. Season the stew with salt and pepper (do not add salt until this time or the lentils may get tough). Serve immediately.

```
• • • • • • • • • • • • • • • • • • • • •
              SHOPPING LIST

                   onion
                  carrots
                   celery
                   garlic
      1 ear corn (or frozen kernels)
                  parsley
               1 lb. lentils
              ground cumin
              dried oregano
                   flour
                 cornmeal
              baking powder
               chicken broth
       16-oz. can Italian tomatoes
                 olive oil
              unsalted butter
               low-fat milk
                   eggs
                dry red wine
• • • • • • • • • • • • • • • • • • • • •
```

TABBOULEH

1. Put the cracked wheat in a large bowl and pour the boiling water over it. Stir to moisten all the grains, cover the bowl and let stand for 2 to 3 hours, until the wheat has expanded and is tender and fluffy.

2. Drain the cracked wheat in a colander, shaking to remove the excess water.

3. Put the drained wheat in a bowl. Add the tomatoes, cucumber, mint, parsley and scallions and mix well. Add the lemon juice and olive oil and season with salt and pepper to taste. Mix well.

By now, many Americans are familiar with this Middle Eastern specialty, having seen it in take-out shops, on the menus of health food stores and, most likely, in a few cookbooks. If you have not made it yourself, we suggest you hesitate no longer. This is a smashing recipe and one that surely will become a family favorite. Its gentle flavor, underscored by mint and lemon juice, and firm, chewy texture combine to make it a side dish every member of the family will adore. It is just as good the second or third day, and so even though the cracked wheat must be soaked for several hours, this should present no problem. Serve it with grilled or broiled fish, meat and poultry.

Serves 6
Preparation time: 15 minutes plus soaking

INGREDIENTS

1¾ cups cracked wheat or bulgur
7 cups boiling water
1 cup seeded, chopped fresh tomatoes
½ cup seeded, diced cucumber
2 tablespoons chopped fresh mint
2 tablespoons chopped fresh parsley
2 tablespoons finely chopped scallions, white part only
2 tablespoons fresh lemon juice
¼ cup olive oil
Salt and freshly ground pepper

Cracked Wheat and Bulgur
Cracked wheat is generally associated with Middle Eastern cooking, where it has been used for centuries to create dishes such as tabbouleh. It's also a staple in Eastern Europe and, in recent years, has become far more readily available in the United States. You may understandably be somewhat confused about the difference, if any, between cracked wheat and bulgur. Yes, there is a difference, but they may nevertheless be used interchangeably. Cracked wheat is made from whole, unprocessed wheat berries, cracked with steel blades. For bulgur, the berries are partly debranned, cooked and dried before they are cracked. These days, the cracking is done in commercial mills; in olden times, you had to crack the berries yourself in a mortar with a pestle. Because of its pre-cooking, bulgur is darker in color than cracked wheat and has a nuttier flavor. Both bulgur and cracked wheat need only to be soaked in hot water before using to make salads such as tabbouleh.

SHOPPING LIST
cracked wheat or bulgur
1 large tomato
1 cucumber
scallions
fesh mint
parsley
1 lemon
olive oil

ROAST TOMATOES
WITH RICE

Using scooped-out tomato cups as containers for zucchini, garlic and rice is a clever way to present vegetables. These can be made ahead of time and served cold, or you can make them an hour or so before supper and serve them at room temperature. We do not include the scooped flesh of the tomato in the recipe since it should be pressed through a sieve to rid it of seeds, which is time consuming. But if you want to go to the trouble, by all means, stir the sieved pulp into the rice mixture.

Serves 4
Preparation time: 15 minutes
Cooking time: 25 to 30 minutes

INGREDIENTS

4 large firm ripe tomatoes
1 medium zucchini cut in ¼-inch dice
1 small clove garlic, finely chopped
1 tablespoon olive oil
2 tablespoons finely chopped fresh basil, or
   2 teaspoons dried combined with 2
   tablespoons finely chopped parsley
¼ cup long-grain rice
Extra virgin olive oil
Lemon wedges, for garnish

1. Heat the oven to 375 degrees. Lightly oil a 9-inch square baking dish.

2. Slice the tops off of the tomatoes, about ½-inch down, and reserve. With a spoon, scoop out the seeds and pulp, leaving the walls of the tomato intact. Turn the tomatoes upside down and allow to drain while preparing the rest of the ingredients.

3. In a medium skillet, heat the oil over medium heat. Add the zucchini and garlic and saute just for 1 minute until heated through, but still crisp. Stir in the basil and remove the pan from the heat.

4. In a small saucepan of boiling salted water, cook the rice for 6 to 8 minutes, until very al dente. Drain the rice and add to the zucchini. Season the mixture with salt and pepper to taste. Spoon the mixture into the tomatoes. Put the tomatoes into the pan. Drizzle a teaspoon of the extra-virgin olive oil over the top of each tomato and cover with the reserved tops. Add about ¼-inch of water to the pan. Bake the tomatoes for 15 to 20 minutes until rice is cooked. Serve the tomatoes hot, warm or cold.

SHOPPING LIST
4 large tomatoes
1 medium zucchini
garlic
lemon
basil (fresh or dried)
olive oil
long-grain rice

ZUCCHINI TIAN

Although you can serve this rice-based zucchini casserole as a side dish, it stands on its own as the main course when you want a light, meatless meal. We suggest accompanying it with a tomato salad or tossed green salad. It is equally good served at room temperature, which makes it a good bet for advance preparation. Make it at night and plan to serve it the next evening for supper.

Serves 4
Preparation time: 30 minutes
Cooking time: 25 minutes

INGREDIENTS

1 quart water
½ cup long-grain rice
¼ cup olive oil
2 medium-size onions, sliced
1½ pounds zucchini, thinly sliced
2 eggs
½ cup grated Gruyere cheese
½ cup grated Parmesan cheese
2 cloves garlic, finely chopped
2 tablespoons chopped parsley
½ teaspoon salt
Freshly ground pepper

1. Bring the water to the boil in a saucepan. Add the rice and cook gently for 15 minutes. Drain in a colander and then put in a bowl.

2. Meanwhile, heat 2 tablespoons of the oil over medium-low heat in a large frying pan. Add the onions and cook for about 20 minutes, stirring occasionally, until very soft. Add to the bowl.

3. Heat the remaining 2 tablespoons of oil in the frying pan and increase the heat to medium-high. Add the zucchini and cook for 10 to 12 minutes, until wilted. Add to the bowl with the rice.

4. Lightly whisk the eggs and add them to the bowl with ¼ cup Gruyere cheese, ¼ cup Parmesan cheese, the garlic, parsley, and salt and pepper to taste.

5. Heat the oven to 375 degrees. Lightly butter an 8- by 10-inch baking dish. Turn the zucchini mixture into the baking dish and smooth the top. Sprinkle with the remaining cheese and bake for 15 minutes. Increase the oven heat to 450 degrees and continue baking for about 10 minutes more until the tian is lightly browned and set.

SHOPPING LIST

long-grain rice
1 ½ lbs. zucchini
onions
garlic
parsley
olive oil
Gruyere cheese
Parmesan cheese
eggs

FALAFEL

Falafel refers to fried balls of spiced chick-peas, although it can also mean a Middle Eastern-style sandwich made with the tasty balls, which is gaining in popularity across the United States. Here, we explain how to form the balls and compose the sandwich. The sandwich is a far cry from peanut butter and jelly, but your kids may like it even better!

Serves 4 to 6
Preparation time: 15 minutes
Cooking time: 5 minutes

INGREDIENTS

2 cups cooked chick-peas
1 slice white bread, crust removed
½ cup water
1 tablespoon flour, plus extra for coating
1 egg, beaten
1 tablespoon tahini (sesame paste)
¼ teaspoon ground cumin
¼ teaspoon ground turmeric
¼ teaspoon dried marjoram
2 cloves garlic, crushed
2 tablespoons finely chopped parsley
Vegetable oil
Shredded lettuce
4 to 6 pita breads, warmed
2 medium tomatoes, chopped
3 to 4 scallions, chopped
4 to 6 tablespoons plain low-fat yogurt, optional

1. Process the chick-peas in a food processor or blender until they are almost smooth but still have some texture. Soak the bread in the water for 1 minute. Squeeze out most of the water, mash the bread and combine it with the chick-peas.

2. Stir the tablespoon of flour and the remaining ingredients into the chick-pea mixture and mix until well combined. Form the mixture into 2-inch balls and coat each with the extra flour.

3. Heat 3 to 4 inches of vegetable oil to 365 degrees in a heavy pot or deep fat fryer. Deep fry the balls, a few at a time, for about 3 minutes until golden brown. Drain on paper towels.

4. Put some shredded lettuce in the pocket of a pita bread. Top with chopped tomatoes and scallions and, if desired, a tablespoon or so of yogurt.

SHOPPING LIST

8 oz. chick-peas
garlic
parsley
lettuce
2 medium tomatoes
scallions
white bread
4 to 6 pita breads
tahini
ground cumin
ground turmeric
dried marjoram
vegetable oil
flour
eggs
plain low-fat yogurt

PITAS STUFFED WITH SPICY LENTILS AND TOMATO SALAD

The ingredient list goes on and on, but since all you do is toss everything together and then stuff it into warm pita bread we thought the recipe ranked among the simple—and delicious! You could dispense with the pita altogether and serve the salad alone with broiled meat or fish.

Serves 4
Preparation time: 30 minutes

INGREDIENTS

2 cups cooked lentils
2 stalks celery, finely chopped
1 small green pepper, stemmed, seeded and finely chopped
2 scallions, thinly sliced
1 carrot, chopped
1 tablespoon curry powder
½ teaspoon ground cumin
1½ teaspoons fresh chopped thyme or ½ teaspoon dried
½ cup finely chopped parsley
4 tablespoons olive oil
2 tablespoons red wine vinegar
Salt and freshly ground pepper
2 tomatoes, seeded and chopped
6 ounces Syrian string or Muenster cheese, shredded
4 individual whole wheat pita loaves, cut open
Spinach leaves, washed and shredded

1. Heat the oven to 300 degrees.

2. Combine the lentils in a bowl with the celery, pepper, scallions, carrot, curry powder, cumin, thyme, parsley, oil and vinegar. Season with salt and pepper to taste. Stir in the tomatoes and cheese.

3. Stack the pitas on a large piece of foil and wrap tightly. Place in the oven for 10 to 15 minutes, until hot.

4. Line each pita with a quarter of the shredded spinach. Fill each with a quarter of the lentil mixture.

SHOPPING LIST

4 whole wheat pita loaves
lentils
celery
1 small green pepper
2 tomatoes
scallions
carrots
parsley
spinach
thyme (fresh or dried)
curry powder
ground cumin
olive oil
red wine vinegar
6 oz. Syrian string or Muenster cheese

MUSHROOM AND BARLEY CASSEROLE

This hearty side dish could also double as a main course.

Serves 4 to 6
Preparation time: 5 minutes
Cooking time: 18 to 21 minutes

INGREDIENTS

4 tablespoons butter or margarine
1½ cups finely chopped onions
1 tablespoon finely chopped shallots
1 pound fresh mushrooms, sliced
1 cup quick-cooking barley
1 cup chicken broth
2 tablespoons chopped fresh parsley
1 teaspoon dried basil, crumbled
¼ teaspoon salt
¼ teaspoon freshly ground pepper

Barley
Barley is sold in supermarkets already pearled, which means its protective hull—a very tough skin indeed—has been removed. If you have never cooked with barley before do not be surprised by its expansion powers. Mixed with liquid, it nearly quadruples in volume.

SHOPPING LIST

onions
shallots
1 lb. mushrooms
parsley
dried basil
quick-cooking barley
chicken broth
butter or margarine

1. Combine the butter, onions and shallots in a 3-quart, microwave-safe casserole. Cover and microwave on High (100 percent) for 4 to 5 minutes, until the onion is softened, stirring once.

2. Stir in the remaining ingredients. Cover and microwave on High (100 percent) for 5 to 6 minutes. Microwave on Low (20 percent) for 9 to 10 minutes, stirring once during the cooking time. Let the casserole stand, covered, for 5 minutes before serving.

QUICK BREADS AND MUFFINS

Baking is a satisfying kitchen chore that need not take a lot of time. High-domed muffins, dense, delicious quick breads and sweet coffee cakes are all easy to make and require minimal time in the oven. As they bake, rich, warm aromas fill the house and cheerfully say "welcome home" to every member of the family.

Keep a supply of flour, cornmeal, sugar and eggs on hand so that, without a moment's hesitation, you can mix up fruit-filled muffins, flaky biscuits or crumbly cornbread on those evenings when nothing else will do. Setting a basket of hot biscuits or puffy popovers on the dinner table turns a simple meal into something special: the baked goods say you care.

The recipes that follow are considered "quick" because they are leavened with baking soda and baking powder, the so-called chemical leaveners. Baking powder is a mixture of an alkali and an acid, which, when moistened, react with each other to form carbon dioxide. The gas raises the batter, reaching its full potential in the heat of the oven. Baking soda, an alkali, reacts further with the baking powder as well as with acidic ingredients such as buttermilk, brown sugar and yogurt. The texture of baked goods raised by chemical leaveners is quite different from those raised by yeast. Each method has its followers, but most folks appreciate both. (Yeast-raised breads and rolls, of course, require several risings and lots of time.)

For the most part the following recipes do not require an electric mixer. A dozen or so firm strokes with a wooden spoon or rubber spatula do the trick, particularly since it is important never to overmix the batters. Ingredients such as nuts and berries are generally stirred in as the last step. One last word about the recipes: we instruct you to "butter" the pans. While you may use butter for this chore, it is perfectly acceptable to use margarine or vegetable oil instead. No doubt by now you are anxious to begin baking and creating that special magic only you and the oven can perform.

CRANBERRY MUFFINS

Cranberries freeze very well and so may be a good choice for these muffins. However, for the utmost flavor, make them with fresh cranberries, available in the markets in the late fall and early winter. Come summer, substitute fresh blueberries for the cranberries for irresistable muffins that you can only dream about in chilly December. When you stir the blueberries into the batter, add them whole—no need to chop them up.

Makes 9 muffins
Preparation time: 10 minutes
Cooking time: 20 minutes

INGREDIENTS

1 cup whole wheat flour
1 cup unprocessed bran
$\frac{1}{4}$ cup packed dark brown sugar
1 teaspoon baking soda
$\frac{1}{2}$ teaspoon salt
1 cup fresh or thawed, frozen cranberries, chopped
1 cup milk
$\frac{1}{4}$ cup vegetable oil
2 tablespoons molasses
1 egg, lightly beaten

1. Position a rack in the upper third of the oven. Heat the oven to 375 degrees. Butter 9 muffin cups.

2. Combine the flour, bran, sugar, soda, salt and cranberries in a bowl and mix to blend. Combine the remaining ingredients and stir into the dry ingredients until just combined—do not overmix.

3. Fill the muffins cups about two-thirds full. Bake for 20 minutes or until risen and lightly browned.

WALNUT-CINNAMON COFFEE CAKE

Welcome back the kind of Sunday morning you thought you could only dream about now that life is so busy. With this recipe it is easy to have homemade coffee cake to munch on while you drink your coffee and peruse the newspaper—no need to run out to the deli for mass-produced bagels or croissants. This cake is just as satisfying baked during the week and served for dessert or packed in lunch boxes for a mid-morning snack.

Makes 1 8-inch-square coffee cake
Preparation time: 15 minutes
Cooking time: 35 minutes

INGREDIENTS

2 ounces (½ cup) walnuts, chopped
2 tablespoons brown sugar
1 teaspoon cinnamon
2 cups all-purpose flour
½ cup sugar
½ teaspoon salt
1½ teaspoons baking powder
½ teaspoon baking soda
½ cup vegetable oil
¾ cup buttermilk
1 medium egg, lightly beaten
1 teaspoon vanilla extract

1. Heat the oven to 350 degrees. Lightly oil an 8-inch-square baking pan.

2. Combine the walnuts, brown sugar and cinnamon in a small bowl. Combine the flour, sugar, salt, baking powder and baking soda in another bowl and mix to blend. Combine the oil, buttermilk, egg and vanilla in a third bowl and add to the dry ingredients. Stir just to combine; do not overmix.

3. Spread half of the batter over the bottom of the baking pan. Sprinkle with half of the walnut mixture. Carefully spread the remaining batter over the walnuts and then sprinkle with the remaining walnut mixture. Bake for about 35 minutes until a knife inserted into the center of the coffee cake comes out clean.

Baking Soda
Baking soda is used with acid ingredients such as buttermilk, yogurt, sour cream, brown sugar, molasses and dried fruits. It combines with the acid to form carbon dioxide which in turn lightens and aerates the dough. You can use it alone or in combination with baking powder.

SHOPPING LIST

chopped walnuts
cinnamon
sugar
brown sugar
baking powder
baking soda
all-purpose flour
vanilla extract
vegetable oil
eggs
buttermilk

OATMEAL DATE MUFFINS

The dates make these muffins chewy and moist, and the oatmeal makes them especially healthful. As most people are aware, oat bran seems to help reduce cholesterol levels.

Makes 9 muffins
Preparation time: 10 minutes
Cooking time: 20 minutes

INGREDIENTS

1 cup all-purpose flour
1 cup quick-cooking oatmeal
$\frac{1}{4}$ cup packed dark brown sugar
2 teaspoons baking powder
1 teaspoon salt
$\frac{1}{2}$ cup chopped dates
1 cup milk
1 egg, lightly beaten
3 tablespoons butter, melted

Chopping Dried Fruit
The easiest way to chop sticky dried fruits such as raisins and dates is to sprinkle them with a little flour. This way, they will not stick to the knife. Mound them on a wooden cutting board and use a heavy, sharp knife. Chilling the fruit first helps a lot, too.

SHOPPING LIST

dates
all-purpose flour
dark brown sugar
baking powder
quick-cooking oatmeal
eggs
butter
milk

1. Position a rack in the upper third of the oven. Heat the oven to 400 degrees. Butter 9 muffin cups.

2. Combine the flour, oatmeal, sugar, baking powder, salt and dates in a bowl. Combine the milk, egg and butter and stir into the dry ingredients until just combined—do not overmix.

3. Fill the muffin cups about two-thirds full. Bake for 20 minutes or until risen and lightly brown.

BUTTERMILK CORNBREAD WITH CORN KERNELS

This recipe is similar to the preceding one, which is not surprising since all cornbreads have a lot in common. Buttermilk is the secret of this bread. Serve it with southern fried chicken or country ham, or with Yankee specialties such as Clam Chowder (page 42) and Cream of Broccoli Soup (page 43).

Serves 6 to 8
Preparation time: 10 minutes
Cooking time: 30 minutes

INGREDIENTS

3 tablespoons butter or margarine
1¼ cups yellow cornmeal
¾ cup all-purpose flour
2 tablespoons sugar
¾ teaspoon salt
1½ teaspoons baking powder
½ teaspoon baking soda
¾ cup fresh or frozen and defrosted corn
   kernels
1 cup buttermilk
2 medium eggs, lightly beaten

1. Heat the oven to 400 degrees. Put 1 table-spoon of butter in a 9-inch cast iron or ovenproof frying pan or a square baking pan and heat the pan in the oven until it is hot and the butter is melted.

2. Meanwhile, combine the cornmeal, flour, salt, baking powder, baking soda and corn kernels in a bowl and mix to blend. Melt the remaining 2 tablespoons of butter and combine with the buttermilk and eggs in a bowl. Pour this mixture into the dry ingredients and stir just to combine (do not overmix). Swirl the butter in the frying pan to coat the sides and pour the batter into the pan. Smooth the top of the batter and bake for 25 to 30 minutes until a knife inserted in the center of the cornbread comes out clean.

Butter
Unsalted butter is used in the preparation of fine sauces, cakes and pastries. It has a better flavor than salted butter.

Clarified butter does not burn as readily as whole butter. To make clarified butter, heat it until it is hot, then strain it through several thicknesses of cheesecloth. Leave it to drip slowly. Do not squeeze the cheesecloth or the butter will become cloudy. Use the butter for dipping lobster and artichokes and for sautéing meats, chicken and fish. Clarified butter will keep in the refrigerator for several weeks.

To make butter curls, dip the curler in cold water before drawing it along the butter to make each curl. If the butter does not form a curl correctly, it may be too salty or too cold.

SHOPPING LIST

fresh or frozen corn kernels
cornmeal
all-purpose flour
sugar
baking powder
baking soda
butter or margarine
buttermilk
eggs

PLUM BREAD

Yogurt and juicy, ripe plums combine in this quick bread to make it especially moist. Serve it for breakfast, lunch or dinner or anytime as a snack. A slice of quick bread is a welcome treat discovered in a lunchbox or briefcase.

Makes 3 loaves
Preparation time: 15 minutes
Cooking time: 35 minutes

INGREDIENTS

3 cups plus 2 tablespoons all-purpose flour
1½ teaspoons baking powder
1½ teaspoons baking soda
½ teaspoon salt
8 tablespoons butter or margarine, softened
1 cup sugar
3 large eggs
2 teaspoons vanilla
⅔ cup plain low-fat yogurt
½ pound plums, pitted, peeled, and sliced
½ cup coarsely chopped walnuts

1. Position a rack in the center of the oven. Heat the oven to 350 degrees. Butter and flour 3 5½-inch- by 3¾-inch loaf pans. Sift 3 cups of the flour along with the baking powder, baking soda and salt through a wire strainer into a bowl.

2. In a large bowl, cream the butter using an electric mixer set at high speed for 1 minute until smooth. Add the sugar gradually, beating constantly for about 2 minutes until the mixture is light. Add the eggs one at a time, beating well after each addition. Add the vanilla, beating until mixed. Using a wooden spoon, stir in the flour mixture, a third at a time, alternating with the yogurt, mixing just until combined.

3. Put the plums and the walnuts into separate bowls. Sprinkle 1 tablespoon of flour over each and toss to coat. Fold the plums and walnuts into the batter. Divide the batter among the pans and bake for 35 to 40 minutes until a toothpick inserted into the center of the loaf comes out clean. Cool the bread in the pans for 10 minutes. Unmold the loaves onto wire racks and cool completely.

Cooling and Storing Quick Breads
If you attempt slicing a quick bread when it is still warm from the oven, it will crumble. Let it cool all the way before taking knife to it, or before wrapping it in foil for storage. A quick bread tastes best, actually, when allowed to mellow for 8 to 24 hours before it is served.

SHOPPING LIST

½ lb. plums
chopped walnuts
all-purpose flour
baking powder
baking soda
sugar
vanilla
butter or margarine
eggs
plain low-fat yogurt

IRISH RAISIN SODA BREAD

These free-form, coarsely textured loaves taste just right with hearty soups on cold autumn evenings. Try a loaf with Mushroom Barley Soup (page 36) or Old-Fashioned Fish Chowder (page 40).

Makes 2 loaves
Preparation time: 15 minutes
Cooking time: 40 minutes

INGREDIENTS

2½ cups all-purpose flour
1½ teaspoons baking powder
½ teaspoon baking soda
½ teaspoon salt
2 tablespoons honey
¾ cup plain low-fat yogurt
¼ cup vegetable oil
1 large egg
½ cup raisins
1½ teaspoons caraway seeds

1. Position a rack in the upper third of the oven. Heat the oven to 375 degrees.

2. Sift the flour, baking powder, baking soda and salt together through a wire strainer into a large bowl. Add the raisins and caraway seeds and toss well.

3. Put the honey, yogurt, oil and egg in a bowl and beat until well combined. Stir the liquid ingredients into the dry ingredients, mixing just until combined. Knead the mixture in the bowl

for about 1 minute, adding additional flour if necessary to make a soft, moist dough.

4. Divide the dough, and with lightly floured hands, form it into rounds. Place the rounds on an ungreased baking sheet. With a sharp knife or single edged razor, cut an "X" about ¼-inch deep on the top of each round. Bake for 35 to 40 minutes until the loaves are golden brown and sound hollow when tapped. Transfer the loaves to a wire rack and cool completely before slicing.

SHOPPING LIST

raisins
caraway seeds
honey
vegetable oil
all-purpose flour
baking powder
baking soda
eggs
plain low-fat yogurt

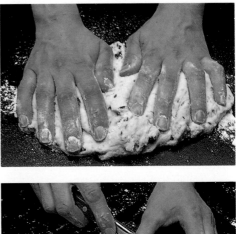

YOGURT BISCUITS

We stirred a good helping of yogurt into this dough to create the tenderest, most flaky biscuits this side of a plantation kitchen. Use a light hand to pat the dough out on the work surface and when you stamp out the biscuits, do not twist the biscuit cutter or upturned glass. Piping hot biscuits are wonderful with summer soups such as the Tuscan Tomato Soup on page 34. Try them, too, with Salmon Scallops with Cucumber Sauce on page 192.

Makes 8 3-inch biscuits
Preparation time: 10 minutes
Cooking time: 20 minutes

INGREDIENTS

2 cups all-purpose flour
2 teaspoons baking soda
1 teaspoon cream of tartar
$\frac{1}{2}$ teaspoon salt
6 tablespoons cold margarine or butter, cut
    into $\frac{1}{4}$-inch pieces
$\frac{3}{4}$ cup plain low-fat yogurt

1. Heat the oven to 425 degrees.

2. Sift the flour, baking soda, cream of tartar and salt together into a large bowl. Add the butter and toss lightly. Using a pastry blender or 2 knives, work the margarine into the flour until the mixture resembles coarse crumbs. Add the yogurt and stir to form a soft dough. Knead the dough very briefly to combine.

3. On a lightly floured surface, pat the dough with lightly floured hands to a thickness of $\frac{1}{2}$-inch. Cut out the biscuits using a 3-inch round cookie cutter or inverted glass. Gather up the scraps, pat out and cut out more biscuits, to make a total of 8. Put the biscuits on an ungreased baking sheet and bake for 18 to 20 minutes, until well risen and golden brown.

VARIATIONS

Add one of the following ingredients to the flour/butter mixture and then proceed with the recipe as instructed.
Scones: $\frac{1}{2}$ cup dark raisins, golden raisins or currants
Herb biscuits: $\frac{1}{4}$ cup chopped fresh dill, basil or parsley
Ginger biscuits: $\frac{1}{4}$ cup very finely chopped crystallized ginger

SHOPPING LIST

all-purpose flour
baking soda
cream of tartar
butter or margarine
plain low-fat yogurt

FRUIT-BRAN MUFFINS

Dried fruit adds good flavor and moisture to bran muffins—everybody's favorite morning treat.

Makes 12 muffins
Preparation time: 15 minutes
Cooking time: 20 minutes

INGREDIENTS

1 cup whole bran cereal
1 cup buttermilk
$\frac{1}{3}$ cup light molasses
$\frac{1}{4}$ cup firmly packed light brown sugar
1 cup sifted all-purpose flour
1 teaspoon baking soda
1 teaspoon baking powder
$\frac{1}{2}$ teaspoon salt
1 egg, lightly beaten
$\frac{1}{4}$ cup vegetable oil
$\frac{1}{2}$ cup chopped softened figs, prunes, raisins or dates

1. Position a rack in the upper third of the oven. Heat the oven to 400 degrees. Butter 12 muffin cups.

2. Stir together the bran cereal, buttermilk, molasses and brown sugar. Sift together the flour, baking soda, baking powder and salt.

3. Stir the egg and vegetable oil into the bran mixture. Combine this mixture with the flour mixture, stirring only until moistened. Gently fold in the fruit.

4. Fill the prepared muffin tins about two-thirds full. Bake for 20 minutes or until risen and lightly browned.

Keeping Muffins
Muffins are at their best eaten straight from the oven. But if this isn't convenient for you, they may be kept in the refrigerator for one or two days, well wrapped in foil. To reheat, loosen the foil and pop them in a 250 degree oven for five to ten minutes. A good alternative, if you don't plan to serve muffins the day they're baked, is to freeze them. Let them cool completely, wrap in foil and put them in the freezer for up to four weeks. (If you freeze them for longer than this they tend to become dry.) To serve, unwrap the foil, rewrap loosely and heat the muffins in a 350 degree oven for 15 to 20 minutes.

SHOPPING LIST

3 oz. figs, prunes, raisins or dates
whole bran cereal
packed light brown sugar
all-purpose flour
baking soda
baking powder
light molasses
vegetable oil
buttermilk
eggs

PEAR-WALNUT MUFFINS

Chopped ripe pears are marvellous in muffins. Look for Anjou or Bosc pears and make sure they are ripe but still firm. Overripe pears will not hold up as well to the oven's heat.

Makes 9 muffins
Preparation time: 15 minutes
Cooking time: 20 to 25 minutes

INGREDIENTS

1½ cups all-purpose flour
½ cup packed brown sugar
2¼ teaspoons baking powder
1 teaspoon cinnamon
½ teaspoon ground ginger
½ teaspoon salt
1 medium unpeeled pear, cored and chopped
1 egg
½ cup plain low-fat yogurt
½ teaspoon vanilla
½ cup vegetable oil

Topping:
3 tablespoons finely chopped walnuts
3 tablespoons packed brown sugar

1. Position a rack in the upper third of the oven. Heat the oven to 350 degrees. Butter 9 muffin cups.

2. Sift the flour, brown sugar, baking powder, cinnamon, ginger and salt together into a large bowl, rubbing the sugar through. Stir in the chopped pear.

3. Whisk together the egg, yogurt, vanilla and oil. Stir into the dry ingredients until just combined—do not overmix. Fill the prepared muffin cups about two-thirds full.

4. Mix together the walnuts and brown sugar. Spoon about ½ teaspoon of the nut mixture onto the top of each muffin. Bake the muffins for 20 to 25 minutes, until risen and lightly browned.

SHOPPING LIST

1 medium pear
cinnamon
ground ginger
vanilla
all-purpose flour
packed brown sugar
baking powder
vegetable oil
eggs
plain low-fat yogurt

ORANGE SPICE MUFFINS

A heady combination of orange and spices make these muffins special enough for a weekend breakfast and sweet enough for dessert on a weekday evening when you want something deliciously satisfying but not overly rich or difficult to make.

Makes 12 muffins
Preparation time: 15 minutes
Cooking time: 25 minutes

INGREDIENTS

1 cup all-purpose flour
1 cup whole wheat flour
1 tablespoon baking powder
1¼ teaspoons cinnamon
¼ teaspoon ground cloves
¼ teaspoon ground nutmeg
¼ teaspoon salt
1 egg
1 cup sour cream or plain low-fat yogurt
¼ cup vegetable oil or melted butter
1 tablespoon frozen orange juice
   concentrate, thawed
1 tablespoon finely grated orange rind
⅓ cup brown sugar
1 tablespoon sugar

1. Position a rack in the upper third of the oven. Heat the oven to 400 degrees. Butter 12 muffin cups.

2. Sift together the flours, baking powder, ¾ teaspoon of the cinnamon, the cloves, nutmeg and salt.

3. Beat the egg with the sour cream or yogurt, the oil or butter and the orange juice concentrate. Stir in the orange rind and brown sugar and mix well.

4. Add the sour cream mixture to the dry ingredients and stir until just combined. Fill the prepared muffin cups about two-thirds full.

5. Combine the remaining 1 tablespoon sugar with the remaining ½ teaspoon cinnamon and sprinkle over the muffins. Bake for 25 minutes until risen and lightly browned.

Sour Cream
If sour cream reaches boiling point it will separate. Watch it carefully to prevent this from happening.

SHOPPING LIST

1 orange
cinnamon
ground cloves
ground nutmeg
all-purpose flour
whole wheat flour
baking powder
brown sugar
sugar
vegetable oil or butter
frozen orange juice
eggs
sour cream or plain low-fat yogurt

APPLE CINNAMON MUFFINS

3. Stir the egg mixture into the flour mixture, alternating with the milk, until just combined.

4. Fill the muffin cups about two-thirds full. Bake for 20 minutes or until risen and lightly browned.

The aromas wafting from the kitchen as these muffins bake will rouse the family from the farthest corner of the house. You may not be able to keep many of them to serve with the meal as they will surely be snatched the moment they come from the oven—but never mind, muffins are a great snack.

Makes 12 muffins
Preparation time: 15 minutes
Cooking time: 20 minutes

INGREDIENTS

2 cups all-purpose flour
1 cup whole wheat flour
4 teaspoons baking powder
1 teaspoon cinnamon
$\frac{1}{4}$ teaspoon salt
1 cup grated apple
$\frac{1}{2}$ cup brown sugar
1 egg, lightly beaten
$\frac{1}{4}$ cup vegetable oil
1 cup milk

1. Position a rack in the upper third of the oven. Heat the oven to 375 degrees. Butter 12 muffin cups.

2. Sift together the flours, baking powder, cinnamon and salt. Combine the apple, brown sugar, egg and oil.

Apples
If apples are peeled and sliced in advance, sprinkle them with lemon juice to prevent discoloration. When preparing apple and other fruit pies, thicken the juices by adding 2 tablespoons of cornstarch dissolved in 2 tablespoons of cold water, or use 3 tablespoons of instant tapioca sprinkled over $\frac{1}{3}$ cup of cold water. The pie can then be cut into compact slices. If the juices are not thickened, the top crust will cave in and the pie will be too juicy.

SHOPPING LIST

1 apple
cinnamon
all-purpose flour
whole wheat flour
baking powder
brown sugar
cinnamon
vegetable oil
eggs
milk

JALAPENO CORN CAKE

Cut this round loaf of cornbread into chunky wedges the next time you make your favorite chili. The jalapenos add zippy flavor and the whole corn kernels give it pleasant texture, which makes it just right with foods with a Tex-Mex flair. As well as chili, we suggest making this when you serve Plymouth Chili (page 150), Arizona Chicken (page 135) or Southwestern Pork Stir Fry (page 166).

Makes 1 8-inch round cake
Preparation time: 15 minutes
Cooking time: 20 to 25 minutes

INGREDIENTS

1 cup yellow cornmeal
1 cup all-purpose flour
2 teaspoons baking powder
½ teaspoon baking soda
½ teaspoon salt
2 teaspoons sugar
1 cup plain low-fat yogurt
1 egg
1½ cups fresh or frozen corn kernels
2 tablespoons vegetable oil
1 tablespoon finely chopped fresh jalapeno
    or 2 tablespoons canned chili pepper
    (optional)
½ cup grated cheddar cheese

1. Heat the oven to 425 degrees. Brush a heavy 8-inch cake pan or cast iron skillet with vegetable oil and place in the oven to heat.

2. Sift together the cornmeal, flour, baking powder, baking soda and salt into a large bowl. Combine the sugar, yogurt, egg and 1 cup corn kernels in a blender or food processor. Blend on high speed to a smooth puree.

3. Add the liquid ingredients together with the ½ cup corn kernels and the chopped jalapeno to the dry ingredients. Stir until just combined.

4. Remove the pan from the oven. Immediately scrape the cornmeal batter into the pan, smoothing the top. Sprinkle the cheese over the top. Return the pan to the oven and bake for 20 to 25 minutes until a toothpick inserted in the center comes out clean and the cake is lightly browned.

APRICOT ZUCCHINI MUFFINS

Muffins in the microwave? Yes. These really work and taste delightfully sweet and moist. The combination of fruit and vegetable make them suitable for breakfast or dinner and the sugary crumb topping makes them just right for brunch or a lunchbox treat. Talk about versatile!

Makes about 18 muffins
Preparation time: 15 minutes
Cooking time: 12 minutes

INGREDIENTS

1 egg
¼ cup sugar
½ cup plus 3 tablespoons packed brown
  sugar
½ cup vegetable oil
½ cup mashed canned apricots
½ teaspoon vanilla extract
¼ teaspoon almond extract
¾ cup whole wheat flour
¾ cup plus 3 tablespoons all-purpose flour
1 teaspoon cinnamon
½ teaspoon salt
½ teaspoon ground nutmeg
1 teaspoon baking soda
½ cup chopped dates
1 cup grated zucchini
3 tablespoons quick-cooking rolled oats
3 tablespoons chopped walnuts
3 tablespoons butter or margarine

1. Stir together the egg, sugar, ½ cup brown sugar, oil, apricots, and the vanilla and almond extracts.

2. Combine the whole wheat flour, ¾ cup all-purpose flour, ¾ teaspoon cinnamon, salt, nutmeg, baking soda, baking powder and dates. Make a well in the center and pour in the egg mixture. Stir until the dry ingredients are just moistened. Fold in the grated zucchini.

3. Line microwave-safe cupcake pans with paper liners. Half fill each with the batter.

4. Combine the remaining 3 tablespoons flour with the rolled oats, the remaining brown sugar, the walnuts and the remaining ¼ teaspoon cinnamon. Cut in the butter until the mixture is crumbly. Top each muffin with 1 tablespoon of the crumb mixture.

5. Microwave 6 muffins at a time on Medium (50 percent) for 4 minutes, rotating the pan a half turn after 2 minutes. Remove the muffins from the pans. Repeat the cooking procedure with the remaining batter. Serve the muffins warm.

SHOPPING LIST

1 zucchini
chopped walnuts
3 oz. dates
canned apricots
quick-cooking rolled oats
sugar
packed brown sugar
baking soda
whole wheat flour
all-purpose flour
vanilla extract
almond extract
cinnamon
ground nutmeg
vegetable oil
eggs
butter or margarine

BANANA NUT BREAD

We don't know anyone who does not like banana bread. Baked in the microwave, this one cooks fast so that the next time you spy an overripe banana in the kitchen, you need not hesitate about how to use it. The bread is tasty served with breakfast, lunch or dinner, and is a great after-school snack that the kids can make themselves. The microwave does not heat up as a conventional oven does and so there is less chance of them burning themselves—just be sure they use potholders when taking the pan from the microwave.

Makes 16 2-inch squares
Preparation time: 10 minutes
Cooking time: 7 to 9 minutes

INGREDIENTS

8 tablespoons butter or margarine, cut into
    pieces and softened
$\frac{3}{4}$ cup packed brown sugar
1 ripe banana, mashed
1 teaspoon lemon juice
2 eggs
$1\frac{1}{4}$ cups all-purpose flour
$\frac{1}{2}$ teaspoon baking powder
$\frac{1}{2}$ teaspoon baking soda
$\frac{1}{2}$ teaspoon salt
$\frac{1}{4}$ teaspoon ground nutmeg
$\frac{1}{2}$ cup chopped pecans or walnuts

1. Combine the butter and sugar in a mixing bowl. Add the banana, lemon juice and eggs and mix well, using a hand-held electric mixer or a large whisk.

2. Sift together the flour, baking powder, baking soda, salt and nutmeg in another bowl. Combine the mixtures, stirring until the flour is just incorporated. Stir in the pecans.

3. Line an 8-inch-square microwave-safe baking dish with wax paper. Pour the batter into the dish and microwave on High (100 percent) for 7 to 9 minutes until a toothpick inserted in the center comes out clean. Rotate the dish a quarter turn every 2 minutes during the cooking time. Remove the bread from the oven and let it rest in the pan for another 5 minutes.

4. Turn the bread out onto a wire rack and let it cool for 10 minutes. Peel off the wax paper and cut the bread into 16 squares.

Cake Cooling Rack
Use a cake cooling rack lined with paper towels for draining bacon and other fried foods. The circulating air keeps the food crisp.

SHOPPING LIST

1 banana
chopped pecans or walnuts
1 lemon
all-purpose flour
packed brown sugar
baking powder
baking soda
ground nutmeg
eggs
butter or margarine

POPOVERS

A basketful of piping hot popovers is a welcome sight on any table. They are easy to make and the batter may rest for as long as 30 minutes before baking. This is helpful for meal organization, since the main thing to remember is to serve popovers as soon as you can after removing them from the oven. If they sit around for long, they will lose their tempting crispness and, since they are full of hot air, literally, will deflate.

Makes 6 popovers
Preparation time: 5 minutes
Cooking time: 30 minutes

INGREDIENTS

1 cup sifted all-purpose flour
½ teaspoon salt
2 eggs
1 cup milk
1 tablespoon vegetable oil

1. Heat the oven to 425 degrees. Butter the popover pans. If using custard cups for baking, heat them in the oven and brush with melted butter just before filling.

2. Combine the flour and salt. Stir in the eggs, milk and vegetable oil, and blend until smooth. Let the batter rest for at least 10 minutes or for as long as 30 minutes.

3. Fill the popover pans or custard cups slightly less than half full. Bake for 30 minutes. Do not open the oven during baking time or the popovers may sink.

Flour
Flour varies in the amount of water that it will absorb, depending on the age of the flour, the method of storage and the method of milling.
Flours cannot be used interchangeably, so recipes should be followed carefully.
Whole wheat flour, rye, buckwheat and other flours are all heavier than all-purpose flour. These flours, and cornmeal, are almost always lightened by being combined with all-purpose flour. Sift flour to be used for baking to aerate and lighten it.

Baking
When baking, do not keep opening and closing the oven door to see how things are getting along. Every time you peer into the oven the temperature drops significantly.

SHOPPING LIST

all-purpose flour
vegetable oil
eggs
milk

CONDIMENTS, JAMS AND SPREADS

We have collected a group of recipes for condiments, jams and spreads that you can make at home in a flash. All will, we hope, add just the right accent and bright flavor to the meal, regardless of how simple it is. For instance, you could try guacamole on a hamburger, pesto with grilled fish, or a quick chutney with lamb chops. It is easy work to make fresh strawberry jam or a low-fat berry spread for fresh, hot muffins or bakery bread toasted to a golden turn.

None of these recipes calls for ingredients not available at the local supermarket. Nor are any difficult to make. We do not expect you to melt paraffin to top off jars of jams, or haul out the canning kettle. In a few recipes, we do suggest using sterile glass jars but if doing so is just too much trouble, even this is not necessary. Jars washed in a good dishwasher are perfectly safe for food that is chilled and consumed within a week or so.

If variety is the spice of life, condiments supply the same panache to a menu. Use them often. They look pretty on a table and round out the meal as no other food will. Your family will enjoy a change from bottles of ketchup and jars of mustard and, with just a little effort, your everyday meals will sparkle.

ORANGE MINT CHUTNEY

Most Americans are familiar with jam-like jarred chutneys such as Major Grey's. As good as these are, chutneys need not have this consistency to be authentic. In India, easy-to-make fresh fruit chutneys appear often on the dining table accompanying the meat course. This one, with its flavors of orange and mint underscored by hot chili peppers and sweet onions, is especially refreshing.

Makes about 1 cup
Preparation time: 10 minutes

INGREDIENTS

1 large seedless orange, peeled and finely
   chopped
1 tablespoon finely chopped red onion
1 tablespoon finely chopped fresh mint or 1
   teaspoon dried mint
1 tablespoon finely chopped fresh green or
   red chili pepper or 2 tablespoons chopped
   canned green chili peppers
1 teaspoon orange juice

Combine all the ingredients in a medium-sized bowl. Cover and refrigerate for 30 minutes to 1 hour. Do not let the chutney stand too long or it will start to lose its fresh flavor and texture.

SHOPPING LIST

1 orange
1 red onion
mint (fresh or dried)
green or red chili pepper (or canned
green chili pepper)
orange juice

LOW-GUILT BERRY SPREAD

We have not been able to take away all the fat and calories but have come up with a creamy, sweet spread that will alleviate the guilt you may experience when you feel the urge to slather butter and preserves on toast, muffins or biscuits. Use your favorite fruit preserves (the "all fruit, no sugar" types cut calories even more), low-fat ricotta and Neufchatel cheese. If you cannot find Neufchatel, use regular cream cheese. A little won't hurt!

Makes about 1 cup
Preparation time: 10 minutes

INGREDIENTS

3-ounce package Neufchatel cheese, softened
½ cup low-fat ricotta cheese
2 tablespoons fruit preserves (not jelly) or
   "no sugar, all-fruit" preserves

1. If necessary, soften the Neufchatel cheese in a microwave oven set at Low (10 percent) power for 1 minute.

2. Put the softened Neufchatel cheese, ricotta and fruit preserves in a bowl and stir until well combined.

SHOPPING LIST

fruit preserves
3 oz. pkg. Neufchatel cheese
low-fat ricotta cheese

FIVE-ALARM SALSA

SANTA FE GUACAMOLE

Don't count the sprinkling of salt (okay, we cheated!) as one of the five ingredients for this exciting condiment so important to Mexican and Tex Mex food. Fresh chili peppers, such as jalapeno and serrano, will make it hotter than canned green chili peppers. Customize the salsa, if you are so inclined, with a cup of thawed corn kernels or some chopped red bell pepper. A tablespoon or so of chopped coriander adds distinctive flavor.

There are endless ways to make guacamole and most involve soft, rich avocados, tomatoes, garlic and lime juice.

Serves 6
Preparation time: 10 minutes

INGREDIENTS

3 ripe medium-size avocados, halved, pitted and skinned
¼ cup finely chopped white or yellow onion
1 ripe medium-size tomato, peeled, seeded and chopped
1 clove garlic, finely chopped
2 tablespoons lime juice
2 tablespoons chopped fresh coriander, optional
1 tablespoon chopped fresh chili pepper or 2 tablespoons chopped canned green chili peppers
Salt

Makes about 2 cups
Preparation time: 10 minutes

INGREDIENTS

2 pounds ripe medium-size tomatoes, peeled, seeded and chopped
2 tablespoons chopped fresh green chili peppers or ¼ cup chopped canned green chili peppers
¼ cup finely chopped white or yellow onion
1 clove garlic, finely chopped
2 tablespoons lime juice
Salt

Mix all the ingredients together in a bowl. Cover and chill for 30 minutes to 1 hour. Do not let stand too long or the salsa will lose its fresh flavor and texture.

1. Mash all the ingredients together in a bowl with the back of a fork until chunky and well mixed. Season with salt to taste.

2. Press a piece of plastic wrap directly on to the surface of the guacamole and chill.

SHOPPING LIST

2 lbs. medium tomatoes
white or yellow onions
garlic
1 lime
green chili peppers (fresh or canned)

SHOPPING LIST

3 medium avocados
white or yellow onions
1 medium tomato
garlic
1 lime
coriander
chili pepper (or canned green chili peppers)

STRAWBERRY JAM

CORIANDER PESTO

Because this jam is lower in sugar than most fruit jams, its consistency will be more liquid than you might expect. We suggest storing the jam in sterile jars. It is easy to sterilize jars: put clean jars in a pot of boiling water for five or ten minutes before draining them and filling them with jam.

Makes about 1 cup
Preparation time: 10 minutes
Cooking time: 20 minutes

INGREDIENTS

1 quart strawberries
1½ cups sugar

1. Hull and rinse the strawberries. Drain in a colander.

2. Combine the berries and the sugar in a heavy pot and mash the berries with a spoon to break them up and release their juices. Bring to the boil, reduce the heat and simmer for 15 to 17 minutes until the fruit is cooked and the juices have reduced. Stir the mixture frequently and be especially careful during the last few minutes of cooking as the jam may begin to stick.

3. Cool and refrigerate in sterile jars.

> **SHOPPING LIST**
>
> *1 qt. strawberries*
> *sugar*

If you like the flavor of coriander, try this version of pesto. The jalapeno peppers and lime juice give it a Southwestern tang—and it tastes awfully good with Tex Mex food.

Makes ½ cup
Preparation time: 15 minutes

INGREDIENTS

2 cups loosely packed coriander leaves, rinsed and dried
⅓ cup mild olive oil or vegetable oil
2 tablespoons pine nuts
½ medium-size jalapeno pepper, stemmed and seeded
1 medium-size clove garlic
1 teaspoon lime or lemon rind
Salt

Combine all of the ingredients and salt to taste in a blender or food processor and process to a paste. Taste and adjust the salt.

> **SHOPPING LIST**
>
> *coriander*
> *1 jalapeno pepper*
> *garlic*
> *1 lime or 1 lemon*
> *pine nuts*
> *olive or vegetable oil*

NEW ENGLAND BARBECUE SAUCE

The sweetness of maple and the tang of bottled chili sauce make this red barbecue sauce just the ticket for slathering on grilled chicken and ribs. It is not a marinade or a basting sauce. Instead, spread it over the food when it is nearly cooked and pass the remaining sauce at the table.

Makes about 2 cups
Preparation time: 10 minutes
Cooking time: 15 minutes

INGREDIENTS

½ medium onion, finely chopped
1 clove garlic, finely chopped
12-ounce bottle chili sauce
⅓ cup maple-flavored syrup
2 tablespoons Dijon mustard
½ teaspoon ground hot pepper
¼ apple cider vinegar

Combine the ingredients in a medium saucepan. Bring to a simmer over medium heat and cook, stirring frequently, for 15 minutes. The sauce may be stored, covered, in the refrigerator for up to a week.

SHOPPING LIST

onion
garlic
Dijon mustard
maple-flavored syrup
apple cider vinegar
ground hot pepper
12-oz. bottle chili sauce

PESTO

Pesto just makes you want to smile. Made when the basil is lush in the garden, fortified with lots of fresh garlic, virgin olive oil and just-grated Parmesan cheese, it has become an American classic. We toss it on pasta and serve it as a main course or a side course, but have you considered using it in soups? On baked potatoes? Alongside grilled chicken or fish? Absolutely delicious.

Makes a scant ⅔ cup
Preparation time: 15 minutes

INGREDIENTS

2 cups loosely packed basil leaves, rinsed
    and dried
⅓ cup olive oil
2 medium-size cloves garlic, crushed
3 tablespoons pine nuts
Salt and freshly ground pepper
3 tablespoons grated Parmesan cheese

Put the basil, oil, garlic, pine nuts and salt and pepper to taste into a blender or food processor and process to a paste. Taste and adjust the seasonings. Stir in cheese.

SHOPPING LIST

basil
garlic
pine nuts
olive oil
Parmesan cheese

FOUR PEPPER RELISH

Here is a snazzy alternative to ordinary hot dog relish. As good as it is on "dogs," try it on turkey burgers or with pork chops.

Makes about 1½ pints
Preparation time: 20 minutes
Cooking time: 15 minutes

INGREDIENTS

1 large red pepper, stemmed, seeded and finely chopped
1 large green pepper, stemmed, seeded and finely chopped
1 large yellow pepper, stemmed, seeded and finely chopped
1 small fresh hot chili pepper, stemmed, seeded and finely chopped
1½ cups finely chopped red onion
⅔ cup white wine vinegar
½ cup sugar
¼ cup chopped fresh coriander
1 teaspoon salt

1. Put the peppers and onion in a heavy enamel or stainless steel saucepan. Add sufficient water to cover and bring to the boil over high heat. Boil for 5 minutes and drain well in a colander.

2. Return the vegetables to the pan and add the remaining ingredients. Bring the mixture to a simmer over low heat and cook for 5 minutes. Serve cold or at room temperature.

SHOPPING LIST

1 large red pepper
1 large green pepper
1 large yellow pepper
1 small hot chili pepper
coriander
1 red onion
sugar
white wine vinegar

CRANBERRY MAPLE RELISH WITH DRIED APPLES

Here is a perfect relish to serve with roast turkey or pork loin. If you plan to serve it right away or in a day or two, no need to bother with sterilizing the jars. For instructions on sterilizing them, however, see the recipe for Strawberry Jam on page 277.

Makes 1 pint
Preparation time: 10 minutes
Cooking time: 30 minutes

INGREDIENTS

½ cup dried apples
½ cup apple cider vinegar
2 tablespoons butter or margarine
¼ cup finely chopped onions
2 cups fresh cranberries
½ cup water
2 tablespoons maple syrup
Salt and freshly ground pepper

1. Combine the apples with the cider vinegar in a heavy enamel or stainless steel saucepan. Bring the mixture to the boil over medium heat. Reduce the heat to low and simmer the mixture for 10 minutes, until the apples become plump.

2. Meanwhile, heat the butter in a heavy enamel or stainless steel saucepan over medium heat. When the butter starts to foam, add the onions and cook for about 5 minutes, stirring frequently, until softened.

3. Combine the apples and their cooking liquid with the onions. Add the remaining ingredients, season with salt and pepper to taste, and bring the mixture to the boil over high heat. Reduce the heat to low and cook for about 20 minutes, stirring occasionally, until the mixture is thickened.

4. Spoon the relish into sterile jars and, when cooled, store in the refrigerator.

SHOPPING LIST

8 oz. cranberries
onions
dried apples
maple syrup
apple cider vinegar
butter or margarine

ONION RAISIN RELISH

For the best results, use tiny pearl onions that are no more than a quarter inch in diameter. You may be able to find these frozen or jarred in the supermarket and already peeled. The search is worth it—this tastes divine with roast pork or ham. It is good, too, with lamb.

Makes about 3 cups
Preparation time: 10 minutes
Cooking time: 30 minutes

INGREDIENTS

1 pound pearl onions, peeled and trimmed,
    if necessary
1 cup raisins
½ cup dark brown sugar
½ cup cider vinegar
1 cup water
4 cloves
2 bay leaves
½ teaspoon ground nutmeg
1-inch piece cinnamon stick

1. Combine all the ingredients in a heavy enamel or stainless steel saucepan. Bring the mixture to the boil over low heat and simmer for about 30 minutes, until the onions are tender and the mixture has thickened.

2. Serve the relish at once or store, covered, in the refrigerator for up to 2 weeks.

Softening Brown Sugar
Once a box of brown sugar has been opened, the sugar will begin to dry out and harden. One way to store brown sugar is to empty it into a zip-locking plastic bag, then seal out as much air as possible. Put the plastic bag of sugar into a glass jar with a screw lid.

Despite your best efforts, the brown sugar may get hard after a few weeks. Use the microwave oven to soften the brown sugar so that it is usable again. Put a piece of bread or a slice of apple into the container of brown sugar, and microwave on high for 15 to 30 seconds. The moisture from the bread or apple will put moisture back into the sugar.

SHOPPING LIST

1 lb. pearl onions
raisins
1-in. piece cinnamon stick
bay leaves
cloves
ground nutmeg
dark brown sugar
cider vinegar

APPLE-PEAR SAUCE

This fruit-filled sauce is terrific on ice cream and sponge cake or layered in a parfait glass with sherbet. Reduce the sugar to ⅓ cup and serve it as a condiment with roast pork.

Serves 6 to 8
Preparation time: 10 minutes
Cooking time: 8 to 10 minutes

INGREDIENTS

3 medium-size, firm, tart apples, peeled, cored and sliced
2 to 3 ripe pears, peeled, cored and sliced
⅓ cup water
⅔ cup sugar
1 teaspoon cinnamon
½ teaspoon ground nutmeg

1. Put the sliced apples and pears together with the water in a 2-quart, microwave-safe casserole and cover with plastic wrap. Microwave on High (100 percent) for 8 to 10 minutes, stirring once halfway through, until the fruit is fork-tender.

2. Add the sugar, cinnamon and nutmeg. Mash with a fork until thoroughly blended. For a very smooth texture, process to a puree in a blender or food processor.

SHOPPING LIST

3 medium tart apples
2–3 ripe pears
cinnamon
ground nutmeg
sugar

HOT BUTTERED RUM RAISIN SAUCE

This sauce is especially tasty with the Bread Pudding on page 302 but is also good with ice cream.

Makes 1¼ cups
Preparation time: 5 minutes
Cooking time: 4 minutes

INGREDIENTS

2 tablespoons sugar
2 tablespoons packed brown sugar
1 tablespoon cornstarch
⅛ teaspoon salt
¾ cup water
⅓ cup dark rum
½ cup raisins
1 tablespoon butter or margarine

1. Combine both the sugars, the cornstarch and the salt in a 1-quart microwave-safe bowl. Stir in the water and rum. Microwave on High (100 percent) for 3 minutes or until thickened, stirring after 1½ minutes.

2. Stir in the raisins and the butter. Microwave on High (100 percent) for 1 minute. Stir again before serving.

SHOPPING LIST

raisins
sugar
packed brown sugar
cornstarch
butter or margarine
dark rum

RASPBERRY SAUCE

Try this warm sauce over chocolate ice cream or a fudge brownie. It turns the everyday into the spectacular.

Makes 1 cup
Preparation time: 5 minutes
Cooking time: 5 minutes

INGREDIENTS

10-ounce package unsweetened frozen
  raspberries, defrosted
2 tablespoons lemon juice
1 to 2 tablespoons superfine sugar
1 tablespoon cornstarch
2 tablespoons water

1. Put the raspberries, sugar to taste and lemon juice in a blender or food processor and process until smooth. Press the puree through a fine strainer to remove the seeds.

2. Pour the mixture into a 1-quart microwave-safe dish and microwave on High (100 percent) for 2 to 2½ minutes, until boiling.

3. Stir the cornstarch and water together to form a smooth paste. Add this to the raspberry mixture, stirring to blend. Microwave on High (100 percent) for 1 to 2 minutes until the sauce is bubbling and thickened. Cover with plastic wrap and let cool.

Ice Cream: What's the Difference?
When you make your weekly (or biweekly) foray to the supermarket, chances are you are impressed by the amazing array of ice creams. You may also be a little bewildered. What does it all mean? Are the so-called designer ice creams really better than the good, old familiar brands? The answer is a qualified "yes." It is definitely a matter of personal taste. For some purposes, less expensive brands of ice cream, usually sold in larger quantities than the high-priced varieties, are just fine. They taste good served with birthday cake and made into ice cream pies, for instance, when the ice cream itself is not the focus of the dish. But these ice creams are often made with poorer quality ingredients than the more expensive brands and, just as significant, contain far more air.

Ice cream is made by incorporating air into a cream and sugar mixture. The amount of air varies from brand to brand, with the more expensive brands incorporating less air—which means more product. You can feel the difference when you balance packages of identical size in your hands. More expensive ice creams are heavier and are always firmer than other brands. You will probably have to let them sit at room temperature for a few minutes before you can scoop them up. But the flavor is worth the wait!

SHOPPING LIST

1 lemon
10-oz. pkg. unsweetened frozen raspberries
superfine sugar
cornstarch

STRAWBERRY SAUCE

BUTTERSCOTCH TOPPING

This no-cook strawberry sauce will bring the taste of June into the winter kitchen every time. Keep large packages of frozen berries in the freezer for quick sauces all year long.

Makes about 1½ cups
Preparation time: 5 minutes

INGREDIENTS

20-ounce package whole frozen unsweetened strawberries, defrosted
¼ cup honey
¼ cup Amaretto, optional

1. Press the strawberries through a fine strainer to remove the seeds.

2. Put the strawberry puree in a bowl and add the honey and, if desired, the Amaretto. Stir to blend and chill until ready to serve.

SHOPPING LIST
20-oz. pkg. whole frozen unsweetened strawberries
honey
Amaretto

A butterscotch sundae is often just what the doctor ordered. With this recipe on hand you can whip one up anytime you feel in the need for the prescribed boost. Watch the sugar and cream mixture in the microwave to see that it does not boil over. Use a large measure, as called for, to eliminate the problem—although with the microwave, clean-up is not a major chore as spilled food does not "bake on" as it does in conventional ovens.

Makes 2 cups
Preparation time: 5 minutes
Cooking time: 4 minutes

INGREDIENTS

1 cup packed brown sugar
½ cup dark corn syrup
½ cup heavy cream
4 tablespoons butter or margarine
5 tablespoons coffee liqueur

1. Combine the sugar, corn syrup, cream and butter in a 4-cup glass measure. Microwave on High (100 percent) for 3 to 3½ minutes until the mixture boils, stirring after 2 minutes.

2. Stir the coffee liqueur into the sauce and allow it to cool. Cover the sauce with plastic wrap and store it in the refrigerator.

SHOPPING LIST
packed brown sugar
dark corn syrup
butter or margarine
heavy cream
coffee liqueur

DESSERTS

Dessert should be more than an occasional indulgence. A bite of something sweet and satisfying after a good meal leaves everyone feeling happy. This final course allows the family to linger at the table and creates a warm and comfortable mood that otherwise would be lost to activities such as rinsing dishes, finishing homework and watching television. Making the effort to prepare dessert also demonstrates to your loved ones that you care about the meal and its completeness—which in turn translates to caring about them.

Most of the desserts on the following pages include fruit, which is low in calories, fat-free and tastes so good that who can object to it? What is more, fruit desserts are frequently easy and fast to prepare and so make ideal candidates for weekday meals when time is not on your side. Try to buy fruit in season and use it sensibly. For instance, unless you have an irrepressible urge for Blueberry Cornmeal Shortcakes do not attempt it in February when blueberries are scarce. Instead, make some Molten Chocolate Sauce and spoon it over frozen yogurt or ice milk—both good stand-ins for richer ice cream.

With these recipes you will be able to treat your family without jeopardizing good health and good sense. They do not call for cup after cup of heavy cream, dozens of egg yolks or rich cheeses. The natural sweetness of the fruit is generally augmented by some sugar and in several recipes we do call for a cup or so of cream, but overall we have kept your family's health and diet in mind—as well as its taste buds. Each of the following desserts is sure to delight the most avid sweet tooth.

Pastry Shell
To make a perfectly shaped pastry shell, fit the rolled pastry into the pie plate, fitting it well into the corners, before trimming. Cover the pastry with a piece of oiled foil, oil side down, touching the pastry. Cover with a single layer of dried beans and fold the edges of the foil over the rim of the pie plate. Bake in a preheated 375-degree oven for 10 minutes until the pastry has "set." Discard the foil. The beans can be reused indefinitely. Prick the bottom of the pastry with a fork to prevent air bubbles from forming. Prick the sides to prevent them from sliding. Return the pastry shell to the oven and cook until crisp. (The time will vary from 8 to 15 minutes, depending on the type of pastry.)

Pastry
To prevent pastry from becoming soggy, cut slits in the top pie crust to allow steam to escape.
Do not cook pastry in the oven at the same time as a roast, or the steam in the oven will prevent the pastry from becoming crisp and flaky.

Pastry Brush
To make a pastry brush flexible, always wet it in cold water and squeeze out the water from the bristles before each use. A paint brush (unused, of course!) can be substituted for a pastry brush.

PEAR AND HAZELNUT CRISP

A crisp is a fruit dessert topped with a sweet, crumbly mixture usually made from flour, butter and sugar. Here, we add chopped hazelnuts to the topping and sprinkle it in generous handfuls over a simple pear filling. If you cannot locate hazelnuts, substitute walnuts or pecans. Both are best if toasted first in a hot oven, as instructed, but neither walnuts nor pecans needs to be skinned.

Serves 4 to 6
Preparation time: 25 minutes
Cooking time: 30 minutes

INGREDIENTS

$\frac{1}{3}$ cup hazelnuts
4 medium pears (about $3\frac{1}{2}$ pounds), peeled, cored and sliced
$\frac{1}{2}$ cup plus 3 tablespoons sugar
2 teaspoons lemon juice
$\frac{1}{2}$ cup all-purpose flour
$\frac{1}{4}$ teaspoon salt
4 tablespoons butter or margarine

1. Heat the oven to 425 degrees. Toast the hazelnuts in a baking dish for 5 to 7 minutes until they become fragrant and their skins begin to crack. Put the nuts in a towel and rub them vigorously to remove the skin (some skin won't come off, but don't worry about it). Coarsely chop the nuts.

2. Reduce the oven heat to 375 degrees. Put the pear slices in a 9-inch pie pan and toss with 3 tablespoons of sugar and the lemon juice.

3. Combine the flour, sugar, salt and hazelnuts in a bowl. Work in the butter until the mixture resembles coarse crumbs. Squeeze together small handfuls of the mixture and then crumble the handfuls over the pears, leaving the topping in fairly large pieces. Bake for about 30 minutes until the fruit is bubbling and the topping is golden brown.

> *Nuts*
> *When chopping nuts in a blender or food processor, add a tablespoon of flour to prevent them from forming clumps.*
> *To toast nuts, spread them on a flat surface and put in a preheated 350-degree oven for 8 to 10 minutes until lightly browned. Stir with a fork to distribute the heat evenly.*
> *Keep opened containers of nuts in the refrigerator so that they will stay fresh.*

SHOPPING LIST
4 medium pears (about 3 ½ lbs.)
1 lemon
hazelnuts
all-purpose flour
sugar
butter or margarine

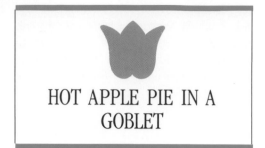

HOT APPLE PIE IN A GOBLET

2. Divide half the cookie crumbs among 4 goblets or wine glasses, sprinkling the crumbs in the bottom of the glasses. Divide the frozen yogurt between the goblets and top each with a quarter of the apples. Sprinkle the top of each with the remaining cookie crumbs and serve immediately.

SHOPPING LIST

*3 large Golden Delicious apples
cinnamon
sugar
16 shortbread cookies
1 pt. low-fat frozen vanilla yogurt*

Here is one your kids will love. Most children, we have found, appreciate individual servings and ingenious containers (consider the popularity of the ice cream cone, for example) and so we created a fruit dessert served in a goblet. Use heavy goblets, not fragile wine glasses, or custard cups for this simple apple "pie." Of course, you can always make it in a larger dish and spoon it out but it will not be as much fun. The dessert calls for store-bought cookies; we suggest Pepperidge Farm Chessman cookies, which taste good and buttery and have no preservatives or cholesterol-laden palm or coconut oil.

Serves 4
Preparation time: 10 minutes
Cooking time: 20 minutes

INGREDIENTS

3 large Golden Delicious apples, peeled, cored and coarsely chopped
$\frac{1}{4}$ cup sugar
$\frac{1}{4}$ cup water
$\frac{1}{2}$ teaspoon cinnamon
16 shortbread cookies, crumbled
1 pint low-fat frozen vanilla yogurt

1. Combine the apples, sugar, water and cinnamon in a medium-sized saucepan and bring to a simmer over medium heat. Cover and cook, stirring occasionally, for 15 minutes. Remove the lid and cook for 5 minutes more, until the apples are soft and the liquid has almost evaporated.

BLUEBERRY CORNMEAL SHORTCAKES

Even summertime's favorite dessert, berry shortcake, can be made healthier with a little forethought. Low-fat yogurt acts with the baking soda to make the lightest shortcake biscuits you ever tasted. Top with whipped cream if you must, but we recommend vanilla-flavored yogurt, which marries perfectly with plump blueberries. If your heart is set on strawberry shortcake, substitute strawberries for the blueberries. Or how about a combination of the two? Mash up a portion of the strawberries without the honey—they do not need extra sweetening, unless you feel a sprinkling of sugar would help.

Makes 8 shortcakes
Preparation time: 20 minutes
Cooking time: 20 minutes

INGREDIENTS

1 pint fresh blueberries, picked over the rinsed
2 tablespoons honey
1½ cups all-purpose flour
½ cup yellow cornmeal
2 tablespoons sugar
2 teaspoons baking soda
1 teaspoon cream of tartar
½ teaspoon salt
6 tablespoons cold butter or margarine, cut into ¼-inch pieces
¾ cup plain low-fat yogurt
Milk, for glaze
1 pint vanilla-flavored yogurt

1. In a medium bowl, combine the blueberries and the honey. Using the back of a fork, crush about one-quarter of the blueberries. Cover and refrigerate until ready to use.

2. Heat the oven to 425 degrees.

3. In a medium bowl, sift together the flour, cornmeal, sugar, baking soda, cream of tartar and salt. Using a pastry blender or two knives, cut in the butter until the mixture resembles coarse crumbs. Add the plain yogurt and stir until a soft dough forms. Lightly knead in the bowl for a brief time until the dough coheres.

4. On a lightly floured surface, pat the dough with floured hands into a ½-inch-thick disk. Using a floured 3-inch round cookie cutter or a glass, cut out rounds of the dough. Gather up the scraps, pat out again and make more rounds. Repeat the procedure to make a total of 8 rounds. Place the shortbreads on an ungreased baking sheet and brush the top of each cake with milk. Bake for 18 to 20 minutes until the cakes are golden brown.

5. Serve the shortcakes topped with the blueberries and a dollop of vanilla yogurt.

SHOPPING LIST

1 pt. blueberries
honey
all-purpose flour
yellow cornmeal
sugar
baking soda
cream of tartar
butter or margarine
plain low-fat yogurt
milk
1 pt. vanilla yogurt

GINGERY STUFFED NECTARINES

What could be easier than slicing up a few ripe, luscious nectarines for dessert? Once cut, we fill the halved fruit with a quick mixture of gingersnap crumbs moistened with a little butter or margarine. After a brief stint in the oven, the nectarines are served with a no-cook strawberry sauce and presto! Dessert is ready. The gingersnaps are easy to find in the market, but for the best nutrition read the label and buy a brand that does not use tropical oils such as palm or coconut, both of which have cholesterol.

Serves 4
Preparation time: 10 minutes
Cooking time: 25 minutes

INGREDIENTS

4 large ripe nectarines, halved lengthwise,
   pits removed
1 cup gingersnap crumbs
¼ cup sugar
2 tablespoons unsalted butter or margarine,
   softened
2 egg whites
Strawberry sauce:
1 pint strawberries, hulled
2 tablespoons sugar, or to taste
2 teaspoons lemon juice
Whole fresh strawberries for garnish

1. Heat the oven to 350 degrees. Lightly butter on 8-inch-square baking dish.

2. Halve the nectarines lengthwise, discarding the pits, and place cut side up in the baking dish.

3. In a small bowl, mix the gingersnap crumbs, sugar, butter and egg whites until combined. Divide the mixture among the nectarines, piling it in the cavities. Bake for about 25 minutes.

4. While the nectarines are baking, prepare the strawberry sauce. Combine the strawberries, sugar and lemon juice in a blender or food processor fitted with the metal chopping blade. Process until smooth. Taste for sugar, adding more if necessary.

5. Serve the nectarines warm or at room temperature with the strawberry sauce.

Strawberries
Rinse strawberries under cold running water and pat them dry gently on paper towels. Do not immerse them in water or they become waterlogged and lose their flavor entirely.

SHOPPING LIST

4 large nectarines
1 pt. strawberries
1 lemon
gingersnaps
sugar
eggs

LACE CREPES

Crepes may seem like an outdated idea, but why put a good recipe out to pasture? They are as versatile and delicious in the 1990s as they ever were. And crepes are so easy to make. What is more, once made, they freeze beautifully stacked with wax paper between each one. Let them defrost on the counter and reheat them in a warm oven or quickly in the crepe pan. Squeeze fresh lemon juice and sprinkle a little sugar over the freshly made crepes, or spread them with Strawberry Jam (page 274).

Makes about 12 crepes
Preparation time: 15 minutes plus chilling
Cooking time: 15 minutes

INGREDIENTS

1 cup all-purpose flour
Pinch of salt
2 tablespoons sugar
2 eggs
1 cup whole milk

1. Combine the flour, salt and sugar in a large bowl. Whisk together the eggs and milk in another bowl.

2. Make a well in the center of the dry ingredients. Pour in the liquid ingredients and whisk briefly to blend. Strain the batter through a sieve and chill for at least 30 minutes.

3. When ready to cook, stir the batter to recombine. Add more milk if necessary to thin it to the consistency of heavy cream. Heat a 7- to 8-inch crepe pan over medium heat and brush lightly with oil. When a drop of water spatters in the pan, pour in about 3 tablespoons of batter. Tilt the pan to coat the bottom with a thin layer of batter and pour off the excess. Cook the crepe for about 30 seconds on each side, until lightly browned. Slide the crepe onto a warm plate and repeat the process until all the batter is used, stacking the crepes as they are cooked.

4. Fold the crepes into quarters and serve warm.

SHOPPING LIST

all-purpose flour
sugar
eggs
milk

SUMMERTIME COBBLER WITH ORANGE BISCUIT CRUST

A bubbling, hot cobbler, bursting with summer's best fruit and berries, is a welcome sight on the table. This one requires a quick toss of fruit right in the baking dish. The crust, made from a simple dough blended together in minutes, is casually draped over the filling to let a little colorful fruit peek around the edges. An easy way to peel peaches is to poach them first for 10 minutes in boiling water and then cool them under cold running water. The skins slip right off.

Serves 4 to 6
Preparation time: 30 minutes
Cooking time: 30 minutes

INGREDIENTS

2 cups sliced, skinned peaches
2 cups sliced nectarines
1½ cups fresh raspberries
1½ cups blueberries
1 cup plus 4 teaspoons all-purpose flour
⅓ cup plus 4 teaspoons sugar
1 tablespoon lemon juice
¼ teaspoon salt
1 teaspoon baking powder
½ teaspoon grated orange rind
4 tablespoons butter or margarine
¼ cup whole milk

1. Heat the oven to 375 degrees.

2. In a 2-quart baking dish, toss the fruit with 4 teaspoons of flour, ⅓ cup of sugar and the lemon juice. Spread the fruit over the bottom of the dish.

3. Combine the remaining cup of flour with the remaining tablespoon of sugar and the salt, baking powder and orange rind in a bowl. Using a pastry blender or two knives, cut in the butter until the mixture resembles coarse crumbs. Add the milk and toss with a fork until the dough holds together.

4. On a floured work surface, pat the dough into a ½-inch-thick round, oval, square or rectangle (depending on the shape of your baking dish). The dough does not need to completely cover the fruit.

5. Position the dough over the fruit and sprinkle with the remaining teaspoon of sugar. Bake for about 30 minutes until the fruit is bubbling and the crust is golden brown.

SHOPPING LIST

3 peaches
3 nectarines
raspberries
blueberries
1 orange
1 lemon
all-purpose flour
sugar
baking powder
butter or margarine
milk

BAKED PEARS

This dessert is about as simple and straight-forward as they get—and absolutely delicious. Use firm, ripe pears that slice easily—overripe fruit will be too soft. You may slice the pears and layer them in the dish an hour or so in advance. Sprinkle fresh lemon juice over them to keep them from turning brown. The lemon will add a dash of good flavor, too.

Serves 4
Preparation time: 15 minutes
Cooking time: 15 minutes

INGREDIENTS

1½ cups light brown sugar
1 cup water
1 whole clove
½ teaspoon cinnamon
½ cup orange or lemon marmalade
4 large, firm, ripe Bosc or Anjou pears
1 teaspoon unsalted butter or margarine

1. Combine the sugar, water and spices in a saucepan over medium heat. Bring to the boil and cook until the sugar dissolves. Turn the heat to low and stir in the marmalade. Cover and simmer for 10 minutes.

2. Meanwhile, peel the pears, halve them lengthwise and core. Slice crosswise into ¼-inch slices.

3. Heat the oven to 400 degrees.

4. Butter a baking dish large enough to hold the slices in a single layer, overlapping slightly. Pour the syrup over the pears and bake for 15 minutes.

SHOPPING LIST

4 large Bosc or Anjou pears
whole clove
cinnamon
light brown sugar
orange or lemon marmalade

ORANGE AND RICOTTA PUDDING

Here is a quick dessert that requires no cooking, just some time in the refrigerator. The sweetness of the orange juice and strawberries play on the mellow flavor of the ricotta. The cream smooths out the dessert so that it deliciously slides over the tongue.

Serves 4 to 6
Preparation time: 20 minutes

INGREDIENTS

1 pint strawberries
⅓ cup orange juice or kirsch
2 pounds fresh ricotta cheese
¼ cup sugar
¼ cup heavy cream
½ cup chopped semisweet chocolate

1. Halve the strawberries and put them in a small bowl with the orange juice or kirsch. Let them soak for 10 minutes.

2. Press the ricotta through a sieve or beat with a whisk until fluffy.

3. Stir the sugar and cream into the ricotta. Fold in the strawberries and their juices. Fold in the chocolate. Spoon the mixture into individual serving dishes and refrigerate for 10 minutes before serving.

```
SHOPPING LIST
1 pt. strawberries
sugar
semisweet chocolate
orange juice (or kirsch)
heavy cream
```

GRAPES AND YOGURT

This is an update of one of the simplest and best of all desserts—grapes in sour cream and brown sugar. The yogurt variation is less guilt-provoking and equally satisfying.

Serves 4
Preparation time: 5 minutes

INGREDIENTS

1 cup plain low-fat yogurt
¼ cup light brown sugar
1½ pounds seedless red or green grapes

1. Combine the yogurt with the sugar in a large bowl.

2. Remove the stems from the grapes. Mound the grapes in a serving dish and spoon the yogurt over the top. Serve at once or chill to serve later.

```
SHOPPING LIST
1 ½ lbs. seedless red or green grapes
sugar
plain low-fat yogurt
```

GRILLED PINEAPPLE

Fresh pineapple is available in the markets most of the year and grilled with a slightly sweetened topping, makes a smashing dessert. Pineapples are surprisingly low in calories, even though they are as sweet as can be. If you use yogurt rather than sour cream, the topping may curdle a little in the broiler— but will still taste good.

Serves 4 to 6
Preparation time: 15 minutes
Cooking time: 5 minutes

INGREDIENTS

1 fresh pineapple
½ cup plain low-fat yogurt or sour cream
Cinnamon

1. Twist the top of the pineapple. Cut the pineapple crosswise into ½-inch-thick slices. Trim the rind from each slice with a large biscuit cutter or a sharp knife. Cut out and remove the core.

2. Heat the broiler.

3. Coat each slice with yogurt or sour cream and sprinkle with cinnamon. Put the slices in a broiler pan and broil on one side only for about 5 minutes, until bubbly and lightly browned.

Fresh Pineapples
Like bananas, pineapples seem to be in the supermarkets nearly all the time. This leads many people to think of them as a "winter fruit"—a fruit from the tropics that we eat fresh during those times of year when we cannot get local produce. It is true; pineapples are easier to find in January than peaches and strawberries are. While they may taste mighty good during the cold of winter, they are at their best in the summer when they have been exposed to longer periods of sun in tropical paradises such as Hawaii and Puerto Rico.

You cannot tell if a pineapple is ripe by wiggling its leaves or by the color of its skin. The only way to determine its ripeness is to taste it, which is why it is important to patronize a reliable market or greengrocer. Some merchants sell pineapples labeled "jet fresh," which means they are flown from the pineapple plantation to the store and so are usually only a few days old when you buy them. These cost more than other pineapples but are, for the most part, better tasting. Pineapples do not ripen after they are harvested and if they are improperly packed or stored—which can happen if they are ocean shipped and trucked overland— they lose moisture and flavor. They may even be spongy or woody and look black around the edges when cut. Once you get fresh pineapple home, it is best to cut it as soon as you can and store the juicy, succulent flesh in a glass jar or bowl in the refrigerator. Uncut pineapples should not be stored for very long or at temperatures lower than 50 degrees.

SHOPPING LIST

1 fresh pineapple
cinnamon
plain low-fat yogurt or sour cream

COTTAGE CHEESE FRITTERS WITH APPLESAUCE

T hese low-fat fritters are simple to fry up and make a pleasing hot dessert on a chilly fall evening. Most likely you have all the ingredients for them in the kitchen right now.

Serves 4
Preparation time: 10 minutes
Cooking time: 10 minutes

INGREDIENTS

1 cup low-fat cottage cheese
5 tablespoons flour
1 teaspoon cinnamon
2 egg yolks
1 egg white
Vegetable oil
Unsweetened applesauce
Plain low-fat yogurt or sour cream

1. Heat the oven to 200 degrees.

2. Combine the cottage cheese, flour, cinnamon and egg yolks in a bowl. In another bowl, beat the egg white with a whisk until stiff, shiny peaks form. Gently fold the egg white into the cheese mixture.

3. Pour the vegetable oil into a skillet to a depth of ¼ inch. Heat over medium-high heat. Drop rounded tablespoons of the cheese mixture into the hot oil and cook for 1 to 2 minutes on each side until golden brown. Drain the fritters on paper towels and keep warm in the oven while you cook the rest.

4. Serve immediately with spoonfuls of applesauce and yogurt or sour cream.

MOLTEN HOT FUDGE SAUCE

This incredible hot fudge sauce will bring you back to the days of drugstore soda fountains. Molten when it is poured over ice cream, it turns fudgy on contact. Try it, too, over pound cake, fruit sherbert or fresh berries. To insure the sauce reaches the proper consistency you will have to use a candy thermometer but do not be put off by the prospect. Thermometers are easy to acquire and simple to use. Be sure the saucepan is big enough to hold the sauce without boiling over or spattering.

Makes about 1½ cups
Preparation time: 10 minutes
Cooking time: 5 minutes

INGREDIENTS

1 tablespoon cocoa powder
1 cup sugar
¾ cup evaporated milk
¼ cup light corn syrup
3 tablespoons margarine or butter
2 ounces unsweetened chocolate, finely
  chopped
Pinch salt
Few drops lemon juice
1 teaspoon vanilla extract

1. In a medium-sized heavy-bottomed saucepan, whisk the cocoa powder, sugar and about one-quarter of the evaporated milk until smooth.

2. Add the corn syrup, margarine, unsweetened chocolate, salt, lemon juice and the remaining evaporated milk. Insert a candy thermometer in the mixture and bring to the boil over medium heat without stirring.

3. Cook at medium heat for 3 minutes until the candy thermometer reaches 236 degrees. Remove the sauce from the heat and stir in the vanilla. The sauce will thicken as it cools.

SHOPPING LIST

1 lemon
cocoa powder
2 oz. unsweetened chocolate
evaporated milk
light corn syrup
vanilla extract
butter or margarine

APPLE BROWN BETTY

In some ways, Apple Brown Betty is more American than apple pie. After all, unlike the pie, betties are a purely American invention and are defined by layering fruit with a crumbly mixture. This one, in the interest of ease and speed, has only one layer of fruit, which is sandwiched by a simple blending of flour, sugar, butter and spices. Could anything be better?

Serves 6
Preparation time: 15 minutes
Cooking time: 35 minutes

INGREDIENTS

1 cup all-purpose flour
½ teaspoon cinnamon
¼ teaspoon salt
¼ teaspoon ground nutmeg
¾ cup sugar
6 tablespoons butter or margarine
4 slices firm-textured bread, crusts removed
1 cup raisins, soaked until plump
3 small apples, peeled and sliced

1. Heat the oven to 350 degrees. Butter an 8-inch-square baking dish.

2. Sift together the dry ingredients. Cut the butter into small pieces and work into the flour mixture, using a fork or pastry blender until the mixture resembles coarse crumbs.

3. Cut the bread into cubes and combine with the raisins and apples.

4. Sprinkle a third of the flour mixture in the baking dish. Add the apple mixture and top with the remaining flour.

5. Bake in the preheated oven for 35 minutes, until crisp. Serve hot or cold.

SHOPPING LIST

firm-textured bread
3 small apples
raisins
cinnamon
ground nutmeg
all-purpose flour
sugar
butter or margarine

APPLE FUDGE BROWNIES

These easy, healthful (for brownies, anyhow!) chocolate treats are custom made for snacking and weekday supper desserts. Try one with a scoop of vanilla ice milk or frozen yogurt.

Makes one 8-inch round
Preparation time: 5 minutes
Cooking time: 12 to 15 minutes

INGREDIENTS

8 tablespoons butter or margarine
2 ounces unsweetened chocolate
1 cup brown sugar
$\frac{1}{2}$ cup unsweetened applesauce
2 eggs, lightly beaten
1 teaspoon vanilla extract
1 cup all-purpose flour
$\frac{1}{2}$ teaspoon baking powder
$\frac{1}{4}$ teaspoon baking soda
$\frac{1}{2}$ teaspoon cinnamon
1 small apple, grated
$\frac{1}{4}$ cup chopped pecans
Confectioners' sugar, optional

1. Put the butter and chocolate in a large glass bowl. Microwave on High (100 percent) for 2 to 3 minutes or until melted. Cool slightly. Stir in the brown sugar, applesauce, eggs and vanilla and beat until smooth.

2. Combine the flour, baking powder, baking soda and cinnamon in a small bowl. Gradually stir the flour mixture into the chocolate mixture until smooth. Stir in the apple and pecans.

3. Pour the mixture into a buttered, 8-inch round glass baking dish. Place an inverted glass pie plate in the oven and set the baking dish on the top. Microwave on Medium (50 percent), rotating the dish twice, for 10 to 12 minutes or until the edges just pull away from the dish. Let stand for 5 minutes.

4. Cool the brownies on a wire rack. Sprinkle with confectioners' sugar, if desired, and cut into wedges before serving.

SHOPPING LIST

1 small apple
chopped pecans
unsweetened chocolate
brown sugar
vanilla extract
all-purpose flour
baking powder
baking soda
cinnamon
confectioners' sugar
unsweetened applesauce
butter or margarine

CHERRY ALMOND FUDGE BROWNIES

These moist, amazingly fudgy brownies seem custom made for anyone who loves chocolate and cherries. They combine the indulgence of chocolate covered cherries with the chewy satisfaction of brownies. Be sure to chop the chocolate fine—use a food processor if you want—before stirring it with the melted butter. Another hint: melt the butter in the microwave for easy cleanup.

Makes 9 brownies
Preparation time: 20 minutes
Cooking time: 35 to 40 minutes

INGREDIENTS

8 tablespoons unsalted butter or margarine, cut into pieces
6 ounces semisweet chocolate, finely chopped
1 cup plus 1 tablespoon all-purpose flour
¼ teaspoon baking soda
¼ teaspoon salt
¾ cup sugar
2 large eggs, at room temperature
1 teaspoon vanilla extract
½ teaspoon almond extract
½ cup pitted fresh or frozen and defrosted sweet cherries
½ cup chopped blanched almonds

1. Position a rack in the center of the oven. Heat the oven to 350 degrees. Lightly butter and flour a 9-inch-square cake pan.

2. Heat the butter in a small saucepan over low heat. Remove the pan from the heat and stir in the chocolate. Let stand for 1 minute and then whisk until smooth. Cool for about 10 minutes until tepid.

3. Sift the cup of flour, the baking soda and salt together through a wire strainer into a large bowl.

4. Whisk the sugar into the chocolate mixture. Whisk in the eggs, one at a time. Beat in the vanilla and almond extracts. Using a wooden spoon, stir in the flour, mixing just until blended.

5. Toss the cherries with the remaining tablespoon of flour and add to the batter along with the almonds. Fold gently until just combined. Turn the mixture into the prepared pan. Bake for 35 to 40 minutes until a toothpick inserted into the center comes out with a moist crumb. Allow the brownies to cool on a wire rack before cutting into squares.

Semisweet and Bittersweet Chocolate
If a recipe calls for semisweet chocolate and you can find only bittersweet, should you panic? Absolutely not. There is little difference between the two, although there do exist differences between brands of both. This may sound contradictory. We admit it is confusing. American manufacturers tend to label dark chocolate (i.e., sweetened chocolate that is not milk chocolate) as semisweet, while Europeans call it bittersweet. Among the various companies exist differences in the proportions of unsweetened chocolate to sugar, so that one manufacturer's bittersweet may taste sweeter than another's semisweet, and vice versa. Use the chocolate you like the best. What you should watch for is that you do not mistakenly purchase unsweetened chocolate or milk chocolate for a recipe that uses semisweet.

POACHED PEACHES WITH ALMOND

Poaching, a gentle form of cooking, enhances the natural sweetness of fruit, which is also heightened by the mildly flavored poaching liquid. Serve these peaches sliced over frozen yogurt and pound cake, or simply by themselves.

Serves 6
Preparation time: 5 minutes
Cooking time: 15 minutes

INGREDIENTS

4 cups water
1 cup sugar
1 tablespoon almond extract
6 ripe peaches

1. Combine the water, sugar and almond extract in a saucepan. Cook on high heat until the sugar has dissolved. Reduce the heat to a gentle simmer and add the peaches. Poach them, uncovered, for 15 minutes.

2. Remove the fruit to a rack. Peel the peaches when they are cool enough to handle.

SHOPPING LIST

6 ripe peaches
sugar
almond extract

BREAD PUDDING

Spoon a generous amount of Hot Buttered Rum Raisin Sauce (page 279) over the pudding for the ultimate in comfort food.

Serves 4
Preparation time: 10 minutes
Cooking time: 5 to 6 minutes plus 5 minutes' standing time

INGREDIENTS

2 tablespoons butter or margarine
2 eggs
1 cup milk
$\frac{1}{3}$ cup sugar
$\frac{1}{4}$ cup raisins
1 teaspoon vanilla extract
$\frac{1}{8}$ teaspoon salt
$1\frac{1}{2}$ cups cubed day-old bread

1. Melt the butter in a 1-quart microwave-safe casserole. Add the eggs and beat well. Stir in the milk, sugar, raisins, vanilla and salt. Add the bread cubes, toss to cover completely, and let the mixture stand for 5 minutes. Stir gently from time to time to ensure that the bread cubes absorb the liquid.

2. Microwave on High (100 percent), uncovered, for 5 to 6 minutes or until set. Stir the pudding after 3 minutes of the cooking time.

SHOPPING LIST
1 loaf bread
raisins
sugar
vanilla extract
eggs
butter or margarine
milk

DRINKS

Family meals are usually accompanied by glasses of cold milk and ice water. Every now and then, a glass of chilled white wine or a mug of frothy beer may find its way to the table, just as may pitchers of iced tea and pots of hot coffee. But there are times when you and your family want to quench a thirst or satisfy a sweet craving with another sort of drink. In this chapter we offer a selection of hot drinks, fruit coolers and sweet shakes and sodas designed to hit the spot every time.

Most of these drinks can be put together in minutes and so provide immediate and delicious gratification. Our quantities are fairly small, since drinks are meant to be made right before consuming. If you want to make a big pitcher of Lemonade Express or Citrus Cooler multiply the ingredients to suit your needs. If, on the other hand, you want only one or two

cups of Hot Chocolate—a perfect antidote for frayed nerves—decrease the amounts.

Consider the glass, cup or mug you select for the drink. While the libation will taste good drunk out of anything, it will taste even better if served in an appropriate container. Tall, clear-glass glasses are best for lemonade; chunky, sturdy mugs are perfect for the Hot Coconut Dream and Hot Chocolate; tall, ribbed soda glasses are great for milkshakes and ice cream sodas and classic Coke glasses are best for Egg Creams.

Enjoying a hot or cool drink together is a nice way to end a day, begin the morning or just take a break from the daily grind. Flip through the following pages and then call your family into the kitchen to sit around the table, sip a glass of something good and talk about the day's events.

Cocktail Party

If you are serving guests at a large cocktail party, prepare several small trays rather than one huge one.

If you are preparing dozens of canapés, the fastest way of handling the situation is to establish a conveyer belt system. Do all the buttering, then all

the whatever comes next. If you are working in a closet or a kitchen with the dimensions of a closet, spread out to the bedroom, living room or erect a series of surfaces to work on.

Allow a minimum of four canapés for each person.

The saltier the hors d'oeuvres, the thirstier will be the guests.

HOT SPICED CIDER

HOT CHOCOLATE

You will love the way the kitchen smells when you make this hot cider drink. And the family will love the way it tastes and how it warms everyone up right to the tips of their toes.

Welcome your children home from an afternoon of sledding or ice skating with a pot of rich, creamy hot chocolate. They may be used to powdered cocoa mixes but once they taste the "real thing" made with melted bittersweet chocolate, they will not want to go back to the convenience food. If you have a microwave, use it to melt the chocolate.

Serves 4
Preparation time: 15 minutes

INGREDIENTS

4 cups apple cider
1 cinnamon stick
1 lemon slice
1 orange slice
6 whole cloves
4 slices fresh ginger
4 cinnamon sticks, for decoration

1. Combine all the ingredients except the 4 cinnamon sticks in a saucepan over high heat. Bring to the boil, cover and remove from the heat. Allow the mixture to sit for 10 minutes.

2. Strain the cider and serve in mugs with a cinnamon stick in each one for stirring.

Serves 4
Preparation time: 10 minutes

INGREDIENTS

2 ounces bittersweet chocolate
2 tablespoons sugar
$\frac{1}{8}$ teaspoon salt
$\frac{1}{2}$ teaspoon vanilla extract
4 cups scalded whole or low-fat milk, kept warm

1. Put the chocolate in the top of a double boiler set over hot, not simmering, water. When the chocolate has melted, add the sugar, salt and vanilla and stir until the sugar dissolves.

2. Add the milk and beat vigorously with a whisk or electric beater for about 3 minutes, until frothy. Serve immediately.

SHOPPING LIST

1 orange
1 lemon
5 cinnamon sticks
whole cloves
fresh ginger
apple cider

SHOPPING LIST

bittersweet chocolate
sugar
vanilla extract
whole or low-fat milk

PARTY PUNCH

INGREDIENTS

$1\frac{1}{2}$ quarts cranberry-apple juice
2 quarts grapefruit juice, chilled
$\frac{1}{2}$ cup superfine sugar
1 quart ginger ale, chilled
1 quart lemon-lime soda, chilled
1 teaspoon almond extract

This recipe makes enough for 12, which is certainly ample for a small party; you may want to make it for a festive family occasion and not wait for an official party. How about mixing up a batch to drink on the last day of school before summer vacation? Or for a birthday supper? Make some for a family bash celebrating a job promotion or raise. The frozen cubes of cranberry-apple juice are not necessary but provide bright color and subtle flavor—as well as fun—to the drink.

Serves 12
Preparation time: 10 minutes plus freezing

1. Pour the cranberry-apple juice into ice cube trays and freeze until solid.

2. Combine the grapefruit juice with the sugar and stir until the sugar dissolves. Pour into a gallon-sized punch bowl and gently stir in the ginger ale, lemon-lime soda and almond extract. Serve over frozen cranberry-apple juice cubes.

SHOPPING LIST

1 ½ qts. cranberry-apple juice
2 qts. grapefruit juice
1 qt. ginger ale
1 qt. lemon-lime soda
almond extract
superfine sugar

HOT COCONUT DREAM

The coconut cream flavors and sweetens this soothing hot milk drink, while the addition of liqueur turns it into a libation certainly not for kids. If your children like the flavor of coconut, omit the liqueur. This is a wonderful treat on a snowy night when the fire is blazing, the kids are sleeping and the winds are howling.

Serves 4
Preparation time: 5 minutes

INGREDIENTS

2 cups whole or low-fat milk
¼ teaspoon vanilla extract
½ cup coconut cream
¼ cup white Creme de Cacao liqueur, optional

1. Heat the milk with the vanilla over medium heat until small bubbles form around the edge.

2. Whisk in the coconut cream, a little at a time. Stir in the liqueur, if using, and serve immediately.

SHOPPING LIST

vanilla extract
coconut cream
whole or low-fat milk
white Creme de Cacao liqueur

LEMONADE EXPRESS

Classic lemonade—nothing quenches thirst on a hot day like it.

Serves 4
Preparation time: 5 minutes

INGREDIENTS

6 lemons
1 cup sugar
4 cups water
4 fresh mint sprigs, for garnish, optional

1. Squeeze the juice from the lemons. Pour into a pitcher and add the sugar and water, stirring until the sugar dissolves.

2. Serve the lemonade in tall glasses over ice, garnished with a sprig of mint, if desired.

SHOPPING LIST

6 lemons
fresh mint
sugar

BANANA ENERGIZER

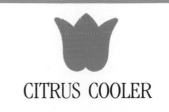

CITRUS COOLER

Do your kids like banana and peanut butter sandwiches? If they do, they will love this banana and peanut butter shake. It is so easy, they can make it themselves as an after-school snack, a morning boost or a sweet drink to sip while they do their homework.

Serves 2
Preparation time: 5 minutes

INGREDIENTS

2 medium-size bananas
2 cups low-fat or skim milk
2 tablespoons creamy peanut butter

Cut the bananas into 1-inch pieces and put them in a blender. Add the milk and peanut butter and blend until smooth. Serve at once.

SHOPPING LIST

3 medium bananas
creamy peanut butter
low-fat or skim milk

This cooler is simply lemonade with a difference. The orange juice lets you reduce the amount of sugar needed for the refreshing drink while adding its own special flavor.

Serves 4
Preparation time: 5 minutes

INGREDIENTS

3 oranges
2 lemons
$\frac{1}{3}$ cup sugar
4 cups water
4 lemon slices or 4 fresh strawberries, optional

1. Squeeze the juice from the oranges and lemons. You should have about 1 cup of juice. Pour into a pitcher. Add the sugar and water and stir until the sugar dissolves.

2. Serve the cooler in tall glasses over ice, garnished with a lemon slice or strawberry, if desired.

SHOPPING LIST

3 oranges
3 lemons
(strawberries optional)
sugar

TROPICAL QUENCHER

COFFEE MILKSHAKE

This tastes like sweet, thick orange juice and goes down ever so smoothly.

Serves 2 to 3
Preparation time: 2 minutes

INGREDIENTS

1 banana
2½ cups orange juice

Cut the banana into 1-inch pieces and put in a blender. Add the orange juice and blend until smooth. Serve at once.

> **SHOPPING LIST**
>
> *1 banana*
> *orange juice*

A coffee shake is a true indulgence, and everyone deserves a splurge once in a while. Substitute chocolate ice cream for a chocolate shake.

Serves 2
Preparation time: 2 minutes

INGREDIENTS

1 cup coffee ice cream
¾ cup cold whole or low-fat milk

1. Put the ice cream and the milk in a blender. Blend for about 1 minute or until very smooth.

2. Serve the shake immediately in chilled glasses.

> **SHOPPING LIST**
>
> *coffee ice cream*
> *whole or low-fat milk*

EGG CREAM

BLACK AND WHITE SODA

No eggs, no cream—just a cool, refreshing drink that will bring back memories of New York City's corner candy stores where egg creams were made famous. But even if you have never been to New York, you will enjoy this easy chocolate drink.

Not too chocolaty and not too plain, black and white sodas were hits with the teens who used to hang out at the Sweete Shoppe— wherever and whenever that was. We predict they will be big hits in your kitchen, as well.

Serves 1
Preparation time: 3 minutes

Serves 1
Preparation time: 5 minutes

INGREDIENTS

1 cup cold low-fat milk
4 tablespoons chocolate syrup
1 cup cold seltzer

INGREDIENTS

4 tablespoons chocolate syrup
1 cup vanilla ice cream
5 to 6 ounces cold seltzer
Whipped cream, optional

1. Pour the milk into a large glass and add the syrup. Add the seltzer, pouring it straight into the glass so that it foams.

1. Pour the chocolate syrup into a tall glass. Add 1 scoop of the vanilla ice cream.

2. Stir the drink with a long-handled spoon. Serve immediately.

2. Fill the glass nearly to the top with seltzer. Top with the remaining scoop of ice cream and a dollop of whipped cream, if desired.

3. Serve the soda with a long-handled spoon and a straw.

```
SHOPPING LIST

chocolate syrup
seltzer
low-fat milk
```

```
SHOPPING LIST

chocolate syrup
seltzer
vanilla ice cream
heavy cream
```

STRAWBERRY SHAKE

1. Put the ice milk or frozen yogurt in a blender. Add the milk and process for 10 to 15 seconds or until smooth.

2. Serve immediately in chilled glasses, garnished with strawberries, if desired.

We made this soda fountain favorite with strawberry yogurt and skim milk to come up with a smooth, rich drink that is easy on the diet.

Serves 2
Preparation time: 5 minutes

INGREDIENTS

1 cup strawberry ice milk or strawberry low-fat frozen yogurt
1 cup skim milk
4 fresh strawberries, optional

SHOPPING LIST

strawberries
strawberry ice milk or strawberry low-fat frozen yogurt
skim milk

Left to right: Strawberry Shake, above; Lemonade Express, page 306; Banana Energizer, page 307.

SNACKS

It is unrealistic—and no fun at all—to dispense with snacks. Everyone feels the need for a little pick-me-up at different points on certain days. Children, with their unpredictable growth spurts and periods of intense activity, need snacks more often than adults. Some experts say that snacking is essential for growing boys and girls, who tend to eat less at meals than adults, and, as they enter adolescence, need more nutrients than their parents. But there is no reason that the term "snack" be synonymous with potato chips and packaged cupcakes.

We understand that an ordinary banana or carrot stick may not hit the spot when you or your children are yearning for a snack. However, there will be times when these healthful, low-fat foods are just right and we suggest keeping fresh, peeled and cut vegetables in the refrigerator and a bowl of fresh fruit on the kitchen counter in plain sight of everyone who wanders into the kitchen in search of "something to eat." Sometimes a handful of raisins does the trick, or how about unbuttered popcorn (which is so easy nowadays with the microwave brands). Other snack foods to consider stocking up on are frozen fruit popsicles, low-fat, low-salt crackers such as Stoned Wheat Thins and Wasa Crispbread, low-salt pretzels (far better than potato chips as they contain only traces of fat), dried fruit such as apples, raisins, currents and apricots (banana chips are too greasy to fit nicely into this category) and low-fat cheeses.

For the occasions when a more elaborate snack is called for, we have a number of good suggestions, too. The recipes that follow are easy and quick to make so that in a very short time you and any hungry youngsters milling about will have something tasty and—for the most part—nutritious to munch on.

GRANOLA

Crunchy granola is good sprinkled on hot cereal or sliced fruit, or simply eaten out of hand. In so many ways, it is the ultimate healthy snack. Kids love it—and parents have been known to dip into the granola jar, too! Since it is cooked very quickly in the microwave, our version is easy to mix up and have around the kitchen all the time. Pack a sack of granola in the morning lunch boxes.

Makes about 3 cups
Preparation time: 5 minutes
Cooking time: 5 to 6 minutes

INGREDIENTS

2 cups quick-cooking oatmeal
½ cup chopped walnuts or pecans
⅓ cup wheat germ
⅓ cup flaked coconut
¼ cup brown sugar
¼ cup vegetable oil
¼ cup honey
1 teaspoon vanilla extract
½ cup raisins or chopped dried apricots

1. Combine the oatmeal, nuts, wheat germ and coconut in a large, microwave-safe baking dish.

2. Stir together the sugar, vegetable oil, honey and vanilla in a small bowl. Combine the raisins with the oatmeal-coconut mixture in the baking dish, pour the liquid mixture over the top and toss thoroughly. Microwave on High (100 percent) for 5 to 6 minutes, stirring twice.

3. Cool completely, stirring occasionally to break up any lumps. Store in an airtight container.

SHOPPING LIST

raisins or dried apricots
chopped walnuts or pecans
quick-cooking oatmeal
wheat germ
flaked coconut
brown sugar
vanilla extract
vegetable oil
honey

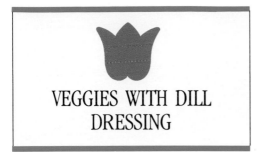

VEGGIES WITH DILL
DRESSING

While you can serve the dressing as a dip with the raw vegetables, try it as a mixed "snacking" salad.

Serves 2
Preparation time: 15 minutes

INGREDIENTS

1 medium-size carrot, peeled and cut
    diagonally into ¼-inch slices
2 small heads broccoli, cut into florets
½ medium-size zucchini, cut into ¼-inch
    slices
¼ medium-size yellow squash, cut into
    ¼-inch slices
¼ medium-size green pepper, cut into strips
Garlic powder
Pepper
½ cup plain low-fat yogurt
¼ teaspoon fresh dill
¼ teaspoon freshly chopped chives

1. Toss the vegetables together in a large bowl. Season with garlic powder and pepper to taste.

2. Combine the yogurt, dill and chives in a bowl. Spoon the dressing over the vegetables and serve or serve the dressing as a dip in a separate bowl.

SHOPPING LIST

carrots
2 small heads broccoli
1 medium zucchini
1 medium yellow squash
1 medium green pepper
fresh dill
chives
garlic powder
plain low-fat yogurt

CRUNCHY SPINACH DIP

The water chestnuts and the cucumber make this dip slightly crunchy, which is a pleasing change from other dips. It is great with crudites or with good, plain crackers.

Makes about 3 cups
Preparation time: 10 minutes plus 4 hours' refrigerating time

INGREDIENTS

8-ounce package cream cheese or
  Neufchatel cheese, softened
¾ cup plain low-fat yogurt
8-ounce can water chestnuts, coarsley
  chopped
¼ cup chopped cucumber
1 tablespoon chopped chives or scallion
  greens
1 tablespoon lemon juice
1 small clove garlic, finely chopped
10-ounce package frozen chopped spinach,
  thawed and squeezed dry

1. Combine the cream cheese, yogurt, water chestnuts, cucumber, chives, lemon juice and garlic in a bowl and mix well.

2. Add the spinach and stir to combine. Cover and refrigerate for 4 hours to develop the flavors. Serve with fresh vegetables such as celery, cherry tomatoes, carrots, broccoli and cauliflower, or with crackers.

SHOPPING LIST

1 cucumber
chives or scallions
1 lemon
garlic
10-oz. pkg. frozen spinach
8-oz. can water chestnuts
8-oz. pkg. cream cheese or Neufchatel cheese
plain low-fat yogurt

CHEESY CAULIFLOWER CRISPIES

These are fun to make since the cauliflower florets are tossed about in a plastic bag—easy cleanup, too. These are delicious with a glass of wine, for the adults in the group, or just as a fast snack anytime of day. You will be surprised to see even the most picky eater in the family actually enjoy the cauliflower!

Makes 15 to 18
Preparation time: 10 minutes
Cooking time: 8 to 10 minutes

INGREDIENTS

1 head cauliflower
$\frac{1}{4}$ cup fresh bread crumbs
$\frac{1}{4}$ cup grated parmesan cheese
2 teaspoons snipped chives
1 teaspoon paprika
4 tablespoons butter or margarine, melted

1. Heat the oven to 300 degrees.

2. Wash the cauliflower and pat it dry. Separate it into bite-sized florets.

3. Combine the bread crumbs, cheese, chives and paprika in a plastic bag. Dip the cauliflower florets into the melted butter, a few at a time, and drop them into the crumb mixture. Shake the bag gently until the cauliflower florets are evenly coated. Repeat with the remaining florets.

4. Spread the florets on a baking sheet and heat for 8 to 10 minutes, until hot.

SHOPPING LIST

1 loaf bread
1 head cauliflower
chives
paprika
butter or margarine
Parmesan cheese

BAKED APPLES WITH GRANOLA

You can make this apple treat with commercial granola, but if you have some of the homemade sort on hand, we recommend it. Serve this as a warming late-afternoon snack with hot cider or, if you prefer, as dessert.

Serves 4
Preparation time: 5 minutes
Cooking time: 5 to 8 minutes

INGREDIENTS

2 large baking apples
2 tablespoons lemon juice
4 teaspoons butter or margarine
4 teaspoons packed brown sugar
4 tablespoons Granola (page 312), slightly
  crushed

1. Cut the apples in half through the stem and remove the cores. Put the apple halves, cut side up, in an 8-by-8-inch microwave-safe baking dish. Sprinkle with lemon juice.

2. Top each apple half with 1 teaspoon butter or margarine and 1 teaspoon brown sugar. Cover the dish with plastic wrap, turning back one corner to vent. Microwave on High (100 percent) for 4 to 6 minutes until the apples are tender, rotating the dish a half turn after 2 minutes.

3. Sprinkle each apple half with 1 tablespoon of granola. Cover and microwave on High (100 percent) for 1 to $1\frac{1}{2}$ minutes. Let the apples stand for 2 minutes before serving.

ZESTY NACHOS

What is a Friday night video without nachos? They are quick to make and gooey to eat—just as a bona fide snack should be. Grownups will appreciate them, too, with frosty margaritas. If you prefer your nachos without the bite of jalapeno peppers, use plain Monterey jack cheese.

Serves 4
Preparation time: 5 minutes
Cooking time: 2 to 3 minutes

INGREDIENTS

Medium-sized bag tortilla chips
4 ounces cheddar cheese, grated
1 ounce Monterey jack cheese with jalapeno
    pepper, grated
2 scallions, sliced

1. Heat the broiler.

2. Spread the tortilla chips on a baking sheet. Sprinkle the grated cheeses and the scallions evenly over the top. Broil for 2 to 3 minutes, until the cheese has melted.

3. Serve immediately, with Five Alarm Salsa (page 273) or Santa Fe Guacamole (page 273).

SHOPPING LIST

medium bag tortilla chips
scallions
cheddar cheese
Monterey jack cheese with jalapeno pepper

JELLED SQUARES

The extra gelatin makes the store bought gelatin dessert firmer than usual so that you can easily cut it into squares for eating out of hand. Or, try cutting it with decorative cookie cutters to delight youngsters.

Makes 64 1-inch squares
Preparation time: 5 minutes plus 2 hours' refrigerating time

INGREDIENTS

2 envelopes unflavored gelatin
2½ cups cold water
6-ounce package fruit-flavored gelatin
   dessert mix

1. Dissolve the unflavored gelatin in 1 cup of water and set aside.

2. Pour 1 cup of water into a saucepan and bring to the boil. Add the gelatin dessert mix, bring back to the boil and remove from the heat. Stir in the unflavored gelatin mixture and the remaining ½ cup of water.

3. Pour into a lightly oiled 8-by-8-inch pan and refrigerate for about 2 hours, until firm. Cut into 1-inch squares and store in the refrigerator in an airtight container.

SHOPPING LIST

2 envelopes unflavored gelatin
6-oz. pkg. fruit-flavored gelatin dessert mix

STUFFED CELERY STICKS

HOMEMADE FRUIT POPS

When they are filled with peanut butter and topped with raisins, these flavorful, satisfying snacks are sometimes called "ants on a log." Either cream cheese or peanut butter is delicious with celery, which is less filling than crackers and ever so easy for small hands to hold.

Makes 16
Preparation time: 5 minutes

INGREDIENTS

4 stalks celery, washed and dried
Cream cheese or peanut butter
Raisins (optional)

1. Cut each celery stalk into 4 short sticks.

2. Fill each stick with cream cheese or peanut butter. Dot the filling with a few raisins, if desired.

SHOPPING LIST

celery
raisins
cream cheese or peanut butter

We suggest orange juice or grape juice, but you may substitute lemonade or another fruit drink. Keep in mind that frozen juices do not taste as sweet as room temperature or chilled juices and you *may* decide to add a little sugar to the juice before freezing. However, we are sure most kids will love them as they come.

Makes 16
Preparation time: 2 minutes plus freezing time

INGREDIENTS

2 cups orange juice or grape juice
6 sturdy plastic drinking straws

1. Pour the fruit juice into an ice tray. Put the ice tray in the freezer.

2. Cut each drinking straw into 3 equal lengths. When the fruit juice cubes are partially frozen, insert 1 length of drinking straw into each cube. Return to the freezer and freeze completely. Use the straws as "popsicle sticks."

SHOPPING LIST

orange juice or grape juice
sturdy plastic drinking straws

MOCK PIZZAS

We know lots of kids who make these English muffin "pizzas" nearly every day after school. They are especially easy with a toaster oven, and they are good without the pepperoni, if you do not happen to have some on hand when you or your children get a "pizza attack."

Makes 8
Preparation time: 5 minutes
Cooking time: 10 minutes

INGREDIENTS

1 cup grated mozzarella cheese
½ pound pepperoni, chopped (optional)
4 English muffins
½ cup commercial spaghetti sauce or Quick Marinara Sauce (page 121)

1. Heat the broiler.

2. Combine the mozzarella cheese and the pepperoni in a bowl.

3. Split the English muffins and toast lightly on both sides, using the broiler or a toaster-oven. Spread the spaghetti sauce evenly on the muffin halves and top with the pepperoni mixture. Broil until the cheese is melted.

SHOPPING LIST

½ lb. pepperoni
4 English muffins
commercial spaghetti sauce

MENUS

Regardless of how good an individual recipe sounds to you when you read it, and despite how much you and your family enjoy it once it is made, there are times when you cannot think of what *else* to serve with it. Throughout the book we have provided serving suggestions, saying, perhaps, that a certain fish dish would taste good with a vegetable dish found in another chapter, and so on.

In this chapter, we have gone a step further, putting together some menus that particularly appeal to us. They are constructed using our recipes, with occasional suggestions for foods not included in the book (sliced strawberries, for instance). We have tried to anticipate your family's needs—devising menus for events such as a child's birthday party, Sunday morning breakfast cooked by Dad, backyard cookouts and picnics at the beach. We also have menus with a seasonal flair for quiet dinners at home, to enjoy after the children are asleep or to share with older children. There are also menus for weekend lunches and quick suppers, which capture the spirit of the book as well as anything else with their sense of fun and easy, good food. You will not be disappointed if you put together meals using these menus but you may also use them as springboards for menus of your own design.

Sunday Morning Breakfast

Menu #1

Potato and Bacon Omelette
Walnut-Cinnamon Coffee Cake
Sliced strawberries (not a recipe)
Banana Energizers

Menu #2

Fish Cakes with Corn
Three-Cheese Omelette
English muffins (not a recipe)
Strawberry Jam

Weekend Brunch

Menu #1

Piperade
Apple Cinnamon Muffins
Hot Spiced Cider

Menu #2

Cheese Bacon and Egg Pie
Orange and Avocado Salad with Citrus
    Vinaigrette
Pear Walnut Muffins

Menu #3

Cheese Blintzes
Beet and Orange Salad with Balsamic
    Vinaigrette
Orange Spice Muffins

Backyard Cookout

Menu #1

Grilled Lemon Chicken or Grilled Tuna with
    Orange Mint Chutney
Tangy Calico Slaw with Yogurt Dressing
Roasted Corn
Blueberry Cornmeal Shortcakes

Menu #2

Barbecued Hamburgers
Lemony Cucumber Salad
Potato and Artichoke Salad
Summertime Cobbler with Orange Biscuit
    Crust

A Picnic at the Beach or in the Park

Cold Arizona Chicken
Gazpacho
Veggies with Dill Dressing
Taco chips (not a recipe)
Cherry Almond Brownies

A Child's Birthday Party

Pizza Joint Pizza
Stuffed Celery Sticks
Make-your-own-sundaes with Molten
  Chocolate Sauce and Butterscotch Topping
Birthday cake (not a recipe)

An Open House

Grilled Sesame Chicken Wings
Santa Fe Guacamole and Five-Alarm Salsa
  with taco chips
Crunchy Spinach Dip with crackers
Cheese Fondue
Curried Yogurt Dressing with crudite

Quiet Dinners at Home

Springtime: Menu #1

Pistou
Fettucine with Asparagus and Walnuts
Salad of soft spring greens with Mustardy Red
  Wine Vinaigrette
Gingery Stuffed Nectarines

Summertime: Menu #2

Tuscan Tomato Soup
Grilled Flank Steak
Artichokes and Basil Butter
Tabbouleh
Poached Peaches with Almonds

Autumn: Menu #3

Walnut Cheese Chicken Breasts
Zucchini Gratin
Stovetop Pilaf
Pear and Hazelnut Crisp

Winter: Menu #4

Baked Cod with Potatoes
Carrot and Scallion Stir Fry
Popovers
Bread Pudding with Hot Buttered Rum-Raisin
  Sauce

Weekend Lunches and Quick Suppers

Menu #1

Minted Pea Soup
Falafel
Baked Apples with Granola

Menu #2

Plymouth Chili
Jalapeno Corn Cake
Salad of crisp greens with Balsamic Vinaigrette
Grilled Pineapple

Menu #3

Old Fashioned Fish Chowder
Salad of crisp greens with Orange Poppyseed
  and Honey Vinaigrette
Irish Raisin Soda Bread
Apple Brown Betty

Menu #4

Zucchini Tian
Salad of soft greens with Curried Yogurt
  Dressing
Buttermilk Cornbread and Corn Kernels
Cottage Cheese Fritters with Apples

Menu #5

Turkey Fajitas
Five Alarm Salsa
Santa Fe Guacamole
Cumin Rice
Ice cream with Raspberry Sauce

Lunch Box and Brown Bag Meals

Menu #1

Meatloaf Sandwich
Tangy Calico Slaw with Yogurt Dressing
Banana Nut Bread

Menu #2

Pitas Stuffed with Spicy Lentils and Tomato
  Salad
Apple Fudge Brownie

Menu #3

Lamb Sandwich with Raita
Lemony Cucumber Salad
Fruit Bran Muffin

GLOSSARY

A la   in the style of; for example, *à la Grecque* means that the food is cooked Greek style.

Acidulate   the process of adding vinegar or lemon juice to another liquid.

Acorn Squash   one of the vine-grown vegetables native to South and North America; a winter vegetable that has recently been miniaturized. It gets its name because of its resemblance to a very large acorn.

Adjust   to add seasoning before serving, after tasting.

Al dente   term used to describe the doneness of pasta.

Allspice   spice combining cinnamon, nutmeg, and cloves from small berries; can be either whole or ground.

Amandine   French term for "garnished with almonds."

Ancho chili pepper   dried chili pepper; when green it is called a poblano chili pepper.

Anchovy   small Mediterranean fish, usually filleted and canned in oil after curing in salt; sold flat and rolled.

Antipasto   selection of small morsels that are eaten before the meal or, literally, before the pasta. It can consist of a variety of sausages, beans, artichokes, cheeses, anchovies, peppers and other vegetables, drizzled with a fine olive oil.

Apéritif   French term for light alcoholic drink served before a meal.

Arborio rice   Italian rice that is shorter and fatter than other grains.

Aromatic vegetables   onions, carrots, and celery that are used to flavor soups, stews, and other long-cooking dishes.

Arrowroot   a white powder used to thicken fine sauces, such as Bigarade for roast duck, or for making a fruit dessert.

Arugula   somewhat bitter green used in salads; popular in Italian cuisine; sold in small bunches.

Aspic   strained broth used in cooking meats, poultry or fish and usually strengthened with the addition of clear gelatin, which sets the liquid when cold into a savory jelly.

Aubergine   French word for eggplant.

Au gratin   method of preparing a sauce in a shallow dish with a topping of bread crumbs, butter, and grated Parmesan cheese, to form a delicate golden crust on the surface.

Avocado   originally found in the tropics; once called an alligator pear; green, thick-skinned fruit now used in many recipes, notably guacamole.

Baba   yeast cake that is soaked in a rum syrup and baked in a tall round mold.

Baguette   traditional long, crusty loaf of French bread.

Bain marie   warm water bath in which delicate dishes such as custard are cooked, surrounded with hot, not boiling, water to maintain an even temperature.

Baking blind term used for the preliminary baking of a pastry shell to firm it before filling it with a custard or other pie filling.

Baking powder combines baking soda, an acid and cornstarch; causes bread or cake to rise when mixed with a liquid.

Baking soda used in baking; when combined with an acid, dough or batter rises.

Barbecue the most ancient form of cooking. Once confined only to roasting meat and birds over hot coals, it is increasingly used for cooking fish and vegetables, using fragrant woods as the source of heat. The food is spread in a single layer on a well-oiled grill and brushed with butter, oil or a marinade as it is cooking.

Barley popular grain used in cereals, breads and soups; varieties include hulled, Scotch, and pearl.

Basil pungent leafy herb used to flavor stews, soups, and many other dishes.

Basmati rice aromatic, long-grained rice popular in India and the Middle East.

Baste to ladle the drippings or a flavored broth over meat or poultry as it is cooking in order to keep it moist.

Bay leaf aromatic herb also called laurel leaf or bay laurel; used to flavor soups, stews, meats, and vegetables; can be fresh or dried.

Bean sprouts germinated beans and seeds popularly used in Chinese cooking.

Béarnaise sauce classic French sauce served with meat, fish, eggs, and vegetables; made by reducing vinegar, wine, tarragon, and shallots, and adding egg yolks and butter.

Beating method of stirring quickly with a wire whisk to form a smooth sauce, with a wooden spoon to make a smooth mixture, or with an electric mixer in order to lighten and thicken two or more ingredients.

Béchamel sauce white sauce.

Beurre blanc French for "white butter," sauce combines wine, vinegar and shallots that are reduced, and cold butter is whisked into mixture until sauce is smooth and thick; served with poultry, seafood, and eggs.

Beurre manié mixture of butter and flour (usually about 2 tablespoons of butter and 1 tablespoon of flour) that is kneaded in the hand to form a smooth paste and added at the last minute to thicken a soup, sauce, or stew to the right consistency.

Blanching plunging just cooked vegetables into a bowl of cold water to stop the cooking process.

Blanquette stew usually made of veal, enveloped in a very rich white sauce to which egg yolks and cream are added.

Bok choy Chinese white cabbage.

Bordelaise sauce French sauce made with wine, brown stock, bone marrow, shallots, parsley and herbs.

Bouillon vegetable, poultry, meat, or fish broth; also available in compressed, flavor-concentrated cubes.

Bouquet garni bunch of herbs (parsley, thyme, bay leaf, etc.) usually tied together and used to flavor soups, stews, or sauces.

Braising browning, then cooking in a small amount of liquid at a low heat.

Bran outer layer of grains; good source of fiber.

Brochette French for "skewer."

Brownies dense, fudge-like chocolate squares — a cross between a cake and a cookie.

Bundt pan cake pan with fluted sides.

Burrito flour tortilla; folded, rolled and filled with a variety of meats, beans, or cheese.

Cabbage   one of the oldest of all cultivated vegetables and known throughout the world; among its relatives are brussels sprouts, broccoli, cauliflower, kale, kohlrabi and collard greens.

Calamari   squid.

Calorie   a unit of heat.

Cannelini bean   large, white kidney bean; available dry or canned.

Caper   salty, pungent berry (or bud) that has been pickled in vinegar; used to flavor sauces and condiments.

Caramelize   to heat granulated sugar with a little added water until it forms an amber liquid.

Caraway seeds   aromatic seeds from an herb in the parsley family; popular in German, Austrian, and Hungarian cuisines.

Cardamom   aromatic spice in the ginger family; native to India.

Cayenne pepper   hot powder made from various chili peppers.

Chervil   mild herb in the parsley family.

Chick-pea   tan bean used in Mediterranean, Indian, and Middle Eastern dishes.

Chicory   curly, bitter green used in salad; similar to endive.

Chiffonade   lettuce, or other leafy green vegetables that are sliced crosswise very thinly and then cooked quickly in hot butter until they are slightly wilted.

Chilies   often thought to be part of the pepper family, they can be mild or very hot, yellow, green, red, or black; available canned, fresh, or dried. Some varieties are: ancho, chipotl, serrano, or jalapeno.

Cilantro   also called coriander.

Cobbler   fruit dessert topped with a cake mixture or with biscuits that are baked separately and then placed on top of the fruit to continue baking until they are browned.

Condiment   spicy, salty, or sharp accompaniment to food, such as ketchup, relish, mustard, etc.

Coriander   leaf related to parsley; also called cilantro.

Cornstarch   fine white powder made from corn that is dissolved in cold water and then added to a liquid to thicken it into a sauce.

Cranberries   clear red berries native to North America.

Creaming   beating together butter and sugar until the mixture is very thick and light in color and the sugar has literally "melted" into the butter.

Cream of tartar   fine white powder that can be added to egg whites when beating or to candy and icing mixtures for creaminess.

Cumin   aromatic spice that is the dried fruit of a plant similar to parsley; available ground or in seeds.

Curdle   to coagulate or separate.

Deglazing   stirring some of the browned morsels that are clinging to the bottom of the pan into a liquid to form a sauce. This is done by adding two or three tablespoons of cold wine or water to the pan, then heating and stirring until the morsels are absorbed.

Dijon mustard   sharp grayish-yellow mustard originally from France; can be mild or hot.

Dill weed   a member of the parsley family.

Egg glaze   two tablespoons of cold milk which are stirred into one egg yolk in a custard cup, and brushed on the surface of the pastry crust at the last minute, so it will become browned and shiny when it is baked.

Eggplant   fruit (not a vegetable) ranging in color from deep purple to white; usually pear-shaped with a smooth, shiny skin; can be prepared in a variety of ways.

Endive   green leafy vegetable; related to chicory; available in three varieties: Belgian endive, curly endive, and escarole; commonly used in salads.

Escalope   a thin piece of meat or poultry that is pounded with a cleaver to make it even thinner, then fried quickly in a combination of hot butter and oil.

Fajitas   favorite of American Southwest cooking; slices of fried skirt steak or other inexpensive cuts of meat which are grilled and usually wrapped in warm tortillas and served with a variety of garnishes.

Farce   stuffing or dressing for a turkey or other poultry or meat.

Fennel   aromatic green plant; some varieties have a licorice flavor; also available in seeds.

Fillet   to remove bones from meat or fish.

Fines herbes   mixture of fragrant herbs including parsley, tarragon, and chives.

Folding   technique used to gently incorporate a lighter ingredient into a heavier mixture.

Frittata   Italian omelet that is cooked very slowly over low heat.

Ginger   tropical plant whose root is pungent and spicy; popular in Indian and oriental cooking; available fresh or ground.

Gluten   component present in wheat flour that becomes developed when dough is kneaded and provides its essential elasticity.

Green peppercorns   immature berries that are pickled in vinegar and used for garnishing such foods as smoked salmon, carpaccio and even deviled eggs.

Guacamole   Mexican specialty made of mashed avocado mixed with lemon or lime juice and seasonings; can be a dip or a sauce.

Gumbo   thin Creole stew made from chicken, shellfish, and vegetables including okra and spices.

Half-and-half   mixture of milk and cream; 10 to 12 percent butterfat.

Hollandaise sauce   rich, creamy sauce made with butter, egg yolks, and lemon juice; served with vegetables, fish, and egg dishes.

Horseradish   herb used in sauces and condiments; also available dried.

Jalapeno chili pepper   dark green chili pepper; ranges from hot to very hot; popular in Mexican dishes; available fresh and canned.

Julienne   to cut into thin strips about 1½ inches in length and ¼ inch in thickness.

Kalamata olive   purple-black olive packed in olive oil or vinegar.

Kohlrabi   member of turnip family; can be steamed or added to soups and stews.

Leek   white-stalked vegetable related to garlic and onion; resembles a large scallion; can be cooked as a vegetable alone or used in a variety of recipes.

Marinade   seasoned liquid in which various foods are soaked to give them flavor.

Marinate   to place meat, fish, or poultry in a shallow dish covered with a sauce either for a short time or for several days.

Medallions   small round circles of meat.

Mozzarella   soft white Italian cheese that melts easily.

Nacho   crisp tortilla chip topped with melted cheese and chili peppers; appetizer or snack.

Nutmeg flavorful seed available ground or whole; can be grated fresh; popular in baked goods, on potatoes or some vegetables.

Oregano pungent herb, sometimes called wild marjoram, popular in Mediterranean cooking.

Orzo form of pasta that looks very much like pine nuts, it is cooked in about eight minutes.

Papaya member of the melon family that grows in tropical climates.

Paprika powder made from red pepper pods; can range from mild to hot.

Parboiling partially cooking food by plunging it quickly into boiling water.

Parsley fresh-flavored herb; available in many varieties; used in recipes or as a garnish.

Peppercorn popular spice from a berry that produces three types: black peppercorn, white peppercorn, and green peppercorn.

Pesto uncooked sauce made with fresh herbs, cheese, and olive oil.

Phyllo thin pastry dough similar to strudel dough; popular in Greek and Near Eastern dishes.

Pissaladière Southern French type of pizza; contains onions, anchovies, black olives, and tomatoes.

Pita type of Middle Eastern round, flat bread of white or whole-wheat flour with a pocket into which various stuffings can be placed.

Poblano chili pepper dark green chili pepper ranging from mild to hot.

Pot pies pastry made from chunks of cooked chicken or small cubes of beef and colorful vegetables enveloped in a sauce and covered with flaky crust.

Pot roasting cooking a large piece of meat or poultry in its own juices with a very small amount of liquid added in a heavy casserole with a tightly fitting lid.

Provençal refers to dishes prepared in the style of Southeastern France; usually contains garlic, onions, tomatoes, olives, and olive oil.

Quiche pastry filled with a type of custard containing eggs, cream, and various seasonings, and baked.

Radicchio red-leafed salad green.

Reduce boiling a liquid gently until the quantity is considerably lessened and the flavor greatly intensified.

Refried beans Mexican cooked red or pinto beans that are mashed, then fried.

Rice vinegar made from fermented rice; used in Japanese and Chinese dishes.

Ricotta grainy cheese smiliar to cottage cheese but smoother and creamier; popular in Italian cooking.

Rosemary aromatic herb in the mint family used as a seasoning in a large variety of foods.

Roux mixture of butter or other fat and flour that is used to thicken a sauce.

Saffron yellow-orange spice available in powder or threads.

Sage pungent Mediterranean herb often used in poultry and pork dishes.

Sauté to cook foods very quickly in a small amount of oil.

Scalding bringing a liquid to simmering point, when small bubbles begin to appear around the edges of the saucepan.

Score to make a series of shallow cuts into the surface of bread, ham, and other meats.

Searing   browning food over very high heat, often in a dry, heavy pan or with a touch of oil, in order to seal in the juices and provide an attractive brown color to it.

Serrano chili pepper   small, very hot pepper; available canned or packed in oil, and fresh.

Sesame oil   light or dark strong, fragrant oil; popular in Indian and oriental dishes.

Shredding   cutting vegetables, and sometimes chicken which has been lightly frozen, into matchstick-thin strips.

Skim   to remove fat from a sauce or stew using a shallow-bowled spoon.

Soybean oil   light yellow oil that is high in polyunsaturated and monounsaturated fats and low in saturated fats; popular in Chinese cuisine.

Soy sauce   dark, salty sauce made from fermented boiled soybeans and roasted wheat or barley; important in oriental cuisine.

Stir fry   to cook in a wok by quickly frying and stirring in very hot oil.

Stock   strained liquid from vegetables, meat, or fish to which water and seasonings have been added.

Taco   a soft tortilla or one that is fried until it is crisp in hot oil or lard. It is folded in half or rolled around a filling made from ground or shredded meat or poultry and served with garnishes.

Tarragon   dark green aromatic herb with a licorice flavor; available fresh, dried and powdered, or in vinegar.

Thyme   member of the mint family; available fresh or dried.

Tortilla   thin flat Mexican pancake made from unleavened corn flour or wheat flour and baked on a griddle or heavy frying pan.

Tostados   tortillas that are fried until they are almost crisp and used like a single slice of bread in making an open-face sandwich.

Tournedos   small beef steaks cut from the loin or tenderloin or filet.

Turmeric   root of a tropical plant similar to ginger; one of the essential components of curry powder and was once known as Indian saffron.

Vinaigrette   basic combination of oil and vinegar, salt, and pepper; other ingredients can be added; popular salad dressing.

Wok   round-bottomed pot used in oriental cooking; various sizes and materials.

Yogurt   dairy product resulting from fermentation and coagulation of milk; available in a variety of flavors or plain.

Zest   outer layer of skin of citrus fruit.

INDEX

M after page number denotes Microwave recipe